Whittier Quad
(Macy Store) 12/3/68

D1179932

INDIA WINS FREEDOM

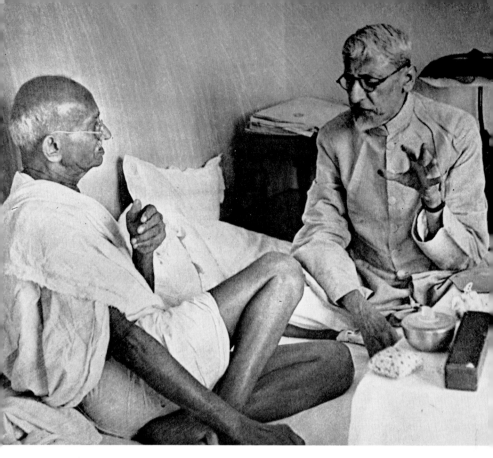

Gandhiji and Maulana Abul Kalam Azad (1946

INDIA WINS FREEDOM

An Autobiographical Narrative

MAULANA ABUL KALAM AZAD

With
Introduction and Explanatory Notes
by
LOUIS FISCHER

LONGMANS, GREEN AND CO.
NEW YORK · LONDON · TORONTO
1960

LONGMANS, GREEN AND CO., INC.
119 WEST 40TH STREET, NEW YORK 18

LONGMANS, GREEN AND CO. LTD.
6 & 7 CLIFFORD STREET, LONDON W 1

LONGMANS, GREEN AND CO.
20 CRANFIELD ROAD, TORONTO 16

PUBLISHED SIMULTANEOUSLY IN THE DOMINION OF CANADA BY
LONGMANS, GREEN AND CO., TORONTO

FIRST AMERICAN EDITION

LIBRARY OF CONGRESS CATALOG CARD NUMBER 60–10882

Printed in the United States of America

For
JAWAHARLAL NEHRU
Friend and Comrade

Preface

WHEN a little over two years ago I approached Maulana Azad with the request that he should write his autobiography, I never for a moment thought that it would be my melancholy duty to write a preface for the volume. He did not like to talk about his personal life and was at first reluctant to undertake the work. It was with great difficulty that he could be persuaded that, as one of the principal actors in the transfer of power from British to Indian hands, he owed a duty to posterity to record his reading of those memorable times. His reluctance was also partly due to his shattered health. He felt that he needed all his energies to cope with the burden of work imposed on him by inescapable political and administrative tasks. He finally agreed on my assuring him that I would do my best to relieve him of the actual burden of writing. This would, of course, mean that the Indian people would be denied the privilege of reading his autobiography in his own words. Indian literature in general and Urdu in particular would be the poorer for this, but even a version in English written under his direction would be better than no record at all.

I think it necessary to describe in some detail how the work has been composed. During these last two years or so, I spent on an average an hour or more every evening with Maulana Azad, except on those occasions when I had to go out of Delhi. He was a wonderful conversationalist and used to describe his experiences in vivid terms. I made fairly copious notes and also asked questions for clarification of a point or elicitation of further information. He consistently refused to speak on personal matters, but, on all questions relating to public affairs, he spoke with the utmost frankness and sincerity. When I had collected sufficient material for a chapter, I prepared a draft in English which I handed over to him at the earliest opportunity. He read each chapter by himself and then we went over it together. At this stage, he made many amendments by addition and alteration, as well as by omission. We proceeded in this way till I was able to give him the first draft of the completed book in September 1957.

When he had the completed text in his hands, Maulana Azad decided that some thirty pages of the text dealing with incidents and reflections mainly of a personal character should not be published for the present. He directed that a copy each of the complete text should be deposited under sealed cover in the National Library, Calcutta, and the National Archives, New Delhi. He was, however, anxious that the exclusion of these passages should not in any way alter either the outline of his picture or his general findings. I carried out the changes according to his instructions and was able to present to Maulana Azad the revised and abridged draft towards the end of November 1957.

He went through it once again during the period when I was away in Australia. After my return we went through the manuscript chapter by chapter and indeed sentence by sentence. He made some minor alterations, but there was no major change. In some cases, a chapter was thus revised three or four times. On Republic Day this year, Maulana Azad said that he was satisfied with the manuscript and it could be sent to the printers. The book as now released represents the text as finally approved by him.

It was Maulana Azad's wish that the book should appear in November 1958 to synchronize with his seventieth birthday. Fate, however, willed otherwise and he will not be with us to see the book when it appears.

As I have already stated, Maulana Azad was not in the beginning very willing to undertake the preparation of this book. As the book progressed his interest grew. In the last six months or so, he rarely missed an evening in the preparation of the manuscript. He was extremely reticent about his personal life, but in the end he volunteered to write a first volume which would have covered the earlier phases of his life and brought the story up to 1937. He did in fact approve a synopsis which, according to his own wishes, is included in this volume as its first chapter. He had also intended to write a third volume to deal with events since 1948. Unfortunately for us, these volumes will now never be written.

The work in connection with this book has been for me a labor of love and I shall feel happy if it helps in forwarding an object that was very dear to Maulana Azad's heart. This is the promotion of greater understanding among the different Indian communities as a first step towards greater understanding among peoples of the world. He also wished that the people of India and Pakistan should look upon one another as friends and neighbors. He regarded the Indian Council for Cultural Relations as an instrument for the achievement of this object and in his presidential address to the Council—his last prepared and printed speech—he made a fervent appeal for the strengthening of the bonds of understanding and sympathy between the people of these two states which till only a decade ago had been one undivided country. I feel that there can be no better use of any income derived from this book than to make it available to the Council for promoting better understanding among the different communities which live in India and Pakistan. Apart from a share to be paid to his nearest surviving relatives, royalties from this book will therefore go to the Council for the annual award of two prizes for the best essay on Islam by a non-Moslem and on Hinduism by a Moslem citizen of India or Pakistan. In view of Maulana Azad's great love and consideration for the young, the competition will be restricted to persons of thirty or below on the 22nd of February in any year.

Before I conclude, I wish to make one other thing perfectly clear. There are opinions and judgments in this book with which I do not agree, but, since my function was only to record Maulana Azad's findings, it would have been highly improper to let my views color the narrative. When he was alive, I often expressed my differences to him, and, with the open-mindedness which was so strong an element in his nature, he has at times modified his views to meet my criticisms. At other times, he smiled in his characteristic way and said, "These are my views and surely I have the right to express them as I will." Now that he is no more, his views must stand in the form in which he left them.

It is difficult for any man to reflect with complete accuracy the views and opinions of another. Even when both use the same language, the change of one word may alter the emphasis and bring about a subtle difference in the shade of meaning. The difference in the genius of Urdu and English makes the task of interpreting Maulana Azad's thoughts still more difficult. Urdu like all other Indian languages is rich, colorful and vigorous. English, on the other hand, is essentially a language of understatement. And when the speaker is a master of Urdu like Maulana Azad, the plight of the writer who seeks to express his thoughts in English can easily be imagined. In spite of these difficulties, I have tried to reflect as faithfully as I could the views of Maulana Azad, and I regard myself as richly rewarded by the fact that the text had met with his approval.

New Delhi,   HUMAYUN KABIR
15 March 1958

Contents

Illustrations

Giants and Men

An Introduction by Louis Fischer,
author of *The Life of Mahatma Gandhi*

UNLIKE the thirteen American colonies, India won national independence not in a revolutionary war but through negotiation. The way to the conference table was prepared by three decades of the Gandhi-led, nonviolent struggle for freedom, and by the five and a half years of Britain's valiant and victorious battle with Hitler, Italy and Japan. The fighting finished, England faced pressing business at home: tending her wounds and mending her economic fences. She had neither the mood nor the might to frustrate India's will to liberty. Within nine months—a very short time—after the end of the global war, therefore, an influential Cabinet Mission, sent by the Attlee Labour government, was in India deliberating with Mahatma Gandhi, Jawaharlal Nehru, Vallabhbhai Patel and Maulana Azad on the terms of Britain's departure. How independence was negotiated and who was responsible for the simultaneous disaster of partition is told in this autobiography of one of the Big Four: Maulana Azad.

Rarely has an insider written with such frankness about events hitherto unrevealed or merely rumored. Nehru and Azad were personally close and politically kin. This book is dedicated, with permission, "For Jawaharlal Nehru, Friend and Comrade." Azad wrote it while Minister of Education in Nehru's Cabinet. He could not have known at the time that he would die before the day of publication. It took courage to blame Nehru, in considerable part, for the partition which Azad opposed from first to last. Courage and honesty are the outstanding characteristics of this book as they were of the man.

An Arabic scholar renowned throughout the Islamic world, Azad

was an Indian nationalist eager to found a free India undiminished
by a Moslem state of Pakistan. For him the vivisection of India was
a public calamity and a personal tragedy. It shattered his entire
lifework for an independent country whose unifying nationhood
would bridge the religious differences between Hindu and Moslem
communities. His heartache was understandable and so, too, the
bitterness against those he holds responsible. He waited ten years
to let his emotions cool and then dictated these memoirs.

It is the irony of fickle politics that Nehru, least Hindu of Hindus,
the westernized agnostic born in the United Provinces (now Uttar
Pradesh), where Moslems and Hindus always coexisted in friendly
affinity, should have acquiesced in the bisection of his beloved India
on religious lines. He did so because he came to the conclusion, as
the very Hindu Patel had a bit earlier in 1947, that it would be impossible to govern free India if the obstructionist Moslem Leaguers,
under Mohammed Ali Jinnah's vengeful inspiration, refused to col-
laborate. Better to stand divided than fall united.

Nehru today regrets the mistake. "Twenty years ago," he told
C. L. Sulzberger in an interview published by the *New York Times*
on March 2, 1957, "I would have said that certainly we should have
some kind of confederation, not federation—independent states with
common defense and economic politics. The difficulty now is if we
talk about it. This upsets our neighbors [Pakistan] because we are
so much bigger. Nevertheless, of course, this remains the logical
future path—confederation with each member nation maintaining
its independence intact."

Such, roughly, was the plan—a confederation consisting of three
regional groupings of autonomous provinces: two Moslem regions
in West and East India, a predominantly Hindu region between
them, each with its own constitution—which the British Cabinet
Mission proposed on May 16, 1946, and which Maulana Azad favored from that date to his dying day.

Nehru, according to Azad, sank the plan in an historic press conference. The Cabinet Mission had considered the advisability of
partition and rejected it. The creation of Pakistan would require the

splitting of two giant provinces, the Punjab and Bengal, "contrary to the wishes of a very large percentage of the inhabitants. . . . Finally there is the geographical fact that the two halves of the proposed Pakistan state are separated by some 700 miles" of Indian territory. "We are therefore unable to advise the British Government," the Mission announced, "that the power which at present resides in British hands should be handed over to two entirely separate sovereign states." Lord Wavell, the British Viceroy, took the same position.

Thwarted, seeing no alternative, Jinnah accepted the Mission's confederation scheme. "Now happened one of those unfortunate events which changed the course of history," Azad writes. The event was a Nehru press interview in Bombay. I attended that fateful question-and-answer period and when it ended I said to Nehru in the presence of Mrs. Vijaya Lakshmi Pandit, his sister, "You have changed the entire basis of the agreement with England."

He smiled and replied, "I am fully aware of that."

Nehru had told the assembled journalists that the Congress party, of which he, Gandhi, Azad and Patel were the leaders, would not be bound by the Cabinet Mission's confederation plan. Actually the All-India Congress Committee had met in the same city of Bombay only two days earlier under Nehru's chairmanship and in Gandhi's presence and voted for the plan. This is fully documented in the minutes; Azad, who participated in the discussions, bears witness to it.

Jinnah read Nehru's press conference statement as the Congress party's withdrawal of the Cabinet Mission's scheme. He accordingly withdrew his approval, too. There followed most cruel, widespread violence, Moslem League intransigence, Congress party despair, and, finally, the British Labour government decision to partition India while unshackling her.

Prime Minister Attlee now sent Lord Mountbatten to "sell" partition to the Indian leaders. After the task had been accomplished he told the Royal Empire Society in London on October 6, 1948, how he did it. "Personally," Mountbatten stated on that occasion, "I was convinced that the right solution for then and still would be to keep a United India" under the Cabinet Mission's plan. But "Mr. Jinnah made it abundantly clear from the first moment that so long as he lived he would never accept a United India. He demanded partition, he insisted on Pakistan." The Congress party, on the other hand, preferred India whole. Its leaders would, however, accept partition to avoid civil war. Mountbatten "was convinced that the Moslem League would have fought."

But the Congress party refused to let large non-Moslem areas go to Pakistan. "That automatically meant," Mountbatten explained at the Royal Empire Society, "a partition of the great provinces of the Punjab and Bengal," which had millions of Hindu and Sikh inhabitants, and more millions of Moslems.

"When I told Mr. Jinnah that I had their [the Congress party leaders] provisional agreement to partition he was overjoyed. When I said it logically followed that this would involve partition of the Punjab and Bengal he was horrified. He produced the strongest arguments why these provinces should not be partitioned. He said that they had national characteristics and that partition would be disastrous. I agreed, but I said how much more must I now feel that the same consideration applied to the partitioning of the whole of India. He did not like that, and started explaining why India had to be partitioned, and so we went round and round the mulberry bush until he finally realized that either he could have a United India with an unpartitioned Punjab and Bengal or a divided India with a partitioned Punjab and Bengal and he finally accepted the latter solution."

It is not startling that Jinnah agreed to partition. He wanted his Pakistan. But how did Mountbatten win over Nehru and Patel and Gandhi—never Azad? "The crucial role in the great decision" to partition India was Nehru's, writes Michael Brecher, professor at Canada's McGill University, in the latest and best biography of the Indian Prime Minister.[1] The biography is laudatory, at times

[1] Michael Brecher, *Nehru, A Political Biography* (New York: Oxford University Press, 1959).

worshipful ("Nehru," Brecher says, "is a giant both as a man and statesman.") but never starry-eyed. Commenting on Nehru's approval of partition, he declares, "For those who have been in opposition most of their political lives, the prize of power is tempting. The Congress leaders had already tasted its fruits [in the Interim Government] and were naturally reluctant to part with it at the moment of triumph"—at the moment when the British announced their readiness to free India. "This," Brecher continues, "applies to Nehru as well." But he sought power primarily to translate his ideals into reality.

Azad had his own views on why Nehru accepted partition and they will give no comfort to the doctrinaire and indoctrinated who believe that men—and women—do not make history. Nehru, Azad says, "is also impulsive and amenable to personal influence." The details fascinate.

There was another factor. Nehru and Krishna Menon told me in India in 1946 that the British were not leaving the country. I found in Indonesia that the nationalist leaders had had the same kind of doubts about Holland's final—1949—decision to quit the Indies. It is extremely difficult for minds conditioned by the prolonged domination of their native land by a powerful imperialism to accept its imminent departure as a reality. When Mountbatten made it clear that, given partition, Britain would indeed leave, Nehru and others eagerly seized the offer lest (who knows?) it be withdrawn.

Azad would have been patient and taken nothing less than an India united as a confederation. Mahatma Gandhi hoped to achieve this by a simple formula. "Hand over power to Mr. Jinnah," he advised Mountbatten in effect at their first meeting.[2] Since the British could not allow the Moslem minority to rule India, however, they would have to stay until Congress accepted power. But the British had decided not to stay. Therefore they would have to yield to the Congress party's condition: no Pakistan.

Mountbatten escaped from this logical pincer by convincing

[2] Pyarelal, *Mahatma Gandhi: The Last Phase* (Ahmedabad, India: Navajivan Publishing House), II, 78.

Nehru and Patel that civil war impended and partition was the only way to avoid it. Nor could Gandhi himself countenance internecine slaughter on a grand scale. Every fiber of his being rebelled against bloodshed. He advanced the slogan, "Peace before Pakistan." But Mountbatten had persuaded Nehru and Patel that there could be no peace without Pakistan. "I felt," Patel explained later, "that if we did not accept partition, India would be split into many bits and would be completely ruined." [3]

The fact is that Congress no longer supported Gandhi on the integrity of India. "Mr. Gandhi," Lord Mountbatten said to the Mahatma in one of their six talks, "today Congress is with me."

"But India," Gandhi replied, "is with me today."

He was wrong. India was about to burst into flames which would burn hundreds of thousands of all races and religions to death. Then a young Hindu shot Gandhi for being pro-Moslem, and India, torn in twain—torn in three really, for there are two Pakistans, one in the east and a second in the west—entered the Nehru era. It has been a difficult, sometimes desperate, period in which the cost of partition multiplied the cost the country must pay for five centuries of stagnation.

What happened was many times worse than that which Nehru and Patel thought they could prevent by bowing to Jinnah-partition. In New York on October 16, 1949, Prime Minister Nehru declared that he would have fought to the end against the establishment of Pakistan had he foreseen the dire consequences that flowed from it. Azad foresaw and warned and yet remained by Nehru's side, a trusted friend during the ten troubled years between independence-plus-partition and his death on February 22, 1958.

Azad was noble and brilliant. His integrity, a stern master, did not prevent him from being generous and gracious. I first met him in Gandhi's ashrama in June, 1942. Azad understood English perfectly and could have spoken it, but to avoid misunderstandings he availed himself of an interpreter. On that first occasion Nehru translated. I asked the Maulana about partition. He said he did not

[3] *Ibid.*, p. 153.

believe in "divorce before marriage." Indians must begin by living in wedlock. If it did not work, they could get a divorce.

Thereafter, on each of my visits to India, he would offer a spread of western food for the spoiled palate of the American and, with none present except Humayun Kabir, his friend and political associate, himself a thoughtful author (now Minister for Cultural Affairs in Nehru's government), and K. R. Kripalani or another secretary, the luncheon conversation—never a sentence of small talk—would proceed meaningfully for two or three hours. If the question required an indiscreet reply about a Cabinet colleague or a government policy, he would indicate agreement by smiling and saying, "You know my views." On one occasion he asked me, "What is India's moral standing abroad?" Nothing more was needed to indicate his displeasure with either the program or, more likely, its spokesman at foreign forums. Usually it was he who cross-examined—on Soviet diplomacy and conditions, Germany, Indonesia, United States policy toward China, yes, even about India. I last broke bread with him a few weeks before his death, when illness had painfully bent his body but left untouched the keen edge of his mind. As ever, he cared for humanity in his own country and in the world. But it was not a cold concern for "masses" or classes. He had warmth, a heart for friendship and an eye for the personal side of politics. His bond with Nehru, his reverence for Gandhi, suffuse the pages of his autobiography. He paints little word pictures of Sir Stafford Cripps, Mountbatten and other British leaders. How does the heat of India's dry plains affect talks on the fate of nations? How did the British arrest respected Indian leaders? What did Azad and Nehru do together in jail? How does it feel to be in prison when your wife dies and not to attend the funeral, yet to go from prison to the Viceroy's palace for negotiations about independence? Threaded between resolutions and texts are delightful human sketches revealing the man and his fellow men. The fight for freedom, under moral leadership, breeds giants. The task of governing, through compromise, cuts them down to normal size.

❋   ❋   ❋

When Maulana Azad's book appeared in India it was a political sensation and immediately became a best seller. Indeed it sold so fast that between printings it occasionally fetched three to four times the published price. Everybody, of course, eagerly awaited Nehru's reaction to Azad's statements and inevitably the matter was brought up at the Prime Minister's press conference. Nehru manifested his customary magnificent magnanimity. He had read the book in manuscript with great care and even made a few minor corrections, one regarding the place where Chiang Kai-shek had stayed in India. Otherwise he insisted on the book's appearing without change, just as it had come from Azad's hand. (The title is Nehru's own formulation.)

An Indian journalist then asked: "Do you think that partition could have been avoided if the proposals brought by Lord Mountbatten could have been brought by some other viceroy? We want to know the exact personal influence which he exercised over your mind."

The Prime Minister replied: "First of all, Maulana Azad has referred to what I said at a Press Conference. Now, I am sorry to confess that I have no very clear ideas of the day to day occurrences in those days; it was a great burden on all of us—a burden of decision, a burden of occurrences, events, happenings, all over, and the tremendous strain under which we were functioning in that Interim Government as it was called, inside the Government, I mean, apart from occurrences outside, because the Moslem League Party were out, as they openly said, to prevent us from functioning satisfactorily. During the period of the interim Government, I think in the first few weeks, I was constantly going to Lord Wavell and telling him that I had had enough of it. I must have done so—I do not know—four or five times in the course of the next two or three months, that is, verbally resigning not actually writing, but saying that I wanted to get out. He said, 'Wait and see' or something like that. So that, it is a little difficult to rely on one's memory of a thing that happened 12 years ago when one was under great strain, in difficulty—not I alone, but all of us. And it is quite conceivable for people to have different recollections as to who influenced whom or what. The real fact is, I think, that personal influences count. How am I to say how I was influenced? I cannot judge. But I think the real facts were, the situation itself and the bitterness and conflicts that were growing in the communal field and the feeling that even if some arrangement could be arrived at to prevent partition, those conflicts and inner disruptions would continue, and might come in the way of any marked progress of the economy of the country later. Because we were anxious naturally to make good, after Independence, in the political and the economic spheres and others—planning and all that—and we felt that if there was some kind of a compulsory union carried on, it would prevent—all our energies would be spent in these inner tugs of war. Whether that was a right analysis or a wrong analysis, I cannot say. I am only saying that it had a powerful effect in our thinking. And, even in the course of the interim Government, we had proposed the appointment of a Planning Commission. It had been opposed by the Moslem League representatives. So that, in every such matter where economic considerations and planning came in, we were likely to come up against inner pulls in different directions. That was, I think—this overwhelming sensation that any kind of a union, if it came about, would first of all not put an end to these inner pulls, secondly, it would leave the Federal Government so weak—with the transfer of power to its various constituent units—the Central Federation would be so weak, that it would not be able to act properly or adopt any effective economic measures. These were the real reasons which ultimately induced us to agree. It was a very, very difficult choice—you can well imagine—and it is frightfully difficult to say now what one could do if one had the same choice. It is very difficult to say; it is very difficult because of what happened subsequently—the terrible things that happened—because when we decided on partition, I do not think any of us ever thought that there would be this terror of mutual killing after the partition. It was in a sense to avoid that, that we decided on partition. So we paid a double price for it, first, you might say, politically, ideologically, second, the actual thing happened that we tried to avoid.

"So, how can I judge how far I was responsible? Mine was certainly part of the responsibility, and Maulana Sahib may be completely right in thinking that I acted wrongly. Only I would say this, that Maulana Sahib thinks too much in individual terms, sometimes, not in terms of historic forces at work. Individuals make a difference and have made a difference but sometimes individuals are only symbols of forces at work." [4]

Now Azad speaks.

[4] Official transcript, Prime Minister Nehru's Press Conference, pp. 7–9.

INDIA WINS FREEDOM

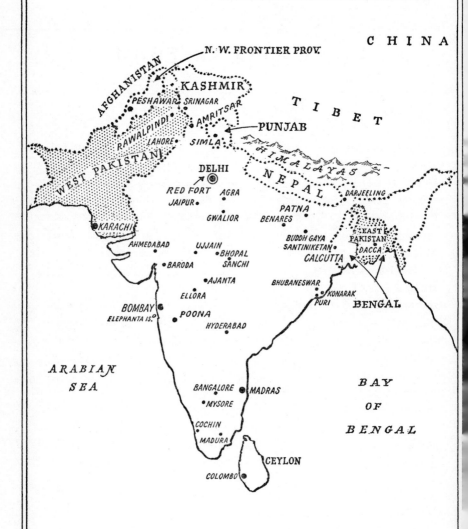

CHAPTER 1

Background

MY forefathers came to India from Herat [a city in Afghanistan] in Babar's [1] days. They first settled in Agra and later moved to Delhi. It was a scholarly family and, in Akbar's [2] time, Maulana [or Moslem scholar] Jamaluddin became famous as a religious divine. After him, the family became more inclined to worldly affairs and several members occupied important civil positions. In Shahjehan's [3] days, Mohammad Hadi was appointed Governor of the Agra Fort.

My father's maternal grandfather was Maulana Munawaruddin. He was one of the last Rukn-ul Mudarassin [or great scholars] of the Moghul period. This post had been first created in Shahjehan's time and was intended to supervise the activities of the State for the promotion of learning and scholarship. The officer had to administer gifts of lands, endowments and pensions to scholars and teachers, and could be compared to a Director of Education in the modern world. Moghul power had by this time declined but these major posts were still retained.

My grandfather died while my father, Maulana Khairuddin, was still very young. My father was therefore brought up by his maternal grandfather. Two years before the Mutiny,[4] Maulana Munawarud-

---

[1] Central Asian ruler (1483–1530), who won dominion over part of Afghanistan, invaded India, and founded the Moghul dynasty.

[2] Akbar (1542–1605) conquered most of northern India in the second half of the sixteenth century. He was the greatest of the Moghul emperors, known for his administrative skill and religious tolerance.

[3] Moghul emperor in Delhi from 1627 to 1658.

[4] The Great Mutiny, or Sepoy Rebellion (1857), of Indian soldiers in the service of the old British East India Company.

1

din was disgusted with the state of affairs in India and decided to
migrate to Mecca. When he reached Bhopal [a state in India],
Nawab Sikandar Jehan Begum detained him. The Mutiny started
while he was still in Bhopal and for two years he could not leave the
place. He then came to Bombay but could not go to Mecca as death
overtook him there.

My father was then about twenty-five. He proceeded to Mecca and
settled there. He built a house for himself and married Sheikh
Mohammed Zaher Watri's daughter. Sheikh Mohammed Zaher was
a great scholar of Medina whose fame had travelled outside Arabia.
My father also became well known throughout the Islamic world
after an Arabic work of his in ten volumes was published in Egypt.
He came to Bombay several times and once came to Calcutta. In
both places many became his admirers and disciples. He also toured
extensively in Iraq, Syria and Turkey.

In Mecca, the Nahr Zubeida was the main source of water for the
people. This was constructed by Begum Zubeida, the wife of Khalif
Harun-al-Rashid. In course of time, the canal had deteriorated
and there was a great shortage of water in the city. This scarcity was
acutest during the Haj [the sacred pilgrimage to Mecca] and pilgrims
had to face great difficulties. My father had this Nahr repaired. He
raised a fund of twenty lakhs [5] in India, Egypt, Syria and Turkey,
and improved the canal in such a way that the Bedouin did not have
an opportunity of damaging it again. Sultan Abdul Majid was then
the Emperor of Turkey and, in recognition of his services, awarded
him the first class Majidi medal.

I was born in Mecca in 1888. In 1890, my father came to Calcutta
with the whole family. Some time before he had fallen down in
Jedda and broken his shin bone. It had been set, but not well, and
he was advised that the surgeons in Calcutta could put it right. He
had intended to stay only for a short time, but his disciples and
admirers would not let him go. A year after we came to Calcutta, my
mother died and was buried there.

My father was a man who believed in the old ways of life. He

[5] A lakh equals 100,000 units of money, population, or the like.

had no faith in western education and never thought of giving me an education of the modern type. He held that modern education would destroy religious faith and arranged for my education in the traditional manner.

Under the old system of education for Moslems in India the boys were first taught Persian and then Arabic. When they had acquired some proficiency in the language, they were taught philosophy, geometry, mathematics and algebra in Arabic. A course of Islamic theology was also required as an essential part of such education. My father had me taught at home, as he did not like to send me to any Madrasa [or Islamic school]. There was, of course, the Calcutta Madrasa, but my father did not have a very high opinion of it. At first he taught me himself. Later he appointed different teachers for different subjects. He wished me to be taught by the most eminent scholar in each field.

Students who followed the traditional system of education normally finished their course at an age between twenty and twenty-five. This included a period when the young scholar had to teach pupils and thus prove that he had acquired mastery over what he had learnt. I was able to complete the course by the time I was sixteen, and my father got together some fifteen students to whom I taught higher philosophy, mathematics and logic.

It was soon after this that I first came across the writings of Sir Syed Ahmed Khan. I was greatly impressed by his views on modern education. I realized that a man could not be truly educated in the modern world unless he studied modern science, philosophy and literature. I decided that I must learn English. I spoke to Maulvi [or learned Moslem scholar] Mohammed Yusuf Jafri, who was then chief examiner of the Oriental course of studies. He taught me the English alphabet and gave me Pyarechand Sarkar's *First Book*. As soon as I gained some knowledge of the language, I started to read the Bible. I secured English, Persian and Urdu versions of the book and read them side by side. This helped me greatly in understanding the text. I also started to read English newspapers with the help of a dictionary. In this way, I soon acquired enough knowledge to read

English books and devoted myself specially to the study of history and philosophy.

This was a period of great mental crisis for me. I was born into a family which was deeply imbued with religious traditions. All the conventions of traditional life were accepted without question and the family did not like the least deviation from orthodox ways. I could not reconcile myself to the prevailing customs and beliefs and my heart was full of a new sense of revolt. The ideas I had acquired from my family and early training could no longer satisfy me. I felt that I must find the truth for myself. Almost instinctively I began to move out of my family orbit and seek my own path.

The first thing which troubled me was the exhibition of differences among the different sects of Moslems. I could not understand why they should be so opposed to one another when all of them claimed to derive their inspiration from the same source. Nor could I reconcile myself with the dogmatic assurance with which each sect branded the others as mistaken and heretical. These differences among the orthodox schools began to raise doubts in my mind concerning religion itself. If religion expresses a universal truth, why should there be such differences and conflicts among men professing different religions? Why should each religion claim to be the sole repository of truth and condemn all others as false?

For two or three years, this unrest continued and I longed to find a solution of my doubts. I passed from one phase to another and a stage came when all the old bonds imposed on my mind by family and upbringing were completely shattered. I felt free of all conventional ties and decided that I would chalk out my own path. It was about this time that I decided to adopt the pen name "Azad," or "Free," to indicate that I was no longer tied to my inherited beliefs. I propose to give a more detailed account of these changes in the first volume of my autobiography.

This was also the period when my political ideas began to change. Lord Curzon [6] was then the Viceroy of India. His imperialist attitude and administrative measures raised the Indian political unrest

[6] Curzon was Governor General or Viceroy from 1899 to 1905.

to new heights. The disturbance was most marked in Bengal, as Lord Curzon paid special attention to this province. It was politically the most advanced part of India, and the Hindus of Bengal had taken a leading part in Indian political awakening. In 1905, Lord Curzon decided to partition the province in the belief that this would weaken the Hindus and create a permanent division between the Hindus and the Moslems of Bengal.

Bengal did not take this measure lying down. There was an unprecedented outburst of political and revolutionary enthusiasm. Shri [or Mr.] Arabindo Ghosh [the Indian philosopher] left Baroda and came to Calcutta to make it the centre of his activities. His paper *Karmayogin* became a symbol of national awakening and revolt.

It was during this period that I came into contact with Shri Shyam Sunder Chakravarty, who was one of the important revolutionary workers of the day. Through him I met other revolutionaries. I remember I met Shri Arabindo Ghosh on two or three occasions. The result was that I was attracted to revolutionary politics and joined one of the groups.

In those days the revolutionary groups were recruited exclusively from the Hindu middle classes. In fact all the revolutionary groups were then actively anti-Moslem. They saw that the British Government was using the Moslems against India's political struggle and the Moslems were playing the Government's game. East Bengal had become a separate province and Bamfield Fuller, who was then Lieutenant-Governor, openly said that the Government looked upon the Moslem community as its favorite wife. The revolutionaries felt that the Moslems were an obstacle to the attainment of Indian freedom and must, like other obstacles, be removed.

One other factor was responsible for the revolutionaries' dislike of Moslems. The Government felt that the political awakening among the Hindus of Bengal was so great that no Hindu officer could be fully trusted in dealing with these revolutionary activities. They, therefore, imported a number of Moslem officers from the United Provinces [7] for the manning of the Intelligence Branch of the Police.

[7] Now called Uttar Pradesh (U.P.), a large state in northern India.

The result was that the Hindus of Bengal began to feel that Moslems as such were against political freedom and against the Hindu community.

When Shyam Sunder Chakravarty introduced me to other revolutionaries and my new friends found that I was willing to join them, they were greatly surprised. At first they did not fully trust me and tried to keep me outside their inner councils. In course of time they realized their mistake and I gained their confidence. I began to argue with them that they were wrong in thinking that Moslems as a community were their enemies. I told them that they should not generalize from their experience with a few Moslem officers in Bengal. In Egypt, Iran and Turkey the Moslems were engaged in revolutionary activities for the achievement of democracy and freedom. The Moslems of India would also join in the political struggle if we worked among them and tried to win them as our friends. I also pointed out that active hostility, or even the indifference of Moslems, would make the struggle for political liberty much more difficult. We must, therefore, make every effort to win the support and friendship of the community.

I could not at first convince my revolutionary friends about the correctness of my diagnosis. But in course of time some of them came round to my point of view. During this period I had also started to work among Moslems and found that there was a group of young men ready to take up new political tasks.

When I first joined the revolutionaries I found that their activities were confined to Bengal and Bihar. I may add that Bihar was then a part of the Province of Bengal. I pointed out to my friends that we must extend our activities to other parts of India. At first they were reluctant and said that the nature of their activities was secret. There were risks in extending their connections and, if branches were established in other provinces, it might be difficult to maintain the secrecy which was essential for success. I was, however, able to persuade them and, within two years of the time that I joined, secret societies were established in several of the important towns of northern India and Bombay. I could tell many interesting as well as amusing stories of the way in which organizations were set up and new members recruited, but the readers must wait for a fuller account till the first volume of my autobiography is ready.

It was during this period that I had an occasion to go out of India and tour in Iraq, Egypt, Syria and Turkey. In all these countries I found great interest in French. I also acquired a taste for the language and started to learn it, but I found that English was fast becoming the most widely spread international language and met most of my needs.

I would like to take this opportunity to correct a mistake that has been given currency by the late Mahadev Desai.[8] When he wrote my biography, he put down a number of questions and asked me to answer them. In reply to one question I had said that when I was about twenty I made a tour of the Middle East and spent a long time in Egypt. In reply to another question I had said that traditional education was unsatisfactory and sterile not only in India, but also in the famous university of al Azhar in Cairo. Somehow Mahadev Desai came to the conclusion that I had gone to Egypt to study in al Azhar. The truth is that I was not a student there for a single day. Perhaps his mistake arose out of his idea that if a man has acquired some learning, he must have gone to some university. When Mahadev Desai found that I had been to no Indian university, he inferred that I must have taken a degree from al Azhar.

When I visited Cairo in 1908, the system in al Azhar was so defective that it neither trained the mind nor gave adequate knowledge of ancient Islamic science and philosophy. Sheikh Mohammed Abdul had tried to reform the system, but the old conservative ulamas defeated all his efforts. When he lost all hopes of improving al Azhar, he started a new college, Dar al-Ulum, in Cairo which exists to this date. Since this was the state of affairs in al Azhar, there was no reason why I should go to study there.

From Egypt I went to Turkey and France and had intended to go

[8] Mahatma Gandhi's chief secretary. Died 1942.

to London. I could not do so, as I received news that my father was
ill. I returned from Paris and did not see London till many years
later.

I have already said that my political ideas had turned towards
revolutionary activities before I left Calcutta in 1908. When I came
to Iraq, I met some of the Iranian revolutionaries. In Egypt I came
into contact with the followers of Mustafa Kamal Pasha. I also met
a group of young Turks who had established a centre in Cairo and
were publishing a weekly from there. When I went to Turkey I
became friends with some of the leaders of the Young Turk movement. I kept up my correspondence with them for many years after
my return to India.

Contact with these Arab and Turk revolutionaries confirmed my
political beliefs. They expressed their surprise that Indian Moslems
were either indifferent to, or against, nationalist demands. They
were of the view that Indian Moslems should have led the national
struggle for freedom, and could not understand why Indian Moslems
were mere camp followers of the British. I was more convinced
than ever that Indian Moslems must cooperate in the work of political liberation of the country. Steps must be taken to ensure that they
were not exploited by the British Government. I felt it necessary to
create a new movement among Indian Moslems and decided that,
on my return to India, I would take up political work with greater
earnestness.

After my return, I thought for some time about my future program
of action. I came to the conclusion that we must build up public
opinion and for this a journal was essential. There were a number of
dailies, weeklies and monthlies published in Urdu from the Punjab
and the U.P. but their standard was not very high. Their get-up
and printing were as poor as their contents. They were produced
by the lithographic process and could not therefore embody any of
the features of modern journalism. Nor were they able to print half-
tone pictures. I decided that my journal should be attractive in get-
up and powerful in its appeal. It must be set up in type and not
reproduced by the lithographic process. Accordingly, I established

the al Hilal [the Crescent] Press and the first number of the journal *al Hilal* was published in June 1912.

The publication of *al Hilal* marks a turning point in the history of Urdu journalism. It achieved unprecedented popularity within a short time. The public was attracted, not only by the superior printing and production of the paper, but even more by the new note of strong nationalism preached by it. *Al Hilal* created a revolutionary stir among the masses. The demand for *al Hilal* was so great that, within the first three months, all the old issues had to be reprinted as every new subscriber wanted the entire set.

The leadership of Moslem politics at this time was in the hands of the Aligarh party. Its members regarded themselves as the trustees of Sir Syed Ahmed's policies. Their basic tenet was that Moslems must be loyal to the British Crown and remain aloof from the freedom movement. When *al Hilal* raised a different slogan and its popularity and circulation increased fast, they felt that their leadership was threatened. They therefore began to oppose *al Hilal* and even went to the extent of threatening to kill its editor. The more the old leadership opposed it, the more popular *al Hilal* became with the community. Within two years, *al Hilal* reached a circulation of 26,000 copies per week, a figure which was till then unheard of in Urdu journalism.

The Government was also disturbed by this success of *al Hilal*. It demanded a security of Rs 2000 [or 2,000 rupees] under the Press Act and thought this might curb its tone. I did not allow myself to be daunted by these pinpricks. Soon the Government forfeited the deposit and demanded a fresh deposit of Rs 10,000. This also was soon lost. In the meantime war had broken out in 1914 and the al Hilal Press was confiscated in 1915. After five months, I started a new press called al Balagh [the Message] and brought out a journal under the same name. The Government now felt that they could not stop my activities by using only the Press Act. Accordingly they resorted to the Defence of India Regulations and in April 1916 externed me from Calcutta. The Governments of Punjab, Delhi, U.P. and Bombay had already prohibited me from entering these prov-

inces under the same regulations. The only place I could go to was
Bihar and I went to Ranchi. After another six months, I was interned
in Ranchi and remained in detention till 31 December 1919. On 1
January 1920 I was, along with other internees and prisoners, released from internment under the King's declaration.

Gandhiji [9] had by this time appeared on the Indian political scene.
When I was an internee at Ranchi, he came there in connection
with his work among the peasants in Champaran. He expressed a
wish to meet me but the Bihar Government did not give him the
necessary permission. It was therefore only after my release in
January 1920 that I met him for the first time in Delhi. There was a
proposal to send a deputation to the Viceroy to acquaint him with
the feelings of Indian Moslems regarding the Khilafat [or Caliphate]
and Turkey's future. Gandhiji participated in the discussions and
expressed his complete sympathy with, and interest in, the proposal.
He declared himself ready to be associated with the Moslems on
this issue. On 20 January 1920, a meeting was held in Delhi. Apart
from Gandhiji, Lokmanya Tilak and other Congress leaders also supported the stand of Indian Moslems on the question of the Khilafat.

The deputation met the Viceroy. I had signed the memorial but
did not go with the deputation as I was of the view that matters had
gone beyond memorials and deputations. In his reply, the Viceroy
said that the Government would offer the necessary facilities if a
deputation were sent to London to present the Moslem point of view
before the British Government. He expressed his inability to do
anything himself.

The question now arose about the next step. A meeting was held
in which Mr. Mohammed Ali, Mr. Shaukat Ali, Hakim Ajmal Khan
and Maulvi Abdul Bari of Firingi-mahal, Lucknow, were also present. Gandhiji presented his program of noncooperation. He said
that the days of deputations and memorials were over. We must
withdraw all support from the Government and this alone would
persuade the Government to come to terms. He suggested that all
Government titles should be returned, law courts and educational

[9] -ji is a suffix of respect and affection.

institutions should be boycotted, Indians should resign from the
services and refuse to take any part in the newly constituted
legislatures.

As soon as Gandhiji described his proposal, I remembered that
this was the program which Tolstoy had outlined many years ago.
In 1901, an anarchist attacked the king of Italy. Tolstoy at the time
addressed an open letter to the anarchists that the method of violence
was morally wrong and politically of little use. If one man were
killed, another would always take his place. In fact, violence always
engendered greater violence. In the Greek legend, 999 warriors
sprouted out of the blood of every warrior killed. To indulge in
political murder was to sow the dragon's teeth. Tolstoy advised that
the proper method to paralyze an oppressive government was to
refuse taxes, resign from all services and boycott institutions supporting the Government. He believed that such a program would com-
pel any government to come to terms. I also remembered that I had
myself suggested a similar program in some articles in *al Hilal.*

Others reacted according to their own backgrounds. Hakim
Ajmal Khan said that he wanted some time to consider the program. He would not like to advise others till he was willing to accept
the program himself. Maulvi Abdul Bari said that Gandhiji's suggestions raised fundamental issues and he could not give a reply
till he had meditated and sought divine guidance. Mohammed Ali
and Shaukat Ali said they would wait till Maulvi Abdul Bari's
decision was known. Gandhiji then turned to me. I said without a
moment's hesitation that I fully accepted the program. If people
really wanted to help Turkey, there was no alternative to the program sketched by Gandhiji.

After a few weeks, a Khilafat Conference was held at Meerut.
It was in this conference that Gandhiji preached for the first time
the noncooperation program from a public platform. After he had
spoken, I followed him and gave him my unqualified support.

In September 1920, a special session of the Congress [party] was
held at Calcutta to consider the program for action prepared by
Gandhiji. Gandhiji said that the program of noncooperation was

necessary if we wished to achieve Swaraj [national independence] and solve the Khilafat problem in a satisfactory manner. Lala Lajpat Rai was the President of this session and Mr. C. R. Das one of its leading figures. Neither of them agreed with Gandhiji. Bipin Chandra Pal also spoke forcefully and said that the best weapon to fight the British Government was to boycott British goods. He did not have much faith in the other items of Gandhiji's program. In spite of their opposition, the resolution for the noncooperation movement was passed with an overwhelming majority.

There followed a period of intensive touring to prepare the country for the noncooperation program. Gandhiji traveled extensively. I was with him most of the time and Mohammed Ali and Shaukat Ali were often our companions. In December 1920, the annual session of the Congress was held in Nagpur. By this time, the temper of the country had changed. Mr. C. R. Das now openly favored the noncooperation program. Lala Lajpat Rai was at first somewhat opposed but, when he found that the Punjab delegates were all supporting Gandhiji, he also joined our ranks. It was during this session that Mr. Jinnah [10] finally left the Congress.

The Government retaliated by arresting leaders throughout the country. In Bengal, Mr. C. R. Das and I were among the first to be arrested. Subhas Chandra Bose and Birenda Nath Sasmal also joined us in prison. We were all placed in the European ward of the Alipore Central jail which became a centre for political discussions.

Mr. C. R. Das was sentenced to six months' imprisonment. I was held under trial for a long time and finally awarded one year's imprisonment. I was in fact not released till 1 January 1923. Mr. C. R. Das was released earlier and presided over the Congress at its Gaya session. During this session, sharp differences of opinion appeared among the Congress leaders. C. R. Das, Motilal Nehru and Hakim Ajmal Khan formed the Swaraj party and presented the Council entry program, which was opposed by the orthodox followers of Gandhiji. Congress was thus divided between no-changers and pro-changers. When I came out, I tried to bring about a reconcilia-

[10] Mohammed Ali Jinnah, subsequently the founder of Pakistan.

tion between the two groups and we were able to reach an agreement in the special session of the Congress in September 1923. I was then thirty-five and was asked to preside over this session. It was said that I was the youngest man to be elected President of the Congress.

After 1923, Congress activities remained mainly in the hands of the Swaraj party. It obtained large majorities in almost all legislatures and carried the fight on the parliamentary front. Congressmen who remained outside the Swaraj party continued with their constructive program but they could not attract as much public support or attention as the Swaraj party. There were many incidents which have a bearing on the future development of Indian politics, but I must ask the reader to wait for a fuller account till the first volume of my autobiography is published.

In 1928, political excitement mounted with the appointment of the Simon Commission [11] and its visit to India. In 1929, Congress passed the Independence resolution and gave the British Government one year's notice of its intention to launch a mass movement if the national demand were not fulfilled. The British refused to comply with our demand, and, in 1930, Congress declared that Salt laws [12] would be violated. Many people were skeptical when the Salt Satyagraha [or civil disobedience. Literally: truth-grasping] began but as the movement gathered strength both the Government and the people were taken by surprise. The Government took strong action and declared the Congress an unlawful organization. It ordered the arrest of the Congress President and his Working [or Executive] Committee. We met the challenge by authorizing each Congress president to nominate his successor. I was elected one of the presidents and nominated my Working Committee. Before I was arrested, I nominated Dr. Ansari as my successor. At first he was not willing to join the movement but I was able to persuade him. In this way, we were able to baffle the Government and keep the movement going.

[11] Led by John Simon, later Sir and Lord.
[12] The British Government had a monopoly on salt production in India.

My arrest was on the basis of a speech I had delivered in Meerut. I was therefore detained in the Meerut jail for about a year and a half.

After the struggle had continued over a year, Lord Irwin [13] released Gandhiji and the other members of the Working Committee. We met first at Allahabad and then at Delhi and the Gandhi-Irwin Pact was signed. This led to a general release of Congressmen and the participation of Congress in the round-table conference. Gandhiji was sent as our sole representative but the negotiations proved abortive and Gandhiji returned empty-handed. On his return from London, Gandhiji was again arrested and a policy of fresh repression was launched. Lord Willingdon was the new Viceroy and he took strong action against all Congressmen. I was at Delhi and detained in the Delhi jail for over a year. This period saw many incidents of great significance in Indian political history but for these also the readers must wait for the first volume.

In 1935, the Government of India Act was passed which provided for provincial autonomy and a federal government at the centre. It is here that the story I wish to tell in the present volume begins.

[13] Later Lord Halifax, Foreign Secretary and Ambassador to Washington.

CHAPTER 2

Congress in Office

IN the first elections held in accordance with the Government of India Act 1935 the Congress won an overwhelming victory. It secured an absolute majority in five of the major provinces and was the largest single party in four. It was only in the Punjab and Sind that the Congress did not achieve comparable success.

This victory of the Congress has to be judged against the Congress' early reluctance to contest the elections at all. The Government of India Act 1935 provided for provincial autonomy but there was a fly in the ointment. Special powers were reserved to the governors to declare a state of emergency, and, once a governor did so, he could suspend the constitution and assume all powers to himself. Democracy in the provinces could therefore function only so long as the governors permitted it. The position was even worse so far as the Central Government was concerned. Here there was an attempt to reintroduce the principle of diarchy which had already been discredited in the provinces. Not only was the Central Government to be a weak federation, but it was also overweighted in favor of the princes [the maharajahs, rajahs, hawabs and other hereditary rulers of more than six hundred states scattered throughout India] and other vested interests. These could generally be expected to side with the British rulers of the country.

It was therefore not surprising that the Congress which was fighting for complete independence of the country was averse to accepting this arrangement. The Congress condemned outright the type of federation proposed for the Central Government. For a long

15

time, the Congress Working Committee was also against the scheme proposed for the provinces. It had a strong section which was opposed even to participating in the elections. My views were quite different. I held that it would be a mistake to boycott the elections. If the Congress did so, less desirable elements would capture the central and provincial legislatures and speak in the name of the Indian people. Besides, the election campaign offered a splendid opportunity for educating the masses in the basic issues of Indian politics. Ultimately the point of view I represented prevailed, and the Congress participated in the elections with results which I have already indicated.

New differences were now revealed within the leadership of the Congress. A section of those who had participated in the elections opposed assumption of office by Congress nominees. They argued that, with special powers reserved to the governors, provincial autonomy was a mockery. Ministries would hold office at the Governor's pleasure. If Congress wished to carry out its election pledges, a clash with the Governor was inevitable. They argued that Congress should therefore try to wreck the constitution from within the Legislature. On this issue also I held the opposite view and argued that the powers given to the provincial governments should be exercised to the full. If a clash with the Governor arose, it should be faced as and when occasion demanded. Without actual exercise of power, the program of the Congress could not be carried out. If, on the other hand, Congress Ministries had to go out on a popular issue, it would only strengthen the hold of the Congress on the popular imagination.

The governors did not wait for the conclusion of this debate. When they found that Congress was hesitating to form the Ministry, they sent for the parties which had the second largest support in the Legislature, even though they did not command a majority. These interim Ministries were formed by non-Congress and, in some cases, anti-Congress elements. Congress indecision about acceptance of office not only indicated divisions of opinion within its ranks, but what is worse it allowed reactionary forces an opportunity to get over the shock of the defeat in the General Elections and retrieve lost ground. During the prolonged negotiations with the Viceroy, an attempt was made to wrest an assurance that the governors would not interfere with the work of the Ministries. After the Viceroy clarified the position, some members of the Working Committee changed their opinion in favor of acceptance of office. Congress had, however, spoken so strongly and insistently against the Government of India Act that, in spite of growing recognition of the need to change the policy, nobody dared to suggest it openly. Jawaharlal [Nehru] was President of the Congress at the time. He had expressed himself in such categorical terms against the acceptance of office that it was difficult for him to propose acceptance now. When the Working Committee met at Wardha, I found a strange reluctance to face facts. I, therefore, proposed in clear terms that Congress should accept office. After some discussion Gandhiji supported my view and Congress decided to form Ministries in the provinces. This was a historic decision, for till now Congress had followed only a negative policy and refused to undertake the responsibility of office. Now, for the first time, Congress adopted a positive attitude towards administration and agreed to take up the burden of government.

One incident happened at the time which left a bad impression about the attitude of the provincial Congress committees. The Congress had grown as a national organization and given the opportunity of leadership to men of different communities. In Bombay, Mr. Nariman was the acknowledged leader of the local Congress. When the question of forming the provincial Government arose, there was general expectation that Mr. Nariman would be asked to lead it in view of his status and record. This was not, however, done. Sardar [an honorary title] Vallabhbhai Patel and his colleagues did not like Nariman and the result was that Mr. B. G. Kher became the first Chief Minister of Bombay. Since Nariman was a Parsee and Kher a Hindu, this led to wide speculation that Nariman had been by-passed on communal grounds. Even if it is not true, it is difficult to disprove such an allegation.

Mr. Nariman was naturally upset about this decision. He raised the question before the Congress Working Committee. Jawaharlal was still President and many hoped that, in view of his freedom from communal [1] bias, he would rectify the injustice to Nariman. Unfortunately, this did not happen. Jawaharlal did not agree with Sardar Patel in many things but he did not also think that Sardar Patel would take a decision on communal considerations alone. He reacted somewhat unfavorably and rejected Nariman's appeal.

Nariman was surprised at Jawaharlal's attitude. He then approached Gandhiji and said that he would place his case in Gandhiji's hands. Gandhiji listened patiently and directed that the charge against Sardar Patel should be investigated by a neutral person.

Since Nariman was himself a Parsee, Sardar Patel and his friends suggested that a Parsee should be entrusted with the enquiry. They had planned their move carefully and prepared the case in a way which clouded the issues. In addition, they exercised their influence in various ways so that poor Nariman had lost the case even before the enquiry began. It was in any case very difficult to establish positively that Nariman had been overlooked only because he was a Parsee. It was therefore held that nothing was proved against Sardar Patel. Poor Nariman was heartbroken and his public life came to an end.

As I reflect on the treatment meted out to Mr. Nariman, my mind goes back to Mr. C. R. Das, one of the most powerful personalities thrown up by the Noncooperation Movement. Mr. Das occupies a very special position in the history of our national struggle. He was a man of great vision and breadth of imagination. At the same time he had a practical mind which looked at every question from the point of view of a realist. He had the courage of his convictions

[1] The word "communal" as it was and is used in India refers to religious communities: Hindu, Moslem, Parsee, Christian and so on. The communal approach contrasts with the attitude of the nationalists (like Azad, Nehru and Gandhi), who regard an Indian as an Indian irrespective of religious affiliation. The Congress party included and includes members of all religious communities, and its politics therefore are not communal. The Moslem League, on the other hand, is restricted to Moslem members and Moslem interests. Similarly, the Hindu Mahasabha caters to Hindu interests. The nationalists desire to integrate the religious communities, the communal organizations seek to segregate them.

and stood up fearlessly for any position he regarded as being right. When Gandhiji placed the noncooperation program before the country, Mr. Das had at first opposed it in the special session held at Calcutta in 1920. A year later, when the Congress met at Nagpur, he joined our ranks and the program of noncooperation was launched. Mr. Das had a princely practice at the Calcutta bar and was one of the most successful lawyers in the country. He was also noted for his fondness for luxury, but he gave up his practice without a moment's hesitation, donned khaddar and threw himself wholeheartedly into the Congress movement. I was greatly impressed by him.

As I have said, Mr. Das had a practical bent of mind. He looked at political questions from the point of view of what was both desirable and practicable. He held that, if India were to win her freedom through negotiations, she must be prepared to achieve it step by step. Independence could not come all of a sudden where the method followed was that of discussion and persuasion. He predicted that the first step would be the achievement of provincial autonomy. He was satisfied that the exercise of even limited power would advance the cause of India's freedom and prepare Indians for undertaking larger responsibilities as and when they were won. It is a measure of Mr. Das's foresight and vision that it was on these lines that the Government of India Act 1935 was passed almost ten years after his death.

In 1921, the then Prince of Wales [2] came to India in connection with the inauguration of the Montagu-Chelmsford scheme of reforms. The Congress had decided to boycott all receptions organized to welcome the Prince. This placed the Government of India in a quandary. The Viceroy had assured the British Government that the Prince would receive a warm welcome in the country. When he learnt of the Congress decision, he took every possible measure to defeat the boycott. The Government did not succeed in its aims and the Prince of Wales was coldly received in almost every town he visited. His last halt was in Calcutta, which was then the most im-

[2] Later King Edward VIII and Duke of Windsor.

portant city of India. The capital had shifted to Delhi but the Viceroy spent every Christmas in Calcutta. A special function had been organized in the city and the Prince of Wales was to open the Victoria Memorial Hall. Elaborate arrangements were, therefore, made for his reception and the Government spared no effort to make his visit to Calcutta a success.

We were then all detained in the Alipore Central jail. Pandit [or scholar, a Hindu title] Madan Mohan Malaviya was trying to arrange a settlement between the Congress and the Government. He met the Viceroy and came back with the impression that if we agreed not to boycott the Prince of Wales in Calcutta, the Government would come to a settlement with the Congress. Pandit Madan Mohan Malaviya came to Alipore Jail to discuss the proposal with Mr. Das and me. The basis of the proposal was that a round-table conference should be called to settle the question of India's political future. We did not give a final reply to Pandit Malaviya as we wanted to discuss the question among ourselves. Both Mr. Das and I came to the conclusion that it was our boycott of the Prince of Wales which had compelled the Government of India to seek a settlement. We should take advantage of the situation and meet in a round-table conference. It was clear to us that this would not lead to our goal but nonetheless it would mark a great step forward in our political struggle. All the Congress leaders except Gandhiji were then in jail. We proposed that we should accept the British offer but at the same time we laid it down as a condition that all Congress leaders must be released before the round-table conference was held.

When next day Pandit Malaviya came to see us again, we informed him of our views. We also told him that he should meet Gandhiji and secure his consent. Pandit Malaviya reported back to the Viceroy and after two days visited us again in the jail. He said that the Government of India was willing to release all the political leaders who were to take part in the discussions. This included the Ali brothers and many other Congress leaders. A statement was prepared by us in which we put down our views in clear terms. Pandit Malaviya took the document and went to Bombay to meet Gandhiji.

To our surprise and regret, Gandhiji did not accept our suggestion. He insisted that all the political leaders, particularly the Ali brothers, must first be released unconditionally. He declared that we could consider the proposal for a round table only after they had been released. Both Mr. Das and I felt that this demand was a mistake. When the Government had agreed that the Congress leaders would be released before the round table, there was no point in such special insistence. Pandit Malaviya went again to Gandhiji with our comments but he did not agree. The result was that the Viceroy dropped his proposal. His main purpose in making the offer had been to avoid a boycott of the Prince of Wales in Calcutta. Since no settlement was made, the boycott was a great success but we had missed a golden opportunity for a political settlement. Mr. Das made no secret of his disapproval and disappointment.

Gandhiji then called a conference in Bombay with C. Sankaran Nair as the Chairman. In this Conference, Gandhiji himself made a proposal for a round-table conference. His terms were almost the same as those brought earlier by Pandit Malaviya. The Prince of Wales had in the meantime left India and the Government had no further interest in the proposal. They paid no attention whatever to Gandhiji's suggestion and rejected it outright. Mr. Das was furious and said that Gandhiji had committed a great mistake. I could not but accept his judgment as correct.

Gandhiji then went on to suspend the noncooperation movement on account of the Chouri Choura incident.[3] This caused a severe political reaction in political circles and demoralized the country. The Government took full advantage of the situation and arrested Gandhiji. He was sentenced to six years' imprisonment and the noncooperation movement slowly petered out.

Mr. C. R. Das used to discuss the situation with me almost every

[3] On February 5, 1922, during a limited civil disobedience movement in a county in Bombay Province, an Indian mob in the small town of Chouri Choura (U.P.), 800 miles from Bombay, killed a number of policemen. Gandhi called it "a brutal murder" and suspended civil disobedience on moral grounds. To "undergo personal cleansing" he fasted five days because he had not been able to "control the unruly elements."

day. He was convinced that Gandhiji had erred grievously in calling
off the movement. This had so demoralized political workers that
it would take many years before public enthusiasm could again
be roused. Besides, Mr. Das held that Gandhiji's direct methods
had failed. He therefore thought that we must adopt other ways
to restore public morale. He was not in favor of waiting and watch-
ing till the situation again improved. He believed in an alternative
program and said that, in the existing situation, direct action must
be given up and the political fight taken inside the legislatures.
Under Gandhiji's influence, the Congress had boycotted the elections
held in 1921. Mr. Das declared that Congress must prepare to capture the legislatures in 1924 and use them to further our political
ends. Mr. Das was hopeful that all active leaders of the Congress
would agree with his analysis and remedy. I thought he was over-
optimistic but I agreed with him that when he was released he
should consult friends and prepare a new program for the country.

Mr. Das came out on the eve of the Gaya Congress. The Reception Committee elected him the President and Mr. Das felt that he
could carry the country with his program. He was encouraged all
the more when he found that Hakim Ajmal Khan, Pandit Motilal
Nehru [father of Jawaharlal] and Sardar Vithalbhai Patel [brother of
Vallabhbhai] agreed with his approach. In his presidential address,
Mr. Das proposed that the Congress should accept the Council
entry program and carry the political struggle into the legislatures.
Gandhiji was at the time in jail. A section of the Congress led by
Shri Rajagopalachari [4] opposed Mr. Das. They felt that, if direct
action was given up and Mr. Das's program accepted, the Govern-
ment would interpret it as a repudiation of Gandhiji's leadership.

I do not think that Shri Rajagopalachari was right in his interpretation. Mr. Das was not seeking a compromise with the Government but only extending the political struggle to another field. He
explained this at length but he did not succeed in converting the
rank and file of the Congress. Shri Rajagopalachari, Dr. Rajendra
Prasad [who was later President of India] and others opposed him

---

[4] Also called Rajaji; later Governor General of independent India.

and defeated his proposal. The Gaya Congress split and Mr. Das tendered his resignation. All the energy of Congressmen was now spent in an internecine struggle between the two groups called the no-changers and the pro-changers.

After another six months, I also came out of jail. I found that the Congress was facing a serious crisis. Instead of the political struggle against the British, the energy of all Congressmen was being dissipated in internecine warfare. Mr. Das, Pandit Motilal and Hakim Ajmal Khan were leading the camp of pro-changers. Rajaji, Sardar Patel and Dr. Rajendra Prasad were the spokesmen for the no-changers. Both groups tried to win me but I refused to identify myself with either camp. I saw that these internal dissensions were dangerous and unless checked in time might break up the Congress. I therefore decided to remain outside both camps and tried to redirect all our attention to the political struggle. I am happy to say that I was successful in my efforts. A special session of the Congress was held at Delhi and I was elected President with the approval of both the groups.

In my presidential address, I stressed the fact that our real object was the liberation of the country. Since 1919, we had been following a program of direct action and this had yielded considerable results. If now some among us felt that we must carry the fight into the legislatures, there was no reason why we should stick rigidly to our earlier decision. So long as the objective was the same, each group should be free to follow the program which it considered best.

The decision of the Delhi Congress was as I had anticipated. It was agreed that pro-changers and no-changers should be free to pursue their own programs. Dr. Rajendra Prasad, Shri Rajagopalachari and their associates took up the constructive program.[5] Mr. C. R. Das, Pandit Motilal and Hakim Ajmel Khan founded the Swaraj party and decided to contest the elections. Their move created great enthusiasm throughout the country. In the central as

[5] This refers to Gandhi's constructive social program: the use of the spinning wheel; wearing of homespun clothing, called khadai or khaddar; basic education; nondiscrimination of untouchables; village uplift, and so on.

well as in all the provincial assemblies, the Swaraj party won a very
large following.

One of the major objections of the no-changers had been that
Gandhiji's leadership would be weakened by the Council entry
program. Events proved that they were wrong. In the Central
Legislature, the Swaraj party proposed a resolution urging the immediate release of Mahatma Gandhi. Before the resolution could be
passed, Gandhiji was released.

I have said that the Swaraj party won a large following in the
central as well as the provincial legislatures. Perhaps its most remarkable achievement was its success in capturing seats reserved for
Moslems.[6] This was largely due to the political realism of Mr. Das,
to which I have referred above. The electorates were communal
[or religiously minded] and only Moslem voters returned Moslem
legislators. The Moslem League and other communal parties were
therefore able to play upon the fears of the Moslems and generally
returned candidates with communal leanings. Mr. Das was able to
overcome the apprehensions of the Moslems of Bengal and was
acclaimed as their leader. The way he solved the communal problem
of Bengal is memorable and should serve as an example even today.

In Bengal, Moslems were the majority community, but for various
reasons they were educationally and politically backward. Even
though they numbered over 50 per cent of the population, they held
hardly 30 per cent of the posts under the Government. Mr. C. R. Das
was a great realist and immediately saw that the problem was an
economic one. He realized that, till the Moslems were given the
necessary assurances for their economic future, they could not be
expected to join the Congress wholeheartedly. He therefore made a
declaration which impressed not only Bengal but the whole of India.
He announced that, when Congress secured the reins of powers in
Bengal, it would reserve 60 per cent of all new appointments for the
Moslems till such time as they achieved proper representation according to population. He went even further in respect of the Cal-

---

[6] Under the law, a minimum number of seats in legislatures were reserved
for the Moslem and other minorities.

cutta Corporation [or Municipality] and offered to reserve 80 per cent of the new appointments on similar terms. He pointed out that, so long as the Moslems were not properly represented in public life and in the services, there could be no true democracy in Bengal. Once the inequalities had been rectified, Moslems would be able to compete on equal terms with other communities and there would be no need for any special reservation.

This bold announcement shook the Bengal Congress to its very foundation. Many of the Congress leaders violently opposed it and started a campaign against Mr. Das. He was accused of opportunism and even partisanship for the Moslems but he stood solid as a rock. He toured the whole province and explained his point of view. His attitude made a great impression on Moslems in Bengal and outside. I am convinced that if he had not died a premature death, he would have created a new atmosphere in the country. It is a matter for regret that, after he died, some of his followers assailed his position and his declaration was repudiated. The result was that the Moslems of Bengal moved away from the Congress and the first seeds of partition were sown.

I must, however, make one fact clear. The Provincial Congress Committee of Bombay erred in denying local leadership to Mr. Nariman and the Working Committee was not strong enough to rectify the wrong. Apart from this one lapse, Congress made every effort to live up to its principles. Once the ministries were formed, necessary measures were taken to ensure justice to all minorities.

This was the first occasion on which Congress was taking up the responsibility of administration. It was thus a trial for the Congress and people watched how the organization would live up to its national character. The Moslem League's [7] main propaganda against Congress had been that it was national [8] only in name. Not content with defaming Congress in general terms, the League also gave out that the Congress Ministries were carrying out atrocities against the

[7] Mr. Jinnah's communal party.

[8] Nationalist as distinguished from communal. Jinnah argued that the Congress was a Hindu party. Maulana Azad's position in the Congress leadership was one of the arguments used to refute this charge.

minorities. It appointed a committee which presented a report making all kinds of allegations about unfair treatment of Moslem and other minorities. I can speak from personal knowledge that these allegations were absolutely unfounded. This was also the view which was held by the Viceroy and the governors of different provinces. As such, the Report prepared by the League carried no conviction among sensible people.

When Congress accepted office, a parliamentary board was formed to supervise the work of the Ministries and give them general guidance on policy. The Board consisted of Sardar Patel, Dr. Rajendra Prasad and myself. I was thus in charge of the parliamentary affairs in several provinces, viz., Bengal, Bihar, U.P., Punjab, Sind and the Frontier. Every incident which involved communal issues came up before me. From personal knowledge and with a full sense of responsibility, I can therefore say that the charges levelled by Mr. Jinnah and the Moslem League with regard to injustice to Moslems and other minorities were absolutely false. If there had been an iota of truth in any of these charges, I would have seen to it that the injustice was rectified. I was even prepared to resign, if necessary, on an issue like this.

The Congress Ministries were in office a little less than two years, but during this short period several important issues were settled in principle. Special mention may be made of the legislation on Zamindari or proprietorship in land, of liquidating agricultural indebtedness and undertaking a vast program of education both for children and adults.

Problems like the abolition of landlordism and the dissolution of agricultural indebtedness were not without difficulty. Many longstanding interests were challenged by such legislation. It is, therefore, not surprising that the vested interests fought Congress at every step. In Bihar, there was strenuous opposition to measures of land reform and I had to intervene personally in order to settle the issue. After prolonged consultations with the landlords, we were able to evolve a formula which allayed their legitimate fears while guaranteeing to the peasants their rights.

That we were able to solve such ticklish problems was largely due to the fact that I had never been identified with any particular section of the Congress. I have already said how I helped to bring together the pro-changers and the no-changers during the early twenties. This conflict was over, but, during the thirties, Congress was sharply divided between what were called the rightists and the leftists. The rightists were regarded as the champions of the vested interests. The leftists, on the other hand, prospered on their revolutionary zeal. I gave due weight to the fears of the rightists but at the same time my sympathies were with the leftists in the matter of reform. I was, therefore, able to mediate between the two extreme points of view and hoped that Congress would carry out its program steadily and without conflict. All plans for the gradual fulfilment of the Congress Election Programme were, however, suspended in 1939 on account of the play of international forces.

CHAPTER 3

War in Europe

THE events related in the last chapter were taking place against the sombre background of impending war. During the entire period under review an international crisis was deepening in Europe. It was becoming more and more evident that war was unavoidable. The incorporation of Austria into the German Reich was followed soon after by demands on Sudetenland.

War seemed almost inevitable when Mr. Chamberlain made his dramatic trip to Munich. There was an understanding between Germany and Britain, and a part of Czechoslovakia came under German occupation without war. For the moment it appeared as if war was averted, but later events proved that the Munich Pact did not help the cause of peace. On the contrary, it brought war nearer and, within a year of Munich, Great Britain was forced to declare war on Germany.

Congress had not been happy over these developments in Europe. At its session held at Tripuri in March 1939, it had passed the following Resolution:

The Congress records its entire disapproval of British Foreign Policy culminating in the Munich Pact, the Anglo-Italian Agreement and the recognition of Rebel Spain. This policy has been one of deliberate betrayal of democracy, repeated breach of pledges, the ending of the system of collective security and co-operation with governments which are avowed enemies of democracy and freedom. As a result of this policy, the world is being reduced to a state of international anarchy where brutal violence triumphs and flourishes unchecked and decides the fate of nations, and in the name of peace stupendous preparations are being made for the most terrible of wars. International morality has sunk so low in Central and South-Western Europe that the world has witnessed with horror the organised terrorism of the Nazi Government against people of the Jewish race and the continuous bombing from the air by rebel forces of cities and civilian inhabitants and helpless refugees.

The Congress dissociates itself entirely from British foreign policy which has consistently aided the Fascist Powers and helped in the destruction of democratic countries. The Congress is opposed to Imperialism and Fascism alike and is convinced that world peace and progress required the ending of both of these. In the opinion of the Congress, it is urgently necessary for India to direct her own foreign policy as an independent nation, thereby keeping aloof from both Imperialism and Fascism, and pursuing her path of peace and freedom.

As the storms gathered on the international scene, a deepening gloom descended on Gandhiji's mind. He was suffering throughout this period from an intense mental crisis. His personal agony was aggravated by appeals made to him by societies and individuals from Europe and America asking him to do something to avert the impending war. Pacifists all over the world looked to him as their natural leader in securing the maintenance of peace.

Gandhiji thought deeply over this question and ultimately suggested to the Congress Working Committee that India must declare its stand in this international crisis. His view was that India must not participate in the impending war in any circumstances, even if such participation meant the achievement of Indian freedom.

I differed from Gandhiji on this issue. My view was that Europe was divided into two camps. One camp represented the forces of nazism and fascism, while the other represented the democratic forces. In a struggle between these two camps, I had no doubt in my mind that India should side with the democracies provided she was free. If, however, the British did not recognize Indian freedom, it was too much to expect that India should fight for the freedom of other nations while she was denied her own freedom. In such a situation India should noncooperate and offer no help whatever to the British Government in its war efforts.

As on various other issues, the Congress Working Committee was divided on this as well. In fact, some of the members were not clear in their views. Pandit Jawaharlal Nehru generally agreed with me but there were many others who felt that they should side with Gandhiji. They, however, realized that, if Gandhiji's policy were followed to its logical conclusion, it would lead to an impasse. They were therefore in a fix and the Congress Working Committee considered the issues without coming to any decision.

While Congress thus hesitated, a crisis was precipitated in India immediately after the declaration of war. When the United Kingdom declared war on Germany on 3 September 1939, she appealed to all members of the Commonwealth to do so. The Dominion Parliaments met and declared war. In the case of India, the Viceroy on his own declared war on Germany without even the formality of consulting the Central Legislature. The Viceroy's action proved afresh, if further proof was necessary, that the British Government looked on India as a creature of its will and was not willing to recognize India's right to decide her course for herself even in a matter like war.

When India was thus unceremoniously dragged into the war, Gandhiji's mental distress reached almost a breaking point. He could not reconcile himself to India's participating in the war in any circumstances. But whatever he felt, a decision of the Viceroy had landed India in the war without any reference to the will of the Indian people.

The views of Congress were clearly expressed in the Resolution passed at the meeting of the Working Committee held at Wardha on 8-15 September 1939. I will quote this resolution in full, as it is one of the clearest statements of the Congress attitude to the war and on the role of the democracies in the international field. The resolution runs as follows:—

The Working Committee have given their earnest consideration to the grave crisis that has developed owing to the declaration of war in Europe. The principles which should guide the nation in the event of war have been repeatedly laid down by the Congress, and only a month ago this committee reiterated them and expressed their displeasure at the flouting of Indian opinion by the British Government in India. As a first step to dissociate themselves from this policy of the British Government, the Committee called upon the Congress members of the Central Legislative Assembly to refrain from attending the next session. Since then the British Government have declared India as a belligerent country, promulgated Ordinances, passed the Government of India Act Amending Bill, and taken other far-reaching measures which affect the Indian people vitally, and circumscribe and limit the powers and activities of the provincial governments. This has been done without the consent of the Indian people whose declared wishes in such matters have been deliberately ignored by the British Government. The Working Committee must take the gravest view of these developments.

The Congress has repeatedly declared its entire disapproval of the ideology and practice of Fascism and Nazism and their glorification of war and violence and the suppression of the human spirit. It has condemned the aggression in which they have repeatedly indulged and their sweeping away of well-established principles and recognised standards of civilised behaviour. It has seen in Fascism and Nazism the intensification of the principles of Imperialism against which the Indian people have struggled for many years. The Working Committee must therefore unhesitatingly condemn the latest aggression of the Nazi Government in Germany against Poland and sympathise with those who resist it.

The Congress has further laid down that the issue of war and peace for India must be decided by the Indian people, and no outside authority can impose this decision upon them, nor can the Indian people permit their resources to be exploited for imperialist ends. Any imposed decision, or attempt to use India's resources, for purposes not approved by them, will necessarily have to be opposed by them. If co-operation is desired in a worthy cause, this cannot be obtained by compulsion and imposition, and the Committee cannot agree to the carrying out by the Indian people of orders issued by external authority. Co-operation must be between equals by mutual consent for a cause which both consider to be worthy. The people of India have, in the recent past, faced great risks and willingly made great sacrifices to secure their own freedom and establish a free democratic state in India, and their sympathy is entirely on the side of democracy and freedom. But India cannot associate herself in a war said to be for democratic freedom when that very freedom is denied to her, and such limited freedom as she possesses taken away from her.

The Committee are aware that the Governments of Great Britain and

France have declared that they are fighting for democracy and freedom and to put an end to aggression. But the history of the recent past is full of examples showing the constant divergence between the spoken word, the ideals proclaimed, and the real motives and objectives. During the war of 1914-18, the declared war aims were, preservation of democracy, self-determination, and the freedom of small nations, and yet the very Governments which solemnly proclaimed these aims entered into secret treaties embodying imperialist designs for the carving up of the Ottoman Empire. While stating that they did not want any acquisition of territory, the victorious Powers added largely to their colonial domains. The present European war itself signifies the abject failure of the treaty of Versailles and of its makers, who broke their pledged word and imposed an imperialist peace on the defeated nations. The one hopeful outcome of that Treaty, the League of Nations, was muzzled and strangled at the outset and later killed by its parent States.

Subsequent history has demonstrated afresh how even a seemingly fervent declaration of faith may be followed by an ignoble desertion. In Manchuria the British Government connived at aggression; in Abyssinia they acquiesced in it. In Czechoslovakia and Spain democracy was in peril and it was deliberately betrayed, and the whole system of collective security was sabotaged by the very powers who had previously declared their firm faith in it.

Again it is asserted that democracy is in danger and must be defended and with this statement the Committee are in entire agreement. The Committee believe that the peoples of the West are moved by this ideal and objective and for these they are prepared to make sacrifices. But again and again the ideals and sentiments of the people and of those who have sacrificed themselves in the struggle have been ignored and faith has not been kept with them.

If the war is to defend the *status quo*, imperialist possessions, colonies, vested interests and privileges, then India can have nothing to do with it. If, however, the issue is democracy and a world order based on democracy, then India is intensely interested in it. The Committee are convinced that the interests of Indian democracy do not conflict with the interests of British democracy or of world democracy. But there is an inherent and ineradicable conflict between democracy for India or elsewhere and imperialism and fascism. If Great Britain fights for the maintenance and extension of democracy, then she must necessarily end imperialism in her own possessions, establish full democracy in India, and the Indian people must have the right of self-determination by framing their own constitution through a Constituent Assembly without external interference and must guide their own policy. A free democratic India will gladly associate herself with other free nations for mutual defence against aggression and for economic co-operation. She will work for the establishment of a real world order based on freedom and democracy, utilising the world's knowledge and resources for the progress and advancement of humanity.

The crisis that has overtaken Europe is not of Europe only but of humanity and will not pass like other crises or wars leaving the essential structure of the present-day world intact. It is likely to refashion the world for good or ill, politically, socially and economically. This crisis is the inevitable consequence of the social and political conflicts and contradictions which have grown alarmingly since the last Great War, and it will not be finally resolved till these conflicts and contradictions are removed and a new equilibrium established. That equilibrium can only be based on the ending of domination and exploitation of one country by another, and on a reorganization of economic relations on a juster basis for the common good of all. India is the crux of the problem, for India has been the outstanding example of modern imperialism and no refashioning of the world can succeed which ignores this vital problem. With her vast resources she must play an important part in any scheme of world reorganization. But she can only do so as a free nation whose energies have been released to work for this great end. Freedom today is indivisible and every attempt to retain imperialist domination in any part of the world will lead inevitably to fresh disaster.

The Working Committee have noted that many rulers [princes or maharajahs] of Indian States have offered their services and resources and expressed their desire to support the cause of democracy in Europe. If they must make their professions in favour of democracy abroad, the Committee would suggest that their first concern should be the introduction of democracy within their own states in which today undiluted autocracy reigns supreme. The British Government in India is more responsible for this autocracy than even the rulers themselves, as has been made painfully evident during the past year. This policy is the very negation of democracy and of the new world order for which Great Britain claims to be fighting in Europe.

As the Working Committee view past events in Europe, Africa and Asia, and more particularly past and present occurrences in India, they fail to find any attempt to advance the cause of democracy or self-determination or any evidence that the present war declarations of the British Government are being, or are going to be, acted upon. The true measure of democracy is the ending of imperialism and fascism alike and the aggression that has accompanied them in the past and the present. Only on that basis can a new order be built up. In the struggle for that new world order, the Committee are eager and desirous to help in every way. But the Committee cannot associate themselves or offer any co-operation in a war which is conducted on imperialist lines and which is meant to consolidate imperialism in India and elsewhere.

In view, however, of the gravity of the occasion and the fact that the pace of events during the last few days has often been swifter than the working of men's minds, the Committee desire to take no final decision at this stage, so as to allow for the full elucidation of the issues at stake, the real objectives aimed at, and the position of India in the present and in the future. But the decision cannot long be delayed as India is being committed from day to day to a policy to which she is not a party and of which she disapproves.

The Working Committee therefore invite the British Government to declare in unequivocal terms what their war aims are in regard to democracy and imperialism and the new order that is envisaged, in particular, how these aims are going to apply to India and to be given effect to in the present. Do they include the elimination of imperialism and the treatment of India as a free nation whose policy will be guided in accordance with the wishes of her people? A clear declaration about the future, pledging the Government to the ending of Imperialism and Fascism alike will be welcomed by the people of all countries, but it is far more important to give immediate effect to it, to the largest possible extent, for only this will convince the people that the declaration is meant to be honoured. The real test of any declaration is its application in the present, for it is the present that will govern action today and give shape to the future.

War has broken out in Europe and the prospect is terrible to contemplate. But war has been taking its heavy toll of human life during recent years in Abyssinia, Spain and China. Innumerable innocent men, women and children have been bombed to death from the air in open cities. Cold-blooded massacres, torture and utmost humiliation have followed each other in quick succession during these years of horror. That horror grows, and violence and the threat of violence shadow the world and, unless checked and ended, will destroy the precious inheritance of past ages. That horror has to be checked in Europe and China, but it will not end till its root causes of Fascism and Imperialism are removed. To that end the Working Committee are prepared to give their co-operation. But it will be infinite tragedy if even this terrible war is carried on in the spirit of imperialism and for the purpose of retaining this structure which is itself the cause of war and human degradation.

The Working Committee wish to declare that the Indian people have no quarrel with the German people. But they have a deep-rooted quarrel with systems which deny freedom and are based on violence and aggression. They do not look forward to a victory of one people over another or to a dictated peace, but to a victory of real democracy for all the people of all countries and a world freed from the nightmare of violence and imperialist oppression.

The Committee earnestly appeal to the Indian people to end all internal conflict and controversy and in this grave hour of peril, to keep in readiness and hold together as a united nation, calm of purpose and determined to achieve the freedom of India within the larger freedom of the world.

CHAPTER 4

I Become Congress President

THE war broke in Europe on 3 September 1939. Before the month was over, Poland lay prostrate under German arms. To add to the misery of the Poles, the Soviet Union had occupied the eastern half of their territory. Once Polish military resistance was crushed, an uneasy lull descended on Europe. France and Germany faced one another across their fortified frontier, but large-scale hostilities were suspended. Everybody seemed to be waiting for something to happen, but their formless fears were vague and undefined.

In India also there was a sense of expectancy and fear. Against this uncertain and threatening background, the question of the Congress presidentship assumed a new importance. I had been pressed to accept the office in the previous year, but had for various reasons declined. I felt that the present occasion was different and I would be failing in my duty if I again refused. I have already indicated my difference with Gandhiji on the question of India's participation in the war. I felt that now that war had started, India must have no hesitation in aligning herself with the democratic powers. The question, however, was: How could India fight for others' freedom when she was in bondage herself? If the British Government made an immediate declaration of India's independence, it would become the duty of all Indians to sacrifice everything for the freedom of the nation. I therefore felt that, in the crisis of the war, it was my duty to serve in any capacity to which I was called. When Gandhiji again requested me to become Congress President, I readily agreed.

There was no real contest for the presidential election, and Mr.

M. N. Roy,[1] who stood against me, was defeated by an overwhelming majority. The session met at Ramgarh and passed a resolution which largely reflected the views I had expressed in my presidential address. The resolution runs as follows:—

This Congress, having considered the grave and critical situation resulting from the war in Europe and British policy in regard to it, approves of and endorses the resolutions passed and the action taken on the war situation by the A.I.C.C. [or All India Congress Committee, a larger body than the Working Committee] and the Working Committee. The Congress considers the declaration by the British Government of India as a belligerent country, without any reference to the people of India, and the exploitation of India's resources in this War, as an affront to them, which no self-respecting and freedom-loving people can accept or tolerate. The recent pronouncements made on behalf of the British Government in regard to India demonstrate that Great Britain is carrying on the War fundamentally for imperialist ends and for the preservation and strengthening of her Empire, which is based on the exploitation of the people of India, as well as of other Asiatic and African countries. Under these circumstances, it is clear that the Congress cannot in any way, directly or indirectly, be party to the War, which means continuance and perpetuation of this exploitation. The Congress therefore strongly disapproves of Indian troops being made to fight for Great Britain and of the drain from India of men and material for the purpose of the War. Neither the recruiting nor the money raised in India can be considered to be voluntary contributions from India. Congressmen, and those under the Congress influence, cannot help in the prosecution of the War with men, money or material.

The Congress hereby declares again that nothing short of complete independence can be accepted by the people of India. Indian freedom cannot exist within the orbit of imperialism and Dominion or any other status within the imperial structure is wholly inapplicable to India, is not in keeping with the dignity of a great nation, and would bind India in many ways to British policies and economic structure. The people of India alone can properly shape their own constitution and determine their relations to the other countries of the world, through a Constituent Assembly elected on the basis of adult suffrage.

The Congress is further of opinion that while it will always be ready,

---

[1] A noted Indian intellectual, formerly an official of the Communist International, but anti-Communist and pro-British during the Second World War.

as it ever has been, to make every effort to secure communal harmony, no permanent solution is possible except through a Constituent Assembly, where the rights of all recognised minorities will be fully protected by agreement, as far as possible, between the elected representatives of various majority and minority groups, or by arbitration if agreement is not reached on any point. Any alternative will lack finality. India's constitution must be based on independence, democracy and national unity, and the Congress repudiates attempts to divide India or to split up her nationhood. The Congress has always aimed at a constitution where the fullest freedom and opportunities of development are guaranteed to the group and the individual, and social injustice yields place to a juster social order.

One of my first tasks on taking over the presidentship from Dr. Rajendra Prasad was to reconstitute the Working Committee. Ten members were common, viz.,

> Shrimati Sarojini Naidu
> Sardar Vallabhbhai Patel
> Seth Jamnalal Bajaj (Treasurer)
> Shri J. B. Kripalani (General Secretary)
> Khan Abdul Gaffar Khan
> Shri Bhulabhai Desai
> Shri Shankar Rao Deo
> Dr. Profulla Chandra Ghosh
> Dr. Rajendra Prasad and myself.

One of the conspicuous absentees in Dr. Rajendra Prasad's Committee had been Jawaharlal Nehru. He had remained aloof after Subhas Chandra Bose resigned from the Congress presidentship owing to his differences with Gandhiji. I brought Jawaharlal back and added Shri C. Rajagopalachari, Dr. Syed Mahmud and Mr. Asaf Ali. A fifteenth name was to be announced later, but soon after the session of the Congress we were arrested and the place remained vacant.

It was a very critical time in the history of Congress. We were affected by the world-shaking events outside. Even more disturbing were the differences among ourselves. I was the Congress President and sought to take India into the camp of the democracies if only she were free. The cause of democracy was one for which Indians felt strongly. The only obstacle in our way was India's bondage. For Gandhiji, however, it was not so. For him the issue was one of pacifism and not of India's freedom. I declared openly that the Indian National Congress was not a pacifist organization but one for achieving India's freedom. To my mind, therefore, the issue raised by Gandhiji was irrelevant.

Gandhiji, however, would not change his view. He was convinced that India ought not to take part in the war in any circumstances. He met the Viceroy and expressed these views to him. He also wrote an open letter to the British people appealing to them that they should not fight Hitler but oppose him by spiritual force. It is not altogether surprising that Gandhiji's appeal found no response in British hearts, for by this time France had already fallen and German power stood at its zenith.

This was a very difficult time for Gandhiji. He saw that the war was devastating the world and he could do nothing to prevent it. He was so distressed that on several occasions he even spoke of suicide. He told me that, if he were powerless to stop the suffering caused by the war, he could at least refuse to be a witness to it by putting an end to his life. He pressed me again and again to lend support to his views. I thought over the matter deeply but I could not bring myself to agree. For me, nonviolence was a matter of policy, not of creed. My view was that Indians had the right to take to the sword if they had no other alternative. It would, however, be nobler to achieve independence through peaceful methods, and, in any case in the circumstances which obtained in this country, Gandhiji's method was right.

The Congress Working Committee was divided on this basic issue. In the earlier stages, Jawaharlal Nehru, Vallabhbhai Patel, Shri Rajagopalachari and Khan Abdul Gaffar Khan [2] sided with me. Dr. Rajendra Prasad, Acharya Kripalani and Shri Shankar Rao Deo were, however, wholeheartedly with Gandhiji. They agreed

[2] Moslem leader of the Congress party in the North West Frontier Province (N.W.F.P.) and widely known as "the Frontier Gandhi."

with him that, once it was accepted that free India could participate in war, the very basis of India's nonviolent struggle for freedom would disappear. I, on the other hand, felt that there was a distinction between an internal struggle for freedom and an external struggle against aggression. To struggle for freedom was one thing. To fight after the country became free was different. I held that the two issues should not be confused.

Matters came to a head during the meeting of the Working Committee and the A.I.C.C. at Poona in July 1940. This was the first meeting of the All India Congress Committee after the Ramgarh Session of the Congress. As President, I placed before the Committee the issue as I saw it. The Committee endorsed my views. Two resolutions were accordingly passed. The first reiterated the conviction of the Congress that nonviolence was the correct policy in attaining India's freedom and must be maintained. The second declared that, in the war between nazism and democracy, India's rightful place was in the democratic camp. She could not, however, participate in the war effort of the democracies till she herself was free. The resolutions as finally accepted were based on my draft.

When the resolution reiterating nonviolence as the basis of India's struggle for freedom was passed, Gandhiji was very pleased. In a telegram of congratulation he sent to me, he said that he was particularly pleased that I had pleaded the cause of nonviolence in the internal struggle. He had felt that in the present temper of the country the A.I.C.C. would readily accept my proposal that India should participate in the war if her freedom was recognized. In view of this he had doubts if I could persuade the A.I.C.C. to pass the resolution on nonviolence in respect of our internal struggle.

The members of the Working Committee, however, began to waver in their attitude towards the war. None of them could forget that Gandhiji was opposed, on principle, to any participation in war. Nor could they forget that the Indian struggle for freedom had attained its present dimensions under his leadership. They were now for the first time differing from him on a fundamental issue and leaving him alone. His firm belief in nonviolence as a creed began to influence their judgment. Within a month of the Poona meeting Sardar Patel changed his views and accepted Gandhiji's position. The other members also started to waver. In July 1940, Dr. Rajendra Prasad and several other members of the Working Committee wrote to me that they firmly believed in Gandhiji's views regarding the war and desired that the Congress should adhere to them. They went on to say that, since I held different views and the A.I.C.C. at Poona had supported me, the signatories doubted if they could continue to remain members of the Working Committee. They had been nominated to the Working Committee to assist the President, but, since they differed on a basic question, they had no option but to offer their resignation. They had considered the matter deeply and, in order not to embarrass me, they were willing to continue as members of the Working Committee so long as their differences did not have any immediate practical application. If, however, the British Government accepted my terms and participation in the war became a live issue, they felt that they would have no option but to resign. They added that, if I agreed to this, they would continue to serve as members of the Working Committee. Otherwise this letter should itself be treated as a letter of resignation.

I was deeply hurt to receive this letter which was signed by all members of the Working Committee except Jawaharlal, Rajagopalachari, Asaf Ali and Syed Mahmud. Even Abdul Gaffar Khan, who had earlier been one of my stanchest supporters, had now changed his views. I had never expected a letter of this kind from my colleagues. I immediately wrote in reply that I fully understood their point of view and accepted the position. The British Government's present attitude held hardly any hope for the recognition of Indian freedom. So long as the British attitude did not change, the question of participation in war was likely to remain an academic issue. I would therefore request them to continue as members of the Working Committee.

In August 1940, the Viceroy invited me to discuss with him the participation of Congress in the Government on the basis of an extended Executive Council with larger powers. Even without con-

sulting my colleagues, I declined the offer. It appeared to me that
there was no common ground between the Congress demand for
independence and the Viceroy's offer of an enlarged Executive
Council. In view of this there was no point in meeting him. I found
that many Congressmen did not agree with my decision. They argued
that I should have accepted the invitation and met the Viceroy but
I was and am still convinced that I took the correct decision.

Gandhiji's reaction to this episode was quite different from that
of the majority of the Congressmen. He wrote a letter to me fully
supporting my decision. In his view my refusal to meet the Viceroy
was a symbol of God's grace. It was not the will of God that India
should participate in this war. In his view this was the reason why
I had refused to meet the Viceroy. This closed the matter, but if, on
the other hand, I had met the Viceroy, Gandhiji feared that there
might have been a settlement and India might have been drawn
into the war.

Soon after this, Gandhiji issued another appeal to the British. He
again asked them to give up arms and oppose Hitler with spiritual
force. Not content with addressing a letter to the British people, he
also met Lord Linlithgow [the Viceroy] and pressed him to accept
his point of view and communicate it to the British Government.

When Gandhiji told Lord Linlithgow that the British people
should give up arms and oppose Hitler with spiritual force, Lord
Linlithgow was taken aback by what he regarded as an extraordinary
suggestion. It was normally his practice to ring the bell for an A.D.C.
to come and take Gandhiji to his car. On this occasion he neither
rang the bell nor sent for the A.D.C. The result was that Gandhiji
walked away from a silent and bewildered viceroy and had to find
his way out to his car all by himself. When Gandhiji met me, he
reported the incident and expressed his surprise that the Viceroy
should forget to do the normal courtesies. I replied, "The Viceroy
must have been so astonished at your suggestion that he did not
remember what his normal practice was." Gandhiji burst into
laughter when he heard this explanation.

Internal debate within the Congress continued. So far as Gandhiji was concerned, Congress was not to participate in the war under any conditions. While we differed in our basic approach, we were agreed that India must withhold all support to the British in the present situation. The conflict between my policy and Gandhiji's creed thus remained a theoretical one. The attitude of the British united us in action even though our basic approach remained different.

The question arose as to what Congress should do in the present context. As a political organization, it could not just sit quiet while tremendous events were happening throughout the world. Gandhiji was at first opposed to any movement as it could be only on the issue of Indian freedom and carry the implication that, once freedom was gained, India would participate in the war. After the meetings at Delhi and Poona, when the British refused the Congress offer of cooperation, Gandhiji thought of a limited civil disobedience movement. He proposed that men and women should protest individually against dragging India into the war. They would dissociate themselves from the war effort publicly and court arrest. I held that there should be a more extensive and active antiwar movement but to this Gandhiji would not agree. Since Gandhiji was not prepared to go further, I finally agreed that at least the individual Satyagraha Movement should start.

Vinoba Bhave [who was Gandhi's spiritual successor and leader of the Bhooden, or Land Gift, Movement] was accordingly selected as the first individual Satyagrahi or civil resister to war. After Bhave, Pandit Nehru offered himself as the second volunteer and Gandhiji accepted him. A number of others followed and soon there was a nation-wide movement of individual Satyagraha. The upshot was that, though I differed radically from Gandhiji in my attitude towards nonviolence, the actual program followed was one on which we both agreed.

There was also occasionally a comic side to such individual Satyagraha. There was a man from the Punjab, Sampuran Singh, who without obtaining the permission of Gandhiji or the Working Committee, offered Satyagraha. When arrested, he put up a defence against the explicit instructions of the Congress. The trying magis-

trate convicted him and fined him one anna,[3] which he paid from
his own pocket, and set him free. This brought such ridicule on the
movement in the Punjab that I had to go there to set matters right.
On my way back, I was arrested at Allahabad. The arrest itself was
not without a touch of humor. I was going to the refreshment room
for an early cup of tea when the Superintendent of Police presented
me with the warrant and his respects. I replied gravely:

I am honoured by the special distinction that you have conferred on
me. You have arrested me even before I had a chance of offering individual Satyagraha.

I was sentenced to imprisonment for two years and detained in
the Naini jail. After some time Dr. Katju [who was a lawyer, a
writer and Minister of Defence in independent India] also joined
me there. We did not, however, serve the full term as two events
of world-shattering importance soon transformed the entire character of the war. The first was Germany's attack on Soviet Russia in
June 1941. Within six months, Japan struck at the U.S.A. at Pearl
Harbor.

Germany's attack on Soviet Russia and Japan's on the U.S.A.
made the war truly global. Before the German attack on Soviet
Russia, the war had been one between Western European countries.
The German attack extended the frontiers of war to vast regions
hitherto untouched. The U.S.A. had been giving substantial help
to the United Kingdom but she was still outside the war. The
American Continent was untouched. The Japanese attack on Pearl
Harbor brought the United States into the turmoil.

The astonishing success of Japan in the earlier stages brought the
war right to India's door. Within a few weeks, Japan had overrun
Malaya and Singapore. Soon Burma, which before 1937 had been
a part of India, was occupied. A situation was created when it
seemed imminent that India herself would be attacked. Japanese
ships had already appeared in the Bay of Bengal and soon the

[3] A small coin worth approximately two cents.

Andamans [islands lying in the Bay of Bengal] and Nicobars fell to the Japanese Navy.

With Japan's entry, the United States had to face direct responsibility with regard to the war. It had even before this period suggested to the British that they should come to terms with India. Now it started to apply greater pressure on the United Kingdom to settle the Indian problem and win India's willing cooperation. Though not known at the time, President Roosevelt, immediately after the Japanese attack on Pearl Harbor, requested the British Government that Indian leaders should be conciliated. The Government of India could not altogether ignore these requests and up to a point it decided to change its policy.

In December 1941, the Viceroy decided that Jawaharlal and I should be released. This decision was intended to test the Congress reaction to the changed war situation. The Government wanted to watch our reactions and then decide whether the others should be released. In any case, it was necessary to release me, for, so long as I was not free, no meeting of the Working Committee could be held.

I was in a state of mental distress when the order of release reached me. In fact, I felt a sense of humiliation when I was set free. On all previous occasions, release from jail had brought with it a sense of partial achievement. On this occasion I felt keenly that, even though the war had been going on for over two years, we had not been able to take any effective steps towards achieving Indian freedom. We seemed to be the victims of circumstances and not the masters of our destiny.

Immediately on my release I called a meeting of the Working Committee at Bardoli. Gandhiji was staying there and had expressed a wish that the meeting might be held there. I went to meet Gandhiji and immediately felt that we had moved further apart. Formerly we had differed on the question of principle alone, but now there was also a basic difference between his reading of the situation and mine. Gandhiji now seemed convinced that the British Government was ready and willing to recognize India as free if India offered full cooperation in the war effort. He felt that, though the

Government was predominantly conservative and Mr. Churchill was the Prime Minister, the war had reached a stage where the British would have no option but to recognize the freedom of India as the price of cooperation. My own reading was completely different. I thought the British Government was sincerely anxious for our cooperation but that they were not yet ready to recognize India as free. I felt that while the war continued, the utmost the British Government would do would be to constitute a new Executive Council with expanded powers and give Congress adequate representation on it. We held long discussions over this issue but I was unable to convince Gandhiji.

Soon after my release, I held a press conference at Calcutta. When I was asked whether Congress was willing to change its policy towards the war, I replied that it depended on the attitude of the British Government. If the Government changed its attitude, so would Congress. I made it clear that the attitude of Congress towards the war was not of the nature of an immutable dogma. I was further asked what Indians should do if Japan invaded India. I replied without a moment's hesitation that all Indians should take up the sword to defend the country. I added, "We can do so only if the bonds which shackle our hands and feet are removed. How can we fight if our hands and feet are tied?"

The Times and the *Daily News* of London commented on this interview and said that this seemed to indicate a difference of opinion between Gandhiji and the Congress leadership. Gandhiji had adopted an unchangeable attitude towards the war which left no room or hope for negotiations. The statement of the Congress President on the other hand held out the hope of agreement.

When the Working Committee met, Gandhiji referred to the press comments in Britain. He admitted that these had influenced him to a certain extent and strengthened his belief that the British Government would be willing to change its attitude if Congress offered cooperation in the war. The debate on what the Congress attitude should be continued for two days but there was no agreed decision. Gandhiji stood firm in his view that nonviolence was a creed and must not be given up in any circumstances. As a corollary to this, he could not, in any circumstances, approve India's entry into the war. I repeated my earlier view that Congress must place greater emphasis on the freedom of India than on nonviolence as a creed.

It was a striking testimony to Gandhiji's capacity for finding a solution to the most difficult of problems that even in this impasse he had a formula which could meet the two opposite points of view. He also had a wonderful capacity of understanding and representing fairly a contrary point of view. When he saw my firm attitude on the question of India's participation in war, he did not press me any longer to change it. On the contrary, he placed before the Working Committee a draft resolution which faithfully reflected my point of view.

Soon there was one other important change in the Indian political situation. Subhas Chandra Bose had, with the outbreak of the war, started a campaign for active opposition to the war effort. His activities led to his imprisonment, but he was released when he undertook a fast. On 26 January 1941, it became known that he had left India. For over a year nothing was heard about him and people were not sure whether he was alive or dead. In March 1942, all doubts were set at rest when he made a speech which was broadcast by the Berlin radio. It was now clear that he had reached Germany and was attempting to organize an anti-British front from there. In the meantime, Japanese propaganda against the British occupation of India also gained in intensity. The steady flow of this propaganda from Germany and Japan affected a large number of people in India. Many were attracted by Japanese promises and believed that Japan was working for Indian freedom and Asian solidarity. They held that, since the Japanese attack weakened British power, it helped our freedom struggle, and we should take full advantage of the situation. There was therefore in the country a section of opinion which grew more and more sympathetic to Japan.

There was another point on which my reading of the situation differed from Gandhiji's. Gandhiji by now inclined more and more to the view that the Allies could not win the war. He feared that it

might end in the triumph of Germany and Japan, or that at the best
there might be a stalemate.

Gandhiji did not express this opinion about the outcome of the
war in clear-cut terms but in discussions with him I felt that he was
becoming more and more doubtful about an Allied victory. I also
saw that Subhas Bose's escape to Germany had made a great impression on Gandhiji. He had not formerly approved many of Bose's
actions, but now I found a change in his outlook. Many of his remarks convinced me that he admired the courage and resourcefulness
Subhas Bose had displayed in making his escape from India. His
admiration for Subhas Bose unconsciously colored his view about
the whole war situation.

This admiration was also one of the factors which clouded the
discussions during the Cripps Mission to India. I shall discuss the
proposal brought by Cripps and the reasons why we rejected it in
greater detail in a later chapter, but here I would like to mention a
report which was circulated about the time of Cripps's arrival.
There was a news flash that Subhas Bose had died in an air crash.
This created a sensation in India and Gandhiji, among others, was
deeply moved. He sent a message of condolence to Subhas Bose's
mother, in which he spoke in glowing terms about her son and his
services to India. Later on it turned out that the report was false.
Cripps, however, complained to me that he had not expected a man
like Gandhiji to speak in such glowing terms about Subhas Bose.
Gandhiji was a confirmed believer in nonviolence, while Subhas
Bose had openly sided with the Axis powers and was carrying on
vigorous propaganda for the defeat of the Allies on the battlefield.

CHAPTER 5

A Chinese Interlude

I HAVE referred to the concern expressed by President Roosevelt about India's participation in the war. The same view was repeatedly urged by Generalissimo Chiang Kai-shek. Since the outbreak of hostilities, he had pressed that the British should come to terms with India and his insistence became greater after Japan attacked Pearl Harbor. A natural result of the Japanese intervention was to increase the importance of the Generalissimo and the Chinese Government. China, like the U.S.A., the U.K., the U.S.S.R. and France, came to be recognized as one of the major powers of the world. Chiang Kai-shek had pressed the British Government throughout to recognize India's independence. He held that, unless India became a voluntary participant in the war, she would not render the help of which she was capable.

A short while before the outbreak of the war, Jawaharlal Nehru had visited South China. Chiang Kai-shek was his host and had thus established close relations with him. He had also thus achieved firsthand knowledge of the Indian political situation. One result of Jawaharlal's visit was that Chiang Kai-shek sent a mission to India and wrote me a letter as the President of the Indian National Congress. In his letter, he expressed full sympathy with Indian aspirations and gave expression to his solicitude for Indian welfare. He now decided that he should himself visit India and meet the Viceroy and the Congress leaders to see if some way of settlement could be found. He hoped that this would lead to an association of the Indian national leaders with the war effort.

I was in Delhi and staying with Asaf Ali when I learnt that Chiang Kai-shek was visiting India in the first half of February 1942. After a few days I received a message from Madame Chiang Kai-shek that she also was accompanying him. An announcement was soon after made by the Government that Generalissimo and Madame Chiang Kai-shek were coming to Delhi as the guests of the Government of India.

The Generalissimo and Madame Chiang Kai-shek arrived in Delhi on 9 February 1942. Two days after his arrival Jawaharlal and I called on him. One difficulty in talking to him was that he knew no foreign language. He had, of course, an interpreter, but naturally this made conversation much slower and a little formal. The Generalissimo made a long opening speech to prove that a dependent nation could achieve freedom in only one of two ways. It could either take to the sword and expel the foreigner, or it could achieve its freedom by peaceful methods. But this meant that advance towards freedom would be gradual. There would be progress towards self-government step by step till the goal was reached. These were the only methods open to a nation which was fighting against either a foreign or a national despot.

China, the Generalissimo said, was a clear example of the validity of this principle. The National Movement in China began in 1911 but it had to pass through many stages before freedom was attained. India would also have to follow the same path. Indians must, of course, decide how they would achieve their goal. The Generalissimo held that there was no alternative to the position that, if freedom could not be attained at one stroke, India should achieve it by gradual stages. He then told me that he had been in touch throughout with the British Government and had sent detailed messages to the British Prime Minister. He had also received a reply from him and he was convinced that, if Indians acted with wisdom and statesmanship, they could fully utilize the war situation and achieve their freedom.

The Generalissimo then asked me, "Where does India rightly belong? Is her place with Nazi Germany or with the democracies?"

I replied that I had no hesitation in saying that, if the obstacles in our way were removed, I would leave no stone unturned to see that India joined the camp of democracy.

The Generalissimo then put a rhetorical question to us. He said that the issue in the world war was freedom or slavery for vast masses of mankind. In view of these high stakes, was it not our duty to side with the U.K. and China without insisting on any conditions?

I replied that we were anxious to join the democratic camp provided we were free and could join the democracies of our own independent choice.

The Generalissimo again said that, so far as India was concerned, his view was that there was no substantial difference between dominion status and complete independence. He dwelt at length on this point and said that if the British Government offered self-government with dominion status, India would be wise to accept it. He added that he knew that Jawaharlal did not agree with his view and wanted complete independence, but, as a well-wisher of India, his advice would be that we should not reject such an offer.

Jawaharlal spoke to me in Urdu and said that, as the Congress President, it was for me to reply to this question.

I told the Generalissimo that if during the war the British Government offered dominion status and agreed that Indian representatives could work with a sense of freedom and responsibility, the Congress would not refuse the offer.

At this stage, Madame Chiang Kai-shek joined us and invited us to tea. Her presence made discussions easier as she was educated in the United States and spoke English with perfect ease.

The Generalissimo said that it was obvious that the British Government would have to shoulder the burden of war. It would not be reasonable to expect that they would give 100 per cent responsibility to Indians so long as hostilities continued.

I replied that a plan could be made for the duration of the war which would be acceptable to both Indian leaders and the British Government. The real issue was, however, the postwar settlement of the Indian question. Once the British Government assured us about Indian freedom after the war, we could come to terms.

Madame Chiang Kai-shek asked me if there would be any objection if our discussions were brought to the notice of the British Government.

I replied that this was the position Congress had taken in public and there could be no objection to our view's being reported to anybody.

During the whole period of Generalissimo Chiang Kai-shek's visit to India, the Government of India was placed in an awkward situation. It did not like such close contacts between the Generalissimo and the Congress leaders. This might create the impression both in India and abroad that the Generalissimo had come to meet us. On the other hand, the Generalissimo had made it clear that he had come to India to discuss the war situation, not only with the Viceroy and the Commander-in-Chief, but with the Congress leaders. The Government could not therefore prevent him from establishing contact with us.

The Generalissimo had expressed a wish to see the Taj [Mahal]. The Government had made a program for an official visit when he would be accompanied by persons chosen by the Government. Madame Chiang Kai-shek, however, said that Jawaharlal should accompany them to Agra. He thus became a member of the party. This also was thoroughly disliked by the Government of India.

From Delhi, the Generalissimo went to Calcutta. The Government of Bengal had arranged that the Generalissimo would stay in the old Government House at Barrackpur. The Generalissimo informed Jawaharlal about this and said that he hoped to meet him in Calcutta again. Jawaharlal did go to Calcutta and had further talks with him. Gandhiji was then staying in Birla Park and the Generalissimo came to meet him there. Their meeting lasted for about two hours with Madame Chiang Kai-shek as interpreter. Gandhiji told him how he had at first started Satyagraha in South Africa and how he had gradually developed the technique of nonviolent noncooperation for the solution of the Indian political problem.

I was not in Calcutta during the Generalissimo's visit. Jawaharlal told me later about the interview. During these days Jawaharlal did not see eye to eye with Gandhiji in all matters. He felt that the way in which Gandhiji had spoken with the Generalissimo had not made a very good impression on him. It is difficult for me to express any opinion on this. It is possible that the Generalissimo had not been able to follow all the implications of Gandhiji's stand. He may also have remained unconvinced by Gandhiji's arguments, but I would be surprised if he was not impressed by the magnetic influence which Gandhiji exercised on foreigners.

The Generalissimo, before he left, made a fervent appeal to Great Britain to give real political power to India as speedily as possible, but it was clear that he had not been able to convince the Viceroy or the British Government about the need of immediate recognition of India as a dominion.

CHAPTER 6

The Cripps Mission

AS the war crisis deepened, people expected that there would be a change in the British Government's attitude to the Indian problem. This actually happened and the outcome was the Cripps Mission of 1942. Before discussing this Mission, it is necessary to refer to a previous occasion when, soon after the outbreak of the war, Sir Stafford Cripps had visited India. During this visit he had many discussions with me. In fact, he spent several days at Wardha during the meeting of the Congress Working Committee. The question of Indian participation in the war effort was naturally one of the most frequent topics in our talks.

During this visit, Sir Stafford Cripps more than once remarked that Gandhiji's views on the war were well known and held out hardly any hope of agreement with the British Government. My views were also widely known and seemed to offer a basis for discussions. He enquired from me if I could assure him that, if the British Government accepted the demand for Indian freedom, the Indian people would accept my views rather than Gandhiji's. I told him that while we all held Gandhiji in the greatest esteem and paid the greatest attention to whatever he said, on this particular issue I was satisfied that the majority of the Congress and the country were with me. I could, therefore, assure him that if India became free, the whole country would wholeheartedly support the war effort. He also enquired from me whether India would accept conscription in such an eventuality. I replied that we would welcome it and see to it that the Indian war effort was total.

Sir Stafford sent me an *aide-mémoire* in which he put down the gist of our discussions and his suggestions for a compromise between the British Government and the Indian people. According to him, the British Government would make an immediate declaration that, with the cessation of hostilities, India would be declared independent forthwith. The declaration would also include a clause that India would be free to decide whether to remain within the British Commonwealth or not. For the duration of the war, the Executive Council would be reconstituted and the members would have the status of ministers. The position of the Viceroy would be that of a constitutional head. It would thus be a *de facto* transfer of power, but the *de jure* transfer could take place only after the war.

Sir Stafford asked for my reaction to his proposal. I replied that I could not commit myself definitely on a hypothetical presentation of such an important issue, but I could assure him that, once the Indian people were convinced that the British Government really meant business, a way to adjust our differences could be found.

From India, Sir Stafford Cripps went as a nonofficial visitor to Russia. Soon after, he was appointed the British Ambassador to Russia. It is sometimes held that he was responsible for bringing Soviet Russia nearer to the Allies. When finally Germany attacked Russia, a great deal of the credit for this break between Hitler and Stalin went to him. This gave him a great reputation and increased his standing in British public life. I have my doubts if he really had any effective influence on Soviet policy, but, in any case, his reputation soared high. When he returned to the U.K., many people even expected that he might replace Mr. Churchill as the head of the Government.

I have already referred to the pressure which President Roosevelt was putting on the British Government for a settlement of the Indian question. After Pearl Harbor, American public opinion became more and more insistent and demanded that India's voluntary cooperation in the war effort must be secured. Even Churchill felt that it was necessary to make a gesture. He decided to take a new step and selected Cripps as the spokesman of a new policy.

After his return from the Soviet Union, Cripps's reputation stood very high. Here was a man who, according to popular opinion, had handled a most delicate mission in Moscow with great success. He was therefore an obvious choice for a mission to India. Besides, his interest in the Indian problem had continued for many years. I have reason to believe that he placed before Churchill the *aide-mémoire* which he had drawn up at Wardha during his last visit to India. My view is that Churchill did not accept the proposals in the *aide-mémoire*, but Cripps formed the impression that the scheme would be acceptable to Churchill. He, therefore, readily agreed to come to India, as, in the light of his earlier discussions with me, he felt that there was a very fair chance of his proposals' being accepted by the Congress.

The announcement by the B.B.C. of the Cripps Mission had a mixed reception in India. While there had been a large spate of speculations, no one knew definitely what exactly the British Government would propose. The announcement was heard in India at 8:00 P.M. on 11 March 1942. Within an hour the press wanted my comments. I said:

> I cannot give a reply without carefully examining what are the exact terms of the offer which Sir Stafford Cripps is bringing. I would, however, welcome him as an old friend and try to meet his views as far as possible.

In spite of great pressure from the press, I refused to commit myself any further.

I was at Wardha when the Viceroy sent me a telegram that the War Cabinet had decided to send Sir Stafford Cripps on a mission to India and that I should come to Delhi to discuss the proposals he was bringing for the settlement of the Indian question. I accepted the invitation and informed the Viceroy accordingly.

Before coming to India, Sir Stafford Cripps had written to the Viceroy that he would like to meet leaders of all the important parties in India. It was perhaps the Government of India which drew up the list, and decided to invite, besides the leaders of the Congress, the leaders of the Moslem League. In addition, invitations

The Congress President, Maulana Azad, arriving at the Viceregal Lodge. *L to R:* Mr A. V. Alexander, Sir Stafford Cripps, Maulana Azad, Lord Pethick-Lawrence. May 5, 1946.

PLATE I

The Congress President and Mr Asaf Ali meet the Cabinet Mission. *L to R:* Lord Pethick-Lawrence, the Maulana, Mr Asaf Ali, Mr A. V. Alexander, Sir Stafford Cripps.

PLATE II

Maulana Azad and Lord Pethick - Lawrence, at the Tripartite Conference in Simla, May 5, 1946.

Lord Wavell, the Viceroy of India, shaking hands with the President of the Indian National Congress at the opening of the Conference.

were sent to representatives of the princes, the Hindu Mahasabha [a communal party] and Khan Bahadur Allah Bux, then Chief Minister of Sind. Khan Bahadur Allah Bux had attained importance in recent months after presiding over the Convention of the Nationalist [as distinguished from communal] Moslems in Delhi. I did not participate in this conference but I had helped in the arrangements from behind the scenes. The conference was held with great éclat and 1,400 delegates came to Delhi from all over India. The session was so impressive that even the British and the Anglo-Indian press, which normally tried to belittle the importance of nationalist Moslems, could not ignore it. They were compelled to acknowledge that this conference was proof that nationalist Moslems were not a negligible factor.

I met Sir Stafford soon after he arrived in New Delhi. The first meeting took place at 3:00 P.M. on 29 March 1942. Sir Stafford had prepared a statement embodying his proposals which may be seen in the Appendix. This he handed to me and said that he was prepared to discuss the proposals further and offer any explanation that might be necessary. When I looked at the statement, I found that it was a proposal for a new Executive Council of the Viceroy. All the existing members would resign. The Congress and other representative organizations would then be requested to send their nominees who together would constitute the new Executive Council. This Council would function for the duration of the war. The British Government would give a solemn pledge that, as soon as hostilities ceased, the question of Indian independence would be taken up.

The net result of the proposal was that in place of the majority of British members in the existing Executive Council, there would be an Executive Council composed of Indians alone. British officers would remain as secretaries, but not as members of the Council. The system of Government would not, however, be changed.

I asked Sir Stafford what would be the position of the Viceroy in this Council. Sir Stafford replied that the Viceroy would function as a constitutional head like the King in the U.K. In order to remove any room for doubt, I asked him to confirm that this would mean

that the Viceroy, as a constitutional head, would be bound by the
advice of the Council. Sir Stafford said that this was the intention.
I said again that the basic question was as to who would exercise
power, the proposed Council or the Viceroy. Sir Stafford repeated
that power would rest with the Council as it rests with the British
Cabinet. I then asked what would be the position of the India Office [1]
in such a picture. Sir Stafford said that this was a matter of detail
which he had not considered so far, but he would like to assure me
that any views the Congress had on the matter would be paid due
regard. Sir Stafford added as an afterthought that the India Office
would remain and there would be a Secretary of State but his
position would be like that of the Dominion Secretary in respect of
the other dominions.

I described in detail how, immediately after the outbreak of the
war, India had repeatedly offered to participate in the war on condition that her freedom was recognized. It was the British who had
failed to take advantage of this offer and were thus responsible for
India's not playing a greater role in the war. Sir Stafford said again
and again that he was sorry for the way things had happened but he
felt convinced that all this would now end if the offer he had brought
on behalf of the British Cabinet was accepted.

Our first interview thus came to an end on a note of optimism.

The meeting of the Congress Working Committee was called on
29 March 1942, and it remained in session till 11 April. This was
perhaps the longest meeting that the Working Committee had till
then held. As was to be expected, the members approached the
proposals in different moods and from different points of view.

Gandhiji was against the acceptance of the proposals from the
very first day. I felt that this was due more to his aversion to war
than to his objection to the proposals as such. In fact, his judgment
of the merits of the proposal was colored by his inherent and unchangeable aversion to anything which might involve India in war.
Proposals however favorable to India, if they meant that India

[1] In effect, the Ministry of Indian Affairs in London, headed by the Secretary
of State for India.

would have to participate in war, went against his grain. He also did not like the last part of the offer which said that after the war the Congress and the Moslem League would be given an opportunity to settle the communal issue.

When Gandhiji met Cripps for the first time during this Mission, Cripps reminded him of the *aide-mémoire* to which reference has already been made. Cripps said that the *aide-mémoire* had been prepared after consultation with Congress leaders, including Gandhiji. Its substance was that during the war there would be complete Indianization of the Executive Council. After the war, India would be declared free. The proposals he had now brought were substantially the same.

Gandhiji said that he had no recollection of the *aide-mémoire*. All that he could remember of his talks with Cripps during his last visit were some discussions about vegetarianism. Cripps replied that it was his misfortune that Gandhiji could remember his talks on food but not the proposals he had so carefully prepared after consulting Gandhiji himself.

During their discussions, Gandhiji and Cripps exchanged many pleasantries, but there were also sharp encounters, though in a friendly spirit. Gandhiji said that the proposals were cut and dried and left hardly any scope for negotiation. He laughingly warned Cripps that I was giving him a long rope but he should take care. Cripps retorted that he knew that I had a rope long enough to hang him.

Jawaharlal was deeply troubled by the developments in Europe and Asia, and was anxious concerning the fate of the democracies. His natural sympathies were with them and he wanted to help them as far as possible. He was therefore inclined to consider the proposals favorably. Indian feeling against the British was so strong at the time that he could not state his position clearly and emphatically. I could, however, read his unspoken thoughts and sympathized generally with his views.

As for the other members of the Congress Working Committee, most of them had no set opinion about the war. They were all look-

ing towards Gandhiji for a lead. The only exception was Shri
Rajagopalachari. He was all for acceptance but his views did not
carry much weight. It was unfortunate that Congress circles looked
upon him as a man hardly distinguishable from a moderate.

The Working Committee debated on the proposals for two days,
but the discussions were inconclusive. I then felt it necessary to seek
further clarification and more detailed information on several points
from Sir Stafford. The basic question involved the powers of the
Executive Council. Sir Stafford had proposed that the Council
would remain but would be constituted with Indian members selected by the political parties. He had verbally assured me that the
Viceroy's position would be that of a constitutional head. The
Working Committee desired that this point should be brought out
clearly in the terms of the agreement itself. Accordingly, on 1
April 1942, I again called on Cripps.

This meeting with Sir Stafford was decisive. Our discussions
continued for some three hours. I found that the position had undergone a radical change since I had last met him. His answers were
now quite different in temper from his replies during the first interview. When I asked him about the status of the Executive Council,
he said that it was his hope that the Council would, even during
the war, work like a cabinet. I enquired if this meant that the
Council would decide all issues by majority and its decisions would
be final. Cripps gave an ambiguous reply. He would not categorically state that the Viceroy would have the final say but the purport
of what he said was that the Council would not have full and unfettered freedom of decision. He tried to explain this by saying that
the position now enjoyed by the Viceroy could not be changed
without a change in the law. However, he stressed again and again
that, whatever might be the position in law, in actual practice the
Viceroy would behave as a constitutional head.

I reminded Sir Stafford that he had been much more categorical
during the first interview. He argued with me and tried to convince
me that his basic position had not changed. What he intended to
convey then was identical with what he was saying now. I reminded

him that, in reply to my question, he had then said categorically that the Executive Council would function exactly like a cabinet. Today, however, he was saying that the legal position would remain unchanged, and he was only trying to reassure me by saying that it was his hope that the Council would function like a cabinet. This was not the impression which I had carried away from the first interview. I also reminded him of our talk about the India Office and the Secretary of State for India. He had then said that the Secretary of State for India would act like the Commonwealth Secretary but he was now saying that any change in the status of the India Office or the Secretary of State for India would require a new parliamentary enactment. Cripps replied that his view was that in practice the India Office would function on a fresh basis but there were practical difficulties in enacting a law which would change the status of the Secretary of State to that of a Commonwealth Secretary.

I then took up the question of the recognition of Indian independence on the cessation of hostilities. Cripps said that the problem of India would be considered from a new angle after the war and she would get the opportunity of deciding her own fate. He added that, as a friend, he would venture to advise that we should not raise any fresh difficulties by asking new questions. India should accept the proposals at their face value and go forward. He had no doubt in his mind that if India cooperated fully with Britain during the war, her freedom after the war was assured.

There has been a great deal of speculation in India and some outside as to why Sir Stafford Cripps changed his position between the first and the second interviews. One possible explanation is that Sir Stafford had hoped to persuade the Congress to accept the proposals, even though there was no change in the basic situation, by his persuasive powers and pleasant manners. That is why he had initially given categorical assurances in order to create a favorable first impression. When, however, the proposals were examined in detail and he was subjected to cross-examination, he felt that he must be cautious and refrain from raising hopes which he was not

in a position to satisfy. An alternative explanation is that, during this
interval, the inner circle of the Government of India had started to
influence him. He was constantly surrounded by the Viceroy and
his entourage. It was perhaps inevitable that their point of view
should at least partially color his vision. A third alternative explanation is that during the interval, messages had passed between Delhi
and London, and the British War Cabinet had sent him fresh instructions which made him feel that if he went too far he might be
repudiated.

It is difficult to give a categorical answer as to what the real
explanation is. It may well be that all the factors mentioned above
had contributed to bring about a change in the situation. Cripps was
essentially an advocate and as such he was inclined to paint things
in a rosier color than was warranted by the facts. He was also inclined to see things from his own point of view and present the
position in as favorable a manner as possible so as to influence his
opponent. When later we sought to pin him down, he was compelled
to retrace his steps. I heard later that in Moscow also he had occasionally exceeded his instructions in a similar manner. A more
charitable explanation may also be offered. As an Englishman, he
was prone to place a greater emphasis on practice and convention
than on written agreements. It is probable that he sincerely believed
that, once his proposals were accepted, conventions would develop
in the way he had indicated in his first interview. Naturally, however, he could not give any formal assurances in this behalf and
hence when we wanted a formal assurance he had to retreat from
his earlier position.

It was therefore a completely new picture which I had to present
to the Working Committee when it met again on the morning of
2 April to consider the result of my second interview with Sir
Stafford Cripps. I tried to sum up the position as follows:—

1. I now clearly saw that the British Cabinet was not prepared to
transfer power to India during the War. The British felt that to do so
would be to take a risk, and they were not prepared to take it.

2. Circumstances of the war and specially American pressure had brought about a slight modification in the British position. Even the Churchill Government now felt that India must be given an opportunity of co-operating in the War on a voluntary basis. This was the reason why they were prepared to set up a purely Indian Executive Council and to give it some more powers. In law the Council would, however, remain only a Council and not a Cabinet.

3. It was possible that in actual practice the Viceroy would adopt a liberal attitude and normally accept the decisions of the Council. The position of the Council would, however, remain subordinate to him, and the final responsibility would rest on him and not on the Council.

4. It therefore followed that the answer to the basic question raised by the Working Committee as to who would have ultimate decision was that it would be the Viceroy.

5. So far as the future was concerned, it was possible that the British Government would, in the words of Cripps, consider the Indian problem from a fresh angle but it could not be said with any certainty that India would become independent with the cessation of hostilities.

6. There was, of course, a strong possibility that after the war there might be a new government in place of the Conservative government headed by Mr. Churchill. It was possible that such a Government would consider the Indian question in a spirit of greater understanding and sympathy but obviously such a contingency could not be a part of the proposals.

7. The result therefore was that if the Congress accepted the Cripps offer, it would be without any clear assurance about the future of India even after the cessation of hostilities.

We discussed these points in the light of the announcement made by the B.B.C. on the occasion of the Cripps Mission. It had then been clearly stated that India would now have an opportunity to decide her own fate. This was also the note which Cripps had struck during the first interview, but, as the negotiations continued, the early mood of confidence and optimism was gradually dissipated.

There were other reasons also for a change in the mood and atmosphere. I have already said that when Sir Stafford came to India, he had asked the Viceroy to issue invitations to a number of political leaders of whom one was the late Mr. Allah Bux. After arriving in India, Cripps appeared to modify his stand, perhaps as a result of the influence of Viceregal Lodge. Allah Bux had come to Delhi on the Viceroy's invitation and was waiting for an interview with Sir Stafford, but the interview was not being fixed. As this was creating an awkward situation, I spoke to Cripps and he said that he would soon meet Allah Bux. In spite of this promise, no interview was actually fixed. Allah Bux at last became disgusted and refused to wait in Delhi any longer. When I heard this, I spoke strongly to Sir Stafford and pointed out that this was an insult not only to Allah Bux but to the strong body of Moslems whom he represented. If Government had any doubts on the point, Allah Bux should not have been invited at all. But since the invitation had been issued, he should be properly met. My intervention resulted in an interview between Sir Stafford and Allah Bux the next day. The interview was for only an hour and was confined to general discussions. This incident created a bad impression on me. I felt that this was not the proper method of dealing with difficult political issues. In my judgment, Cripps had not behaved like a statesman.

There was another incident which left me with a disagreeable taste. As soon as the text of the War Cabinet's proposals was released, there was a large volume of criticism in the Indian press. The most critical were the papers which generally expressed the Congress point of view. While the Congress Working Committee was still in session, Cripps sent me a letter in which he said that, though "the Hindu press" had not welcomed the offer, he hoped that I would consider the proposal from a broader point of view. This reference to the Hindu press appeared very odd to me. It also occurred to me that perhaps he was putting the emphasis on the Hindu press because I am a Moslem. If he did not like the comments made by the press, he could easily have referred to the Indian press, or a section of it. I replied that I was surprised at his reference to the Hindu press and did not think that there was any justification for drawing such a distinction among the different sections of the Indian press. I assured him that the Congress Working Committee would consider the proposals only from an Indian point of view and it would take into consideration all sections of opinion before it came to a decision.

During this long session of the Working Committee from 29 March to 11 April, I was with the Committee for practically the whole day. I also met Cripps almost every evening after 2 April. At most of these meetings Jawaharlal was also present. As soon as I had received the intimation of Cripps's proposed visit, I had sent a circular letter to all members of the Working Committee that nobody should meet him separately. The reason for this was that such separate meetings may and sometimes do lead to confusion and misunderstanding. I further said that, if a member of the Working Committee wanted to meet Cripps on some special issue or because of his past associations with Cripps, he should first inform me of his intention.

Cripps complained to me that, during his last visit to India, he had met many members of the Working Committee. This time he found that I had put a restraint on them and not one was willing to meet him. They would not even express an opinion if they met him at some social function, for they felt that the Congress President might take objection to such action.

I told Cripps that, when a responsible organization was negotiating with the Government, it must do so only through its accredited representatives. The Working Committee had decided that the Congress President should carry on the negotiations. It would therefore not be proper for other members of the Working Committee to negotiate separately. If, however, Cripps wanted to meet any member of the Working Committee for any reason, I would gladly arrange it.

Cripps said that he was particularly anxious to meet Bhulabhai Desai. He had stayed with him during his last visit to India. Pointing to the khadi[2] suit he was then wearing, Cripps said with a smile, "Even these clothes I am now wearing are a gift of Bhulabhai Desai."

I asked Bhulabhai Desai to meet Sir Stafford and he did so.

The debate on the offer continued in the Working Committee.

[2] Homespun cotton cloth. Gandhi advocated its universal use. Nehru called it "the livery of independence."

Gandhiji was against acceptance. Jawaharlal favored the proposal. I differed from both of them. Gandhiji was opposed to the proposal because of his opposition to war. Jawaharlal was in favor because of his attachment to the democracies. He was also influenced by the appeal which Generalissimo Chiang Kai-shek had addressed to the Indian people. He was therefore for acceptance of the proposals if this could be done without compromising the Congress position.

As for me, I had only one test by which to judge the proposals. Was the offer of the British Government leading to the freedom of India? If so, we should accept the offer gladly and without any mental reservations. If not, we should reject it categorically. For me, the only test was the issue of Indian freedom.

My attempt throughout the negotiations was to get the Cripps offer in a form which we could accept. I wanted a convention to be created by which the Council would work like a *de facto* Cabinet and the Viceroy like a constitutional head. If we were satisfied on this one point, we could accept the offer and should not insist on a *de jure* transfer of power during the war.

As I have said earlier, these negotiations continued for two long weeks. The Working Committee met during the day, I met Cripps in the evening and reported next morning to the Working Committee. Cripps had discussions with the Viceroy while the Working Committee was in session. I also later came to know that during this period, Cripps had consulted Churchill on three occasions. He may also have consulted other members of the War Cabinet.

Cripps kept on insisting that during the war the decisive factor must be the conduct of the war. The war had now reached a stage where geographical considerations alone placed a heavy burden on India. It was, therefore, necessary that the Executive Council should have a say in the matter and even the British War Cabinet must rely on the Indian Executive Council. He argued that in such a situation it was not necessary to insist on an expansion of the legal powers of the Council or lay it down in clear terms that it would have the final decision. The force of circumstances would place the responsibility increasingly on the Indian leaders who formed the

Executive Council. Lord Wavell [3] was then the Commander-in-Chief in India. Cripps had several discussions with him and suggested that I should also meet him. His feeling was that if I met Wavell and received from him a report on the war situation, this would have a desirable effect. He accordingly wrote to me to meet Wavell. I readily agreed and Cripps arranged an interview.

Cripps personally took Jawaharlal and me to Wavell but after a formal introduction he left us and we talked with Wavell for over an hour. Nothing, however, emerged from these discussions which could offer a reply to our basic question. On this occasion, Wavell spoke more like a politician than a soldier and insisted that, during the war, strategic considerations must take precedence over all other issues. I did not deny this but pointed out that our concern was as to who would exercise power in the administration of India. Wavell could throw no light on this question.

As a result of our insistence, it had been proposed that one of the members of the Executive Council would deal with problems relating to the war. Cripps tried to persuade us that this would ensure Indian participation in the responsibility for the conduct of the war. He could not, however, clearly say what would be the relation between the Indian member and the Commander-in-Chief. It was mainly to discuss this question that he arranged for my interview with Wavell. When I asked Wavell if the role of the Indian member of the Council would be that of a responsible Cabinet Minister, he could give no direct reply. The conclusion I drew from my talk with him was that the Indian member would have responsibility but no power. He would be in charge of Canteens, Commissariat and Transport, but would have little say about the fighting forces.

The position may be briefly summed up as follows. The Cripps offer stressed that, after the war, Indian independence would be recognized. During the war, the only change was that the Executive Council would be entirely Indian and consist of leaders of the political parties. Regarding the communal problem, Cripps said that

[3] General, poet and biographer of Lord Allenby, his World War I commander. Later, Viceroy.

after the war the provinces would have the option to decide whether to join the Union or not.

I had not objected to Cripps's basic principle that independence would be recognized after the war. I felt, however, that, unless *de facto* power and responsibility were given to the Council during the war, the change would not be significant. During my first interview with him, Cripps had given me an assurance on this point and said that the Council would act like a cabinet. In the course of discussion, it became clear that this was a poetic exaggeration. His real offer was quite different.

An even greater snag was the option given to the provinces to stay outside the Union.[4] This, as well as the solution of the communal problem suggested by Cripps, had greatly disturbed Gandhiji. He had reacted violently against it. When I met him after my first interview with Cripps, I immediately realized that Gandhiji regarded the Cripps offer as totally unacceptable. He felt that it would only add to our difficulties and make a settlement of the communal problem impossible.

I discussed in detail the implication of this item with Cripps. I asked him to tell us what exactly he and his colleagues in the War Cabinet had in view. Cripps tried to persuade me that the Indian political problem could not be solved till the communal problem was settled. This could be done in one of two ways. One was to settle it forthwith. The other was to defer a decision till after the war, when power would be in Indian hands. Cripps said that in his opinion it would be wrong to raise the issue at present. It would only add to the difficulties. The only feasible thing was, therefore, to wait for the end of the war. He assured me, however, that, if the Hindus and the Moslems could come to an agreement, a solution could be reached even now.

I told Cripps that the right given to the provinces to opt out

---

[4] See Paragraph C of the Cripps Draft Declaration in the Appendix. Any province would have the right not to accept the new federal constitution and to make its own treaty arrangements with the British government.

meant opening the door to separation. Cripps tried to defend his
position by pointing out that the right was given to a province as a
whole and not to any particular community. He was convinced that
once the right of the provinces to opt out was recognized, no
province would, in fact, demand that right. Not to concede the
right would on the other hand rouse suspicion and doubt. The
provinces would be able to look at the question objectively only
when they felt that they had perfect freedom to decide as they chose.

After we had discussed this issue one morning, Cripps telephoned
to me in the evening and said that Sir Sikandar Hayat Khan was
coming to meet him the next day. Cripps hoped that Sir Sikandar
would prove helpful in the solution of the communal problem.
Punjab was a Moslem majority province and, if Punjab decided to
remain with India, this would give a lead to the other Moslem
majority provinces. I told him that I was doubtful if Sir Sikandar
could solve the problem but, since he was coming to Delhi, I would
be glad to see him.

Sir Sikandar came to Delhi the next day and after meeting Cripps
he saw me. He was of the view that the Cripps offer was the best
possible solution of the communal problem. He was convinced that,
if the matter were put to the vote of the Punjab Assembly, its
decision would be on national and not communal lines. I conceded
that, if the vote were now taken, his forecast was likely to be right,
but as to what would happen after the end of the war was more than
he or I could say. I told him that I could not accept that he would
have the same influence then as he had now.

Regarding the Indian states, the Cripps offer gave to the representatives of the states full freedom to decide their future. This
included the power to opt out like the provinces. I must, in fairness
to Cripps, point out that in his discussions with the representatives
of the states, he was clear and forthright. He told the Maharaja of
Kashmir that the future of the states was with India. No prince
should think for a moment that the British Crown would come to
his help if he decided to opt out. The princes must therefore look

to the Indian Government and not to the British Crown for their future. I remember that most of the representatives of the states looked crestfallen after their interview with Cripps.

The Working Committee had already approved a draft resolution on the proposals brought by Cripps. This was sent to him on 2 April, but not released to the press till the negotiations finally broke down. Apart from the general question of the transfer of power to India, the major difficulty had arisen over the definition of the powers of the Commander-in-Chief and the Indian member of the Executive Committee in charge of defence. Cripps had suggested that the Indian member would be responsible mainly for public relations, demolibization, postwar reconstruction and amenities for the members of the defence forces. Congress regarded these functions as totally insufficient and made a counterproposal that the Defence Minister would be in charge of all functions excepting those to be exercised by the Commander-in-Chief for the purpose of the conduct of the war. Cripps made certain countersuggestions, but these also proved unsatisfactory as he wanted to reserve all important functions to the Commander-in-Chief.

I had a further meeting with Cripps in the late afternoon of 9 April and on the morning of the 10th reported to the Working Committee the result of my discussions. We came regretfully to the conclusion that the British Government's proposals as they stood were not acceptable.

Accordingly on 10 April 1942, I wrote to Sir Stafford that the approach to the Indian problem in the Draft Declaration was not only wrong but was likely to lead to greater complications in the future. He wrote an answer on 11 April in which he tried to argue that his proposals offered the best possible solution of the Indian problem and insisted that he had not changed his position at any stage. He now tried to shift the blame onto Congress and wanted to publish his letter. I replied on the same day refuting his contention and pointing out that the correspondence would convince any impartial observer that the fault for the failure of his mission lay with him and not with Congress. The main points in my two letters

are given below, but interested readers may find the whole correspondence in the Appendix.

Briefly, this is what I wrote to Sir Stafford in my two letters of
10 and 11 April 1942. The Draft Declaration laid much greater
emphasis on the future than on the immediate present, while India
demanded changes in the present system. In spite of its objections
to some of the proposals for the future, Congress was still willing
to come to a settlement with the Government for the sake of
national defence. In order to rouse enthusiasm and create a mass
psychology of resistance to the invader, it was necessary to have a
national government. People must be made to feel that they were
free to defend their own freedom and their own country.

My letters also pointed out that Congress had no intention of
interfering with the technical and operational sides of war and was
even prepared to accept some limitations on the powers of the
Indian Defence Minister for the duration of the war, but we could
not forget that the defence of the country was the supreme demand
of the moment. During the war, civil administration is bound to be
subordinated to the demands of defence. To reserve defence solely
for the Viceroy or the Commander-in-Chief meant that all powers,
including those ostensibly transferred to Indian hands, would be
denied to India.

Another point emphasized by me was that Congress was very
much alive to the importance of solving the communal problem.
We recognized that in tackling the political question in India,
communal questions were bound to arise at some stage or other
and would have to be solved. I assured him that as soon as the main
political problem was settled, the responsibility of finding a satisfactory solution to the communal and other problems would be
ours. I was confident that we could find a satisfactory solution to the
communal problem as soon as the political question was settled.

I then pointed out with regret that the first impression of the
picture created as a result of my earlier interviews with Sir Stafford
gradually became blurred as the discussions on material points
proceeded from stage to stage. When I last met him on the night

of 9 April the picture had completely changed and hopes of a settlement had faded out.

Since Sir Stafford had said that he proposed to publish his letter to me, I wrote back that presumably he would not object if I released the entire correspondence as well as the resolution we had passed. Cripps wrote back to say that he had no objection. Accordingly these were released to the press on 11 April.

The resolution was in the following terms:—

The Working Committee have given their full and earnest consideration to the proposals made by the British War Cabinet in regard to India and the elucidation thereof by Sir Stafford Cripps. These proposals, which have been made at the very last hour because of the compulsion of events, have to be considered not only in relation to India's demand for independence, but more specially in the present grave war crisis, with a view to meeting effectively the perils and dangers that confront India and envelop the world.

The Congress has repeatedly stated, ever since the commencement of the War in September 1939, that the people of India would line themselves with the progressive forces of the world and assume full responsibility to face the new problems and shoulder the new burdens that had arisen, and it asked for the necessary conditions to enable them to do so to be created. An essential condition was the freedom of India, for only the realization of present freedom could light the flame which would illumine millions of hearts and move them to action. At the last meeting of the All India Congress Committee after the commencement of the War in the Pacific, it was stated that: "Only a free and independent India can be in a position to undertake the defence of the country on a national basis and be of help in the furtherance of the larger causes that are emerging from the storm of war."

The British War Cabinet's new proposals relate principally to the future upon the cessation of hostilities. The Committee, while recognising that self-determination for the people of India is accepted in principle in that uncertain future, regret that this is fettered and circumscribed and certain provisions have been introduced which gravely imperil the development of a free and united nation and the establishment of a democratic State. Even the constitution-making body is so constituted that the people's right to self-determination is vitiated by the introduction of non-representative elements. The people of India have as a whole clearly demanded full independence and the Congress has repeatedly declared that no other status except that of independence for the whole of India could be agreed to or could meet the essential requirements of the present situation. The Committee recognise that future independence may be implicit in the proposals but the accompanying provisions and restrictions are such that real freedom may well become an illusion. The complete ignoring of the ninety millions of the people of the Indian States and their treatment as commodities at the disposal of their rulers is a negation of both democracy and self-determination. While the representation of an Indian State in the constitution-making body is fixed on a population basis, the people of the State have no voice in choosing those reprsentatives, nor are they to be consulted at any stage, while decisions vitally affecting them are being taken. Such States may in many ways become barriers to the growth of Indian freedom, enclaves where foreign authority still prevails and where the possibility of maintaining foreign armed forces has been stated to be a likely contingency, and a perpetual menace to the freedom of the people of the States as well as of the rest of India.

The acceptance beforehand of the novel principle of non-accession for a province is also a severe blow to the conception of Indian unity and an apple of discord likely to generate growing trouble in the provinces, and which may well lead to further difficulties in the way of the Indian States merging themselves in the Indian Union. The Congress has been wedded to Indian freedom and unity and any break in that unity, especially in the modern world when people's minds inevitably think in terms of ever larger federations, would be injurious to all concerned and exceedingly painful to contemplate. Nevertheless the Committee cannot think in terms of compelling the people in any territorial unit to remain in an Indian Union against their declared and established will. While recognising this principle, the Committee feel that every effort should be made to create conditions which would help the different units in developing a common and co-operative national life. The acceptance of the principle inevitably involves that no changes should be made which result in fresh problems being created and compulsion being exercised on other substantial groups within that area. Each territorial unit should have the fullest possible autonomy within the Union, consistently with a strong national State. The proposal now made on the part of the British War Cabinet encourages and will lead to attempts at separation at the very inception of a union and thus create friction just when the utmost co-operation and goodwill are most needed. This proposal has been presumably made to meet a communal demand, but it will have other consequences also and lead politically reactionary and obscurantist groups among different communities to create trouble and divert public attention from the vital issues before the country.

Any proposal concerning the future of India must demand attention and scrutiny, but in today's grave crisis, it is the present that counts, and even proposals for the future are important in so far as they affect the present. The Committee have necessarily attached the greatest importance to this aspect of the question, and on this ultimately depends what advice they should give to those who look to them for guidance. For this present the British War Cabinet's proposals are vague and altogether incomplete, and it would appear that no vital changes in the present structure are contemplated. It has been made clear that the Defence of India will in any event remain under British control. At any time defence is a vital subject; during wartime it is all important and covers almost every sphere of life and administration. To take away defence from the sphere of responsibility at this stage is to reduce that responsibility to a farce and a nullity, and to make it perfectly clear that India is not going to be free in any way and her Government is not going to function as a free and independent government during the pendency of the War. The Committee would repeat that an essential and fundamental prerequisite for the assumption of responsibility by the Indian people in the present is their realisation as a fact that they are free and are in charge of maintaining and defending their freedom. What is most wanted is the enthusiastic response of the people which cannot be evoked without the fullest trust in them and the devolution of responsibility on them in the matter of defence. It is only thus that even at this grave eleventh hour it may be possible to galvanise the people of India to rise to the height of the occasion. It is manifest that the present Government of India as well as its provincial agencies, are lacking in competence, and are incapable of shouldering the burden of India's defence. It is only the people of India, through their popular representatives, who may shoulder this burden worthily. But that can only be done by present freedom, and full responsibility being cast upon them.

The Committee, therefore, are unable to accept the proposals put forward on behalf of the British War Cabinet.

I also held a press conference on 11 April 1942 when I met a large number of journalists and explained to them the reasons which had led to our rejection of the Cripps offer. I need not repeat them at length, for they are embodied in both the Resolution and the correspondence. I laid special stress on the point that, as the discussions proceeded, we found that the rosy picture at first drawn by Sir Stafford gradually faded. This change in the atmosphere was also reflected in my interview with Lord Wavell. In the course of our talks, Sir Stafford Cripps had repeatedly emphasized the technical difficulties in the way of transferring defence to an Indian member. It was at his suggestion that we had met Lord Wavell, because he could explain the technical side of the question much better. Curiously enough, throughout our interview with the Commander-in-Chief, at which other military officers were also present, not a word was spoken about any technical difficulty. The entire discussion proceeded on political lines. It did not strike me for a moment that we were interviewing a military expert, for Lord Wavell spoke like an expert politician.

During the press conference, I also felt it necessary to clarify the position created by certain speculations in a section of the press regarding Mahatma Gandhi's part in the discussion. Gandhiji's views on the subject of participation in any war were well known and it would be entirely untrue to suggest that the Working Committee's decisions were in any way influenced by those views.

Gandhiji made it clear to the Working Committee that we were perfectly free to come to our own decisions on the merit of the proposals. He did not want to participate even in the earlier sittings of the Working Committee and it was only because of my insistence that he agreed to stay on for several days. Eventually, he felt that he could not stay any longer and all my persuasion failed to move him.

I also informed the press that the Working Committee's decision was at every stage unanimous.

I concluded by saying that it was a matter for deep regret that the goal which all of us had passionately desired was not reached, but it should be placed on record that discussions were carried on in a friendly atmosphere. In spite of profound differences, which at times led to heated controversy, Sir Stafford and we had parted as friends and the cordiality of the talks was maintained to the last.

So far as Congress was concerned, this was the way the Cripps Mission came to an end. It was not, however, the case with Jawa-

harlal and Rajagopalachari. Before passing on to the next phase in
the story of India's struggle for freedom, I would like to make a
special reference to their reaction to these events.

Jawaharlal gave an interview to the representative of the *News
Chronicle* soon after Cripps left. The whole tone and attitude of the
interview appeared to minimize the difference between Congress
and the British. He tried to represent that, though Congress had
rejected the Cripps offer, India was willing to help the British.

I also learnt that there was a proposal that Jawaharlal should
make a broadcast from All-India Radio. From what I knew of his
attitude, I was afraid that his statement might create confusion in
the public mind. Jawaharlal had already left for Allahabad and I
had also made arrangements for returning to Calcutta. I decided
that I would stop on the way and have a further talk with him. I
did so and told Jawaharlal clearly that, now that the Working
Committee had passed a resolution, he must be very careful regarding what he said. If he gave a statement which created the impression that Congress was not going to oppose the war effort, the whole
effect of the Congress Resolution would be lost. The Congress
stand was that India was willing to help Britain but could do so
only as a free country. I was sure that this was also his attitude. If
he said anything which created the impression that India was
willing to support the war effort regardless of the British attitude,
the Congress Resolution would become meaningless. I therefore
requested him to refrain from making any statement. At first he
argued with me but in the end he saw my point of view. I was very
glad when he declared that he would make no statement at all and
would cancel the broadcast which he had promised to make.

I want to make it absolutely clear that Jawaharlal's attitude was
not due to any doubt regarding India's freedom. His attitude was a
natural result of his understanding of the international situation.
He was from the beginning a confirmed anti-Facist. His visit to
China and his discussions with Chiang Kai-shek had strengthened
his antipathy to fascism. He was so impressed by China's struggle
against Japan that he felt that the democracies must be supported

at any cost. In fact he felt genuine grief that India should not be fighting by the side of the democracies.

I may also mention that Jawaharlal has always been more moved by international considerations than most Indians. He has looked at all questions from an international rather than a national point of view. I also shared his concern for the international issues, but to me the question of India's independence was paramount. I preferred the democracies to the fascist powers but I could not forget that, unless the democratic principle was applied to India's case, all professions of democracy sounded hollow and insincere. I also remembered the course of events since the First World War. Britain had then declared that she was fighting German imperialism to protect the rights of the smaller nations. When the United States entered the War, President Wilson formulated his famous Fourteen Points and pleaded for the self-determination of all nations. Nevertheless the rights of India were not respected. Nor were the Fourteen Points ever applied to India's case. I, therefore, felt that all talk about the democratic camp was meaningless unless India's case was seriously considered. I made all these points in an interview I gave to the *News Chronicle* about a week later in Calcutta.

During the whole of this period, Jawaharlal was living under a terrible mental strain. He had recently returned from China where he had been greatly influenced by Generalissimo and Madame Chiang Kai-shek. It was clear to him that India's help was essential if China were to resist Japan successfully. One evening during the meeting of the Working Committee, Jawaharlal came to me and our discussion convinced me that he was in favor of accepting the Cripps offer even though there was no change in the British stand. He argued that in view of the favorable assurances given by Cripps, we should not hesitate. Jawaharlal did not say this in so many words but this was the trend of all his arguments.

I was greatly disturbed as a result of this talk and could not sleep till almost two o'clock in the morning. As soon as I woke, I went to Shrimati [Mrs. or Madam] Rameshwari Nehru's [5] house where

---

[5] The wife of Jawaharlal Nehru's first cousin.

Jawaharlal was staying. We discussed the various issues for over an hour. I told him that the trend of his thought was against our best interests. If real power were not transferred to India and only a new Executive Council were formed, then the only thing we should receive from Cripps was a promise which would be valid after the war. In the existing circumstances, such a promise had little value. Who knew what would be the end of the war? We were prepared to participate in the war as a free country. The Cripps offer gave us nothing on that point. Even the decision to participate in the war was not ours, but the Viceroy's. Cripps was asking us to accept this decision of the Viceroy without giving us the opportunity of deciding for ourselves. If we still accepted the offer, it would mean that all of our decisions till now had been wrong.

I further argued that the world was bound to change after the war. No one who was aware of the world's political situation could doubt that India would become free. Hence the offer of Cripps really gave us nothing. If we accepted his offer, we might have cause to rue it in the future. In case the British went back on their word, we should not even have the justification for launching a fresh struggle. War had given India an opportunity for achieving her freedom. We must not lose it by depending upon a mere promise.

Jawaharlal was greatly depressed by all that was happening. It was clear that he was not sure of his position. The struggle in his mind made him feel helpless. He remained silent for some moments, then said: "I do not for a moment want to decide according to my personal inclinations. Remove all doubt from your mind on this point. My decision will be the same as that of my colleagues."

Jawaharlal's nature is such that, when there is some tension in his mind, he talks even in his sleep. The day's preoccupations come to him as dreams. When I came out, Shrimati Rameshwari Nehru told me that for the last two nights Jawaharlal had been talking in his sleep. He was carrying on a debate and was sometimes muttering and sometimes speaking loudly. She had heard Cripps's name, sometimes references to Gandhiji and sometimes my name. This was added proof of how great was the strain under which his mind was working.

The second person on whom the negotiations had a profound effect was Shri Rajagopalachari. He had for some time been deeply disturbed by the deteriorating communal situation in the country. It was his view that the independence of India was held up because of the differences between the Congress and the League. My reading of the situation was that the British did not wish to take any risks during the period of the war and the differences among the communities gave them a pretext for keeping the power in their hands. Rajagopalachari did not agree and soon after the rejection of the Cripps offer, he began to say openly that if only the Congress would accept the League's demands, the obstacles to Indian freedom would be removed. Not content with expressing this view generally, he sponsored a resolution in the Madras Congress Legislature party to the following effect:

The Madras Legislature Congress Party notes with deep regret that the attempts to establish a National Government for India to enable her to face the problems arising out of the present grave situation have failed and that, as a result of this, Nationalist India has been placed in a dilemma. It is impossible for the people to think in terms of neutrality or passivity during an invasion by an enemy power. Neither is it practicable to organize any effective defence independently and un-co-ordinated with the defence measures of the Government. It is absolutely and urgently necessary in the best interests of the country at this hour of peril to do all that the Congress can possibly do to remove every obstacle in the way of the establishment of a national administration to face the present situation, and, therefore, as much as the Muslim League has insisted on the recognition of the right of separation of certain areas from United India upon the ascertainment of the wishes of the people of such areas as a condition precedent for a united national action at this moment of grave national danger, this party is of opinion and recommends to the All-India Congress Committee that to sacrifice the chances of the formation of a National Government at this grave crisis for the doubtful advantage of maintaining a controversy over the unity of India is a most unwise policy and that it has become necessary to choose the lesser evil and acknowledge the Muslim League's claim for separation; should the same be persisted in when the time comes for framing a constitution for India and thereby remove all doubts and fears in this regard and to invite the Muslim League for a consultation for the purpose of arriving at an agreement and securing the installation of a National Government to meet the present emergency.

Rajagopalachari had not consulted me before he sponsored this resolution. Nor, as far as I was aware, had he consulted any of our other colleagues. I was greatly disturbed when I read of the resolution in the papers. If one of my colleagues in the Working Committee went about preaching against the decision of Congress, it would not only weaken the discipline of the organization but create confusion in the public mind and give a handle to the imperial power. I accordingly felt that the matter should be discussed by the Working Committee.

I told Rajagopalachari that the resolutions passed by the Madras Legislature were not consistent with the declared policy of the Congress. As a responsible member of the Working Committee, he should have avoided all association with such resolutions. If he felt strongly on the subject, he should have discussed the matter with his colleagues in the Working Committee before giving expression to his views. If the Working Committee did not agree with him it was open to him to resign and then propagate his views.

Rajagopalachari admitted that he should have talked the matter over in the Working Committee before the resolutions were moved in the Madras Legislature. He was, however, unable to withdraw the two resolutions, as they represented his considered view. He addressed a letter to me in which he expressed his regret for publicly ventilating his views on a highly controversial question before consulting the President. I give the text of his letter below:

19, Edmostone Road,
Allahabad
April 30, 1942.

Dear Maulana Saheb,

With reference to your observation on the resolutions passed on my motion by the Madras Congress Legislative party, I admit that I should have talked the matter over with you and other colleagues of the Working Committee before moving the resolutions, knowing as I did their disagreement on the subject. I write this to express my regret.

I have explained to you already how strongly I feel. I believe that I should be failing in my duty if I do not endeavour to get people to think and act in the direction which my conviction leads to. I feel that in the public interests I should move the resolutions already notified by Mr. Santanam, I desire, therefore, to request you to permit me to resign my place in the Working Committee.

Let me tender my grateful thanks for the unqualified trust and affection bestowed on me by you and the other colleagues during all these many years that I have served in the committee.

Yours sincerely,
C. Rajagopalachari

CHAPTER 7

Uneasy Interval

THE failure of the Cripps Mission led to widespread disappointment and anger in the country. Many Indians felt that the Churchill Cabinet had sent Sir Stafford only because of American and Chinese pressure, but that in fact Mr. Churchill had no intention of recognizing Indian freedom. The long-drawn-out negotiations with many parties were intended merely to prove to the world outside that Congress was not the true representative of India and that the disunity of Indians was the real reason why the British could not hand over power to Indian hands. Since there was misunderstanding and confusion even among Congressmen, I decided to call a meeting of the All India Congress Committee. This was held from 29 April to 2 May 1942 at Allahabad and was preceded by a meeting of the Working Committee from 27 April to 1 May.

In opening the proceedings of the All India Congress Committee, I said that a month and a half ago we had met at Wardha. At that time it was known that the British Government had decided to make a new approach to the Indian problem. It was announced that Sir Stafford Cripps, a member of the War Cabinet, would proceed to India with fresh proposals for the settlement of the Indian problem. The Working Committee at Wardha decided that, as the Congress President, I should meet Sir Stafford on behalf of Congress. I had a series of interviews with Sir Stafford and told him that the draft declaration he had brought was disappointing. It offered nothing here and now and referred to an uncertain future. The proposals regarding the present were not only vague but yielded nothing to popular control. Defence was to be the sole responsibility of His Majesty's Government in England. This reservation reduced to nullity the supposed transfer of power from British to Indian hands. In wartime, defence covered every sphere of civil administration.

I paid a public tribute to the patriotism and loyalty of my colleagues and informed the Committee that all our decisions were unanimous. I also pointed out that we had a clear idea of the lines on which the communal and other problems were to be solved, but we did not allow this to influence our attitude to the Cripps offer. We judged the offer by only one test: would it or would it not transfer power from British to Indian hands? I had no doubt that we would have produced a satisfactory solution of the communal problem if the question of the transfer of political power had first been satisfactorily settled.

I then dealt with the view expressed by some that the Cripps Mission, though it did not produce a settlement of the Indo-British problem, had succeeded in changing the attitude of the people towards the war. I held this view to be absolutely wrong and misleading. If anything, the Mission had done almost irreparable injury to Indo-British understanding. It had raised hopes only to disappoint them. It had confirmed the faith that an enslaved India will have nothing to do with the war. Only a free India could defend herself. Sir Stafford Cripps was now saying that the initiative in dealing with the Indian situation must henceforth lie with the leaders of the Indian people and not the British Government. I declared that Congress had gone as far as it possibly could and would take no further initiative in the matter.

I then referred to the imminent peril of invasion by Japan. I sharply criticized those who believed or said that Japan would give India freedom. National self-respect demanded that we should not think in terms of a change of masters. We would resist the Japanese aggression in spite of our difference with the British. There could be no welcome for Japan, whether active or passive. Had we been free, we would have resorted to armed resistance if any country attacked us. Armed resistance was denied to us but we had the weapon of nonviolence. This was a weapon we had used for the last twenty-two years. No one could take it away from us.

The All India Congress Committee endorsed the stand of the Working Committee and reaffirmed the resolution on the Cripps Mission passed by it. It also decided that the Working Committee should be authorized to take such further action as might be necessary for continuing our struggle for Indian freedom.

I returned to Calcutta from Allahabad and was disturbed to see the deterioration in the situation on all hands. The majority of the people were now convinced that the British would lose the war and some seemed to welcome a Japanese victory. There was great bitterness against the British which at times was so intense that they did not think of the consequence of a Japanese conquest of India.

After Cripps departed, I also found a marked change in Gandhiji's attitude. I have already said how much opposed he was in the beginning to any movement during the war. He had held that India should stand for nonviolence and not deviate from it for any reason. That is why, in spite of my efforts, he would not consent to any mass movement, for he felt such a movement might lead to violence. In fact it was with the greatest difficulty that I could persuade him to agree to the individual Satyagraha or Civil Disobedience Movement. Even then he laid down so many conditions that the movement could be nothing more than a moral gesture.

Gandhiji's mind was now moving from the extreme of complete inactivity to that of organized mass effort. The process had perhaps begun earlier but it became clear only after Cripps left. In June 1942, I went to visit him at Wardha and stayed with him for about five days. During my talks with him I saw that he had moved far away from the position he had taken at the outbreak of the war.

I now began to sense that the Government anticipated a Japanese attack on India. The Government seemed to be of the view that, even if the whole country were not invested, the Japanese would make an attempt to occupy Bengal. They thought that the Japanese would attack by sea and advance on Calcutta from Diamond Harbor. I came to know that the Government had decided to abandon Calcutta in such a contingency. A secret circular had been issued to selected officers instructing them about the stages at which they should leave Calcutta, Howrah and the 24 Parganas [a district near Calcutta] and the routes they should follow. The Government had also taken certain necessary precautionary measures. They had worked out a plan of resistance at different places and even prepared provisional orders about the line of retreat in case a withdrawal became necessary. According to this, the first line of resistance would be along the river Padma, the second between Asansol and Ranchi and the last near Allahabad. The Government had also decided that, in case of a Japanese attack, something like the scorched earth policy must be followed. They had also prepared measures for the blowing up of important bridges and the destruction of factories and industrial installations in order to deny them to the Japanese. Plans for the destruction of the Iron and Steel Factory at Jamshedpur [which was owned by the Tata Company] had somehow become known and there was great anxiety and unrest in the whole area.

I reported all these developments to Gandhiji. I also told him that it was my conviction that, once the Japanese set foot on Indian soil, it would become our sacred duty to oppose them with every means at our disposal. I felt that it would be intolerable to exchange an old master for a new one. In fact it would be far more inimical to our interests if a new and virile conqueror replaced the old Government which in course of time had become effete and was gradually losing its grasp. I was convinced that it would be far more difficult to oust a new imperialism like that of the Japanese.

I had already taken some steps in anticipation of a possible Japanese attack on India. I had asked the Congress organization to carry on propaganda to build up public resistance against the Japanese. I had divided Calcutta into a number of wards and started to recruit and organize bands of volunteers pledged to oppose Japan. These volunteers were instructed to place every possible obstacle in the way of the Japanese army if it should advance. The scheme I had in view was that, as soon as the Japanese army reached Bengal and the British army withdrew towards Bihar, the Congress should step in and take over the control of the country. With the aid of our volunteers, we should capture power in the interregnum before the Japanese could establish themselves. In this way alone could we hope to oppose the new enemy and gain our freedom. In fact, most of my time during May and June 1942 was spent in developing and carrying out this new line.

I was surprised to find that Gandhiji did not agree with me. He told me in unqualified terms that if the Japanese army ever came into India, it would come not as our enemy but as the enemy of the British. He said that, if the British left immediately, he believed that the Japanese would have no reason to attack India. I could not accept his reading and in spite of long discussions we could not reach agreement. I found that Sardar Patel held the same view and perhaps he had influenced Gandhiji. We therefore parted on a note of difference.[1]

[1] Of his attitude towards the Japanese, Gandhi wrote to Miss Slade (Mira-behn) as follows:

". . . Remember that our attitude is that of complete non-cooperation with the Japanese army, therefore we may not help them in any way, nor may we profit by any dealings with them. Therefore we cannot sell anything to them. If the people are not able to face the Japanese army, they will do as armed soldiers do, i.e. retire when they are overwhelmed. And if they do so, the question of having any dealings with the Japanese does not and should not arise. If, however, the people have not the courage to resist the Japanese unto death and the courage and capacity to evacuate the portion invaded by the Japanese, they will do the best they can in the light of instructions. One thing they should never do—to yield willing submission to the Japanese. That will be a cowardly act, and unworthy of a freedom-loving people. They must not escape from one fire only to fall into another and probably more terrible. Their attitude therefore must always be of resistance to the Japanese. No question, therefore, arises of accepting British currency notes or Japanese coins. They will handle nothing from Japanese hands. So far as dealings with our own people are concerned they will either resort to barter or make use of such British currency as they have, in the hope that the National Government that may take the place of British Government will take up from the people all the British currency in accordance with its capacity. . . .

". . . If the British have retired in an orderly manner, leaving things in Indian hands, the whole thing can work splendidly and it might even be made difficult for the Japanese to settle down in India or any part of it in peace, because they will have to deal with a population which will be sullen and

In the first week of July, there was a meeting of the Working Committee at Wardha. I reached Wardha on 5 July and Gandhiji spoke to me for the first time about the "Quit India" Movement. I could not easily adjust my mind to this new idea. I felt that we were facing an extraordinary dilemma. Our sympathies were with the Allied powers but the British Government had taken up an attitude which made it impossible for us to cooperate with them. We could side with the British only as a free country but the British wanted us as mere camp followers. On the other hand, the Japanese had occupied Burma and were advancing towards Assam. I felt that we must refrain from any word or action which could offer encouragement to the Japanese. It seemed to me that the only thing we could do was to wait upon the course of events and watch how the war situation developed. Gandhiji did not agree. He insisted that the time had come when Congress should raise the demand that the British must leave India. If the British agreed, we could then tell the Japanese that they should not advance any further. If in spite of this they advanced, it would be an attack on India and not on the British. If such a situation developed we must oppose Japan with all our might.

I have already said that I had been in favor of organized opposition to the British at the outbreak of the war. Gandhiji had not then agreed with me. Now that he had changed, I found myself in a peculiar position. I could not believe that with the enemy on the Indian frontier, the British would tolerate an organized movement of resistance. Gandhiji seemed to have a strange belief that they would. He held that the British would allow him to develop his movement in his own way. When I pressed him to tell us what exactly would be the program of resistance, he had no clear idea. The only thing he mentioned during our discussions was that, unlike previous occasions, this time the people would not court imprison-

---

resistant. It is difficult to say what can happen. It is enough if people are trained to cultivate the power of resistance, no matter which power is operating—the Japanese or the British. . . ." (Pyarelal, *Towards New Horizons* [Ahmedabad: Navajivan Press, 1959], pp. 192–93.)

ment voluntarily. They should resist arrest and submit to the Government only if physically forced to do so.

I was skeptical of the Japanese attitude and held that we could not place any trust in Japanese professions. It seemed to me most unlikely that they would stop their victorious march when they saw the British withdraw. To me it seemed that instead of stopping them, such a step might encourage them in their march to India. Would they not regard the British withdrawal as the most favorable opportunity for occupying India? I could not give categorical answers to these questions and I therefore hesitated to adopt Gandhiji's line.

Gandhiji held that the British would regard his move for an organized mass movement as a warning and not take any precipitate action. He would therefore have time to work out the details of the movement and develop its tempo according to his plans. I was convinced that this would not be the case. The Government would not wait but arrest Gandhiji and other Congress leaders as soon as Congress passed any resolution for launching a mass movement. In the absence of the leaders, the country would be paralyzed and the people so dejected that they would be unable to take action against the Japanese if they should attack India. The people were now responding to the Congress call because of their faith in Gandhiji but, when he and his colleagues were in jail, they would not know what to do. After a great deal of thought, I came to the conclusion that something must be done to keep up the people's spirit. If Gandhiji were allowed to develop the movement in his own way, it would naturally proceed along nonviolent lines. If, however, we were all arrested, the people must not be allowed to fall into a state of inertia but be encouraged to carry on the movement as best as they could without bothering too much about violence or nonviolence.

When the Working Committee began its discussions, I elaborated these points in detail. Among members of the Working Committee only Jawaharlal supported me and then only up to a point. The other members would not oppose Gandhiji even when they were not fully convinced. This was not a new experience for me. Apart from Jawaharlal, who often agreed with me, the other members were generally content to follow Gandhiji's lead. Sardar Patel, Dr. Rajendra Prasad and Acharya Kripalani had no clear idea about the war. They rarely tried to judge things on their own, and in any case they were accustomed to subordinate their judgment to Gandhiji. As such, discussion with them was almost useless. After all our discussions, the only thing they could say was that we must have faith in Gandhiji. They held that if we trusted him he would find some way out. They cited the example of the Salt Satyagraha Movement in 1930. When this had begun, nobody knew what was going to happen. The Government themselves were contemptuous of the move and had openly ridiculed it. In the end, however, the Salt Satyagraha Movement had proved a great success and compelled the British to come to terms. Sardar Patel and his colleagues held that this time also Gandhiji would have the same success. I confess that this kind of reasoning did not satisfy me.

Gandhiji's idea seemed to be that, since the war was on the Indian frontier, the British would come to terms with the Congress as soon as the movement was launched. Even if this did not take place, he believed that the British would hesitate to take any drastic steps with the Japanese knocking at India's doors. He thought that this would give the Congress the time and the opportunity to organize an effective movement. My own reading was completely different. I was convinced that in this critical stage of the war, the Government would not tolerate any mass movement. It was a question of life and death for the British. They would, therefore, act swiftly and drastically. I clearly saw that, as soon as we decided on a movement, the Government would arrest all Congress leaders and then nobody could say what would happen.

I had a strong conviction that a nonviolent movement could not be launched or carried out in the existing circumstances. A movement could remain nonviolent only if the leaders were present and able to guide it at every step and I was convinced that the leaders would be arrested at the first suggestion of a movement. If, of course, the Congress decided to abjure nonviolence, there was scope for a movement. Even a leaderless people could disrupt communications, burn stores and depots and in a hundred ways sabotage the war effort. I also recognized that such a general upheaval might lead to a deadlock and force the British to come to terms. It would, however, be a great risk but I held that, if the risk were to be taken, it should be done with open eyes. On the other hand, I could not for a moment see how the nonviolent movement of Gandhiji's conception could be launched or maintained in war conditions.

Our discussions started on 5 July and continued for several days. I had on earlier occasions also differed from Gandhiji on some points but never before had our difference been so complete. Things reached a climax when he sent me a letter to the effect that my stand was so different from his that we could not work together. If Congress wanted Gandhiji to lead the movement, I must resign from the presidentship and also withdraw from the Working Committee. Jawaharlal must do the same. I immediately sent for Jawaharlal and showed him Gandhiji's letter. Sardar Patel had also dropped in and he was shocked when he read the letter. He immediately went to Gandhiji and protested strongly against his action. Patel pointed out that if I resigned from the presidentship and both Jawaharlal and I left the Working Committee, the repercussions on the country would be disastrous. Not only would the people be confused, but Congress would be shaken to its very foundation.

Gandhiji had sent me this letter early on the morning of 7 July. At about midday he sent for me. He made a long speech whose substance was that he had written in the morning in haste. He had now thought further over the matter and wanted to withdraw his letter. I could not but yield to his persuasion. When the Working Committee met at three in the afternoon, the first thing Gandhiji said was that the penitent sinner has come back to the Maulana!

We began to discuss in greater detail the various elements of the proposed movement. Gandhiji made it clear that like other movements, this would also be on the basis of nonviolence. All methods short of violence would, however, be permissible. During the discussions, Jawaharlal said that what Gandhiji had in view was in fact an open rebellion even if the rebellion were nonviolent. Gandhiji liked the phrase and spoke of an open nonviolent revolution several times. On 14 July 1942, the Working Committee passed the following resolution on the national demand:—

Events happening from day to day, and the experience that the people of India are passing through, confirm the opinion of Congressmen that British rule in India must end immediately, not merely because foreign domination, even at its best, is an evil in itself and a continuing injury to the subject people, but because India in bondage can play no effective part in defending herself and in affecting the fortunes of the war that is desolating humanity. The freedom of India is thus necessary not only in the interest of India but also for the safety of the world and for the ending of nazism, fascism, militarism and other forms of imperialism, and the aggression of one nation over another.

Ever since the outbreak of the world war, the Congress has studiedly pursued a policy of non-embarrassment. Even at the risk of making its satyagraha ineffective, it deliberately gave it a symbolic character, in the hope that this policy of non-embarrassment, carried to its logical extreme would be duly appreciated, and that real power would be transferred to popular representatives, so as to enable the nation to make its fullest contribution towards the realization of human freedom throughout the world, which is in danger of being crushed. It has also hoped that negatively nothing would be done which was calculated to tighten Britain's stranglehold on India.

These hopes have, however, been dashed to pieces. The abortive Cripps proposals showed in the clearest possible manner that there was no change in the British Government's attitude towards India and that the British hold on India was in no way to be relaxed. In the negotiations with Sir Stafford Cripps, Congress representatives tried their utmost to achieve a minimum, consistent with the national demand, but to no avail. This frustration has resulted in a rapid and widespread increase of ill-will against Britain and growing satisfaction at the success of Japanese arms. The Working Committee view this development with grave apprehension as this, unless checked, will inevitably lead to a passive acceptance of aggression. The Committee hold that all aggression must be resisted, for any submission to it must mean the degradation of the Indian people and the continuation of their subjection. The Congress is anxious to avoid the experience of Malaya, Singapore, and Burma and desires to build resistance to any aggression on or invasion of India by the Japanese or any foreign power.

The Congress would change the present ill-will against Britain into goodwill and make India a willing partner in a joint enterprise of securing freedom of the nations and peoples of the world and in the trials and tribulations which accompany it. This is only possible if India feels the glow of freedom.

The Congress representatives have tried their utmost to bring about a solution of the communal tangle. But this has been made impossible by the presence of the foreign power whose long record has been to pursue relentlessly the policy of divide and rule. Only after the ending of foreign domination and intervention can the present unreality give place to reality, and the people of India, belonging to all groups and parties, face India's problems and solve them on a mutually agreed basis. The present political parties, formed chiefly with a view to attract the attention of and influence the British power, will then probably cease to function. For the first time in India's history, realization will come home that princes, jagirdars, zamindars and propertied and monied classes derive their wealth and property from the workers in the fields and factories and elsewhere, to whom essentially power and authority must belong. On the withdrawal of British rule in India, responsible men and women of the country will come together to form a provisional Government, representative of all important sections of the people of India which will later evolve a scheme whereby a Constituent Assembly can be convened in order to prepare a constitution for the Government of India acceptable to all sections of the people. Representatives of free India and representatives of Great Britain will confer together for the adjustment of future relations and co-operation of the two countries as allies in the common task of meeting aggression. It is the earnest desire of the Congress to enable India to resist aggression effectively with the people's united will and strength behind it.

In making the proposal for the withdrawal of British rule from India, the Congress had no desire whatsoever to embarrass Great Britain or the Allied Powers in their prosecution of the war, in any way to encourage aggression on India or increased pressure on China by the Japanese or any other Power associated with the Axis Group. Nor does the Congress intend to jeopardise the defensive capacity of the Allied Powers. The Congress is therefore agreeable to the stationing of the armed forces of the Allies in India, should they so desire, in order to ward off and resist Japanese or other aggression, and to protect and help China.

The proposal of withdrawal of the British Power from India was never intended to mean the physical withdrawal of all Britishers from India, and certainly not of those who would make India their home and live there as citizens and as equals. The Working Committee refer them to the All-India Congress Committee for final decision. For this purpose the A.I.C.C. will meet in Bombay on 7 August 1942.

CHAPTER 8

Quit India

WHEN the resolution of the Working Committee was published, it created an electric atmosphere in the country. People did not pause to consider what were the implications, but felt that at last Congress was launching a mass movement to make the British quit India. In fact, very soon the resolution came to be described as the "Quit India" Resolution by both the people and the Government. The masses, like some of the members of the Working Committee, had an implicit faith in Gandhiji's leadership and felt that he had some move in his mind which would paralyze the Government and force it to come to terms. I may here confess that there were also people who thought that Gandhiji would bring freedom for India by some magic or superhuman method and did not therefore think it necessary to make any special personal effort.

After passing the resolution, the Working Committee decided that it would wait for Government reaction. If the Government accepted the demand or at least showed a conciliatory attitude there would be scope for further discussions. If, on the other hand, the Government rejected the demand, a struggle would be launched under Gandhiji's leadership. I had little doubt in my mind that the Government would refuse to negotiate under duress. My anticipation was justified by the course of events.

A very large concourse of the foreign press had come to Wardha as they were anxious to know what the Working Committee would decide. On 15 July, Gandhiji held a press conference. In reply to a question, he said that if the movement were launched, it would be a nonviolent revolution against British power.

After the resolution was passed, Mahadev Desai (who was Gandhiji's secretary) told Miss Slade that she should go and meet the Viceroy and explain to him the purport of the resolution. Miss Slade was the daughter of a British admiral but had adopted the Indian way of life under Gandhiji's influence. Popularly known as Mira Ben [or Mirabehn], she was one of his stanchest disciples and lived for many years in his ashrama.[1] It was suggested that she should also try to give an account of the nature of the proposed movement and how it would work. Miss Slade left Wardha to meet the Viceroy and requested an interview. The private secretary to the Viceroy replied that, since Gandhiji had declared that he was thinking in terms of rebellion, the Viceroy was not prepared to grant her an interview. He made it clear that the Government would not tolerate any rebellion during the war, whether it was violent or nonviolent. Nor was the Government prepared to meet or discuss with any representative of an organization which spoke in such terms. Mira Ben then met the private secretary to the Viceroy and had a long talk with him. I was at the time in Delhi and she reported her conversation to me. She then went back to Wardha and described the interview to Gandhiji.

Soon after this, Mahadev Desai issued a statement that there appeared to be some misunderstanding about Gandhiji's intentions. He said that it was not correct to say that Gandhiji had decided to launch an open nonviolent rebellion against the British. I confess that Mahadev Desai's statement somewhat surprised me. The fact is that after Jawaharlal coined the phrase, Gandhiji had talked of nonviolent revolution. He may have given some special meaning to it in his own mind, but to the general public his statement meant that Congress was now resolved to force the British Government to give up their power by adopting all methods short of violent insurrection. I have already said that I had anticipated the likely British

[1] A place, usually a village or a suburb, where a group of disciples live with their mentor.

reaction and was not therefore surprised by the Viceroy's refusal to
meet Gandhiji or his representative. As already decided by the
A.I.C.C., a meeting of the A.I.C.C. was called at Bombay on 7
August 1942 to consider the situation further.

From 14 July to 5 August, my time was taken up in a series of
meetings with Congress leaders from different parts of the country.
I wanted to impress on them that if the Government accepted our
demand, or at least allowed us to function, the movement must
develop strictly according to Gandhiji's instructions. If, however, the
Government arrested Gandhiji and other Congress leaders, the
people would be free to adopt any method, violent or nonviolent,
to oppose the violence of the Government in every possible way. So
long as the leaders were free and able to function, they were responsible for the course of events, but, if the Government arrested them,
the Government must take the responsibility for the consequences.
Naturally, these instructions were secret and never made public.
The picture as it presented itself to me was that Bengal, Bihar, the
United Provinces, the Central Provinces, Bombay and Delhi were
fully prepared and the movement would be strong in these provinces. Assam was then the centre of the British war effort and was
full of army officers and men. As such, no direct action was possible
there. Assam could, however, be reached only through Bengal and
Bihar, which gave an added importance to the program in these two
provinces. Regarding the other provinces, I did my best to create
a proper atmosphere but I must confess that the picture was not
very clear to me.

The refusal of the Viceroy even to receive Mira Ben made
Gandhiji realize that the Government would not easily yield. The
confidence he had in this regard was shaken but he still clung to
the belief that Government would not take any drastic action. He
thought that he would have enough time after the A.I.C.C. meeting
to prepare a program of work and gradually build up the tempo
of the movement. I could not share his optimism. On 28 July, I
wrote a detailed letter to him in which I said that the Government
was fully prepared and would take immediate action after the

Bombay meeting of the A.I.C.C. Gandhiji replied that I should not draw any hasty conclusions. He also was studying the situation and he still believed that a way out might be found.

On 3 August, I left Calcutta for Bombay. I was not absolutely sure but I had a premonition that I was leaving Calcutta for a long time. I had also received some reports that the Government had completed its plans and proposed to arrest all the leaders immediately after the resolution was passed.

The Working Committee met on 5 August and prepared a draft resolution which was placed before the A.I.C.C. on the 7th. In my opening remarks, I gave a brief survey of the developments since the last meeting of the Committee. I also explained at some length the reasons which had led the Working Committee to change its attitude and call upon the nation to launch a struggle for India's freedom. I pointed out that the nation could not watch passively while its fate hung in the balance. India had sought to cooperate with the democracies but the British Government made it impossible to offer honorable cooperation. Faced with the imminence of Japanese invasion, the nation was seeking to gain strength to resist the aggressor. The British could, if they wished, withdraw from India as they had withdrawn from Singapore, Malaya and Burma. Indians could not withdraw as it was their own homeland and must therefore develop the strength to shake off the British chain and withstand any attack by any new aggressor.

Except a handful of communists [2] who opposed the move, all members of the A.I.C.C. welcomed the resolution drafted by the Working Committee. Gandhiji also addressed the meeting, and, after two days' discussions, a resolution endorsing the stand of the Working Committee was passed with an overwhelming majority late on the evening of 8 August. The text of the resolution will be found in the Appendix.

During my visits to Bombay I generally stayed with the late Bhulabhai Desai. I did so on this occasion as well. He was then ill

[2] Since Hitler had invaded the Soviet Union in June, 1941, the communists were now prowar and supported the British war effort.

and had been unwell for some time. I was therefore a little surprised when, on my return after the meeting of the A.I.C.C., I found he was waiting for me. It was very late and I was tired and thought that he must have retired. I gently admonished him for staying up so late, but he told me that Mohammed Taher, one of my relations, who has his business in Bombay, had called for me and waited a long time. When I did not return, he had left a message with Bhulabhai Desai. Mohammed Taher had a friend in the Bombay Police and had learnt from him that all the Congress leaders would be arrested early next morning. Taher's friend also told him that he did not know it for certain but it was reported that we would all be transported out of India, perhaps to South Africa.

I had heard similar rumors in Calcutta before I left. Later I came to know that the rumor was not without foundation. When the Government decided that we should all be arrested, they also thought that it would not be politic to keep us in the country. In fact, approaches had been made to the Government of South Africa. There must have been some last-minute hitch, for later the decision was changed. We soon found out that the Government had planned that Gandhiji should be detained at Poona while the rest of us should be imprisoned in the Ahmednagar Fort jail.

Bhulabhai was greatly disturbed by this news and that is why he was waiting for me. I was very tired and in no mood to listen to such rumors. I told Bhulabhai that if the news was true, I had only a few hours of freedom. It was better that I should have my dinner quickly and go to sleep so that I could face the morning better. I would rather sleep than spend my few hours of freedom in speculating about rumors. Bhulabhai agreed and soon I lay down to sleep.

I have always been in the habit of waking very early. This morning also I got up at 4:00 A.M. I was, however, still very tired and had a feeling of heaviness in my head. I took two aspirins and a cup of tea and settled down to work. It had been decided that we should send a copy of the resolution we had passed along with a covering letter to President Roosevelt. We felt that this was the least we could do in view of the interest he had been taking in the question of Indian freedom. I began to draft a letter to President Roosevelt but could not finish it. Perhaps because I was tired or perhaps because of the aspirin, I again felt drowsy and lay down to sleep.

I do not think I could have slept for more than fifteen minutes when I felt someone touch my feet. I opened my eyes and found Dhirubhai Desai, son of Bhulabhai, standing with a sheet of paper in his hand. I knew what it was even before Dhirubhai told me that the Deputy Commissioner of Police, Bombay, had brought this warrant for my arrest. He also told me that the Deputy Commissioner was waiting on the verandah. I told Dhirubhai to inform the Deputy Commissioner that I would take a little time to get ready.

I had my bath and then dressed. I also gave the necessary instructions to my private secretary, Mohammed Ajmal Khan, who had by now joined me. I then came out on the verandah. Bhulabhai and his daughter-in-law were talking with the Deputy Commissioner. I smiled at Bhulabhai and said that the information his friend brought last evening had proved correct. I then turned to the Deputy Commissioner and said, "I am ready." It was then 5:00 A.M.

I got into the Deputy Commissioner's car. A second car picked up my belongings and followed us. We drove straight to the Victoria Terminus. It was time for the local trains but the station was completely empty. Perhaps all trains and passengers had been temporarily stopped. As soon as I got down from the car, I saw Asoka Mehta [a prominent Socialist intellectual]. He also had been arrested and brought to the Victoria Terminus. I realized that the Government had arrested not only the members of the Working Committee but also local leaders of the Congress in Bombay. I assumed that this was being done throughout India. There was a train waiting on the platform to which I was brought. An engine was then attaching a dining car to the train. It was a corridor train which usually ran on the Bombay-Poona line. I was taken to a compartment where I sat down by the window.

Almost immediately Jawaharlal, Asaf Ali and Dr. Syed Mahmud appeared on the scene. Jawaharlal told me that Gandhiji had also been brought to the station and put in another compartment. A European military officer came up to us and asked if we wanted tea. I had already had my cup but ordered some more.

At this stage a second military officer appeared and began to count us. Something was obviously puzzling him, for he counted us several times. As he came up to our compartment, he said aloud, "Thirty." When this had happened twice or thrice, I responded equally loudly and said "Thirty-two." This seemed to confuse him further and he started to count once again. Soon, however, the guard blew his whistle and the train started to move. I noticed Mrs. Asaf Ali standing on the platform. She had come to see her husband off. As the train started to move, she looked at me, and said, "Please don't worry about me. I shall find something to do and shall not remain idle." Later events showed that she had meant what she said.

I have already said that ours was a corridor train, Mrs. [Sarojini] Naidu [3] now came to our compartment and said that Gandhiji wanted to meet us. We walked down the corridor to his compartment which was some distance away. Gandhiji was looking very depressed. I have never seen him looking so dejected. I understood that he had not expected this sudden arrest. His reading of the situation had been that the Government would take no drastic action. I had, of course, warned him again and again that he was taking too optimistic a view but obviously he had placed greater faith in his own judgment. Now that his calculations had proved wrong, he was uncertain as to what he should do.

After we had talked for a minute or two, Gandhiji said, "As soon as you reach your destination, you should inform the Government that you wish to continue to function as Congress President. You should ask for your private secretary and other necessary facilities for the purpose. When you were arrested last time and detained in Naini jail, the Government had provided you with these facilities.

[3] An Indian poet and Congress leader.

You should ask for the same facilities again, and if necessary make an issue of it."

I could not agree with Gandhiji. I told him that the situation now was completely different. We had chosen our path with open eyes and must take the consequences. I could understand if he wanted me to fight on the issues which had been adopted by Congress, but did not see how I could fight on a minor issue like the extension of certain personal facilities to me. I did not think that I would be justified in asking that my private secretary should be allowed to be with me so that I might carry on Congress work. This was hardly an issue on which I could fight in the present situation.

While we were talking the Police Commissioner of Bombay, who also was in the train with us, came up. He asked us to return to our own compartment. He told me that only Mrs. Naidu could stay with Gandhiji. Jawaharlal and I then returned to our compartment. The train was now moving fast towards Kalyan. It did not stop there but took the route for Poona. I thought that perhaps we would be detained there, and my belief became stronger when the train stopped.

It seemed that the news of our arrest had somehow reached Poona. The platform was full of police and no member of the public was allowed on it. There was, however, a large crowd on the overbridge. As the train steamed in, they started to shout "Mahatma Gandhi ki Jai" ["Long live Mahatma Gandhi"]. No sooner was this slogan raised than the Commissioner ordered the police to make a lathi charge [4] on the people. The Commissioner said that he had received Government orders that no demonstrations or slogans would be permitted.

Jawaharlal was sitting by the window. As soon as he saw that the police were making a lathi charge, he jumped out of the compartment and rushed forward crying, "You have no right to make a lathi charge." The Police Commissioner ran after him and tried to bring Jawaharlal back into his compartment. Jawaharlal would not, however, listen to him and spoke angrily. By this time, another

[4] A running attack in which the police wield bamboo staves.

member of the Working Committee, Shankar Rao Deo, had also come out on the platform. Four policemen surrounded him and asked him to return to the train. When he refused to do so, they lifted him up bodily and carried him back. I called out to Jawaharlal that he should return. Jawaharlal looked angry but carried out my request. The Police Commissioner came up to me and said two or three times, "I am very sorry sir, but these are my orders and I must carry them out."

From my window I saw that Mrs. Naidu and Gandhiji were taken out of the train. We later learnt that they were detained in the Aga Khan's house, popularly known as Aga Khan Palace. Another arrested man from Bombay who had also got down wanted to go out on the platform, but the police prevented him. He would not desist till the police physically stopped him. I believe he was trying to act according to Gandhiji's instructions. It will be remembered that Gandhiji had said that on the occasion of the present movement, nobody should court arrest voluntarily. It was only when physical force was applied that men should agree to go to prison.

After Gandhiji had been taken away, the train again started to move. I now realized we were being taken to Ahmednagar. We reached the station at about 1:30 P.M. The platform was completely empty except for a handful of police officers and a single army officer. We were asked to get down and were put in waiting cars. They started immediately and did not stop till we arrived at the gate within the Fort. An army officer was standing there. The Commissioner of Police brought out a list and handed it to him. The army officer called out our names one by one and asked us to enter. The Police Commissioner was in fact handing us over to the military authorities. From now on we were under military control.

CHAPTER 9

Ahmednagar Fort Jail

NINE other members of the Working Committee were brought to Ahmednagar with me, viz., Jawaharlal, Sardar Patel, Asaf Ali, Shankar Rao Deo, Govind Ballabh Pant [later Home Minister of independent India], Dr. Pattabhi Sitaramayya, Dr. Syed Mahmud, Acharya Kripalani and Dr. Profulla Ghosh. Rajen Babu [or Rajendra Prasad, later President of independent India] was also a member of the Working Committee but, as he did not attend the meeting at Bombay, he was arrested in Patna and detained there.

We were taken inside the Fort and brought to a building which looked like a military barrack. There was an open courtyard about 200 feet long surrounded with rooms. We learnt later that foreign prisoners had been kept here during the First World War. A jailor from Poona who was transferred checked our luggage as it was brought in. I had a small portable radio which I always carried with me. My other belongings were sent in but the radio was taken into custody and I did not see it again till my release.

Dinner was served to us soon after on iron platters. We did not like them and I told the jailor that we were accustomed to eat from china plates. The jailor apologized and said that he could not supply us with a dinner set then but it would be obtained next day. A convict from Poona had been brought to serve us as our cook. He could not prepare food according to our taste. He was soon changed but the new cook was no better.

The place of our detention was kept a secret. This seemed to me foolish, for it was obvious that the facts could not be concealed for long. The Government action did not, however, surprise me. Perhaps all governments act foolishly on such occasions. After two or three days, the Inspector-General of Prisons, Bombay, came to visit us. He told us that Government orders were that we could not write even to our relations nor receive letters from them. Nor should we be supplied with any newspapers. He was very apologetic and said that these were strict orders which he had to carry out. He would, however, be glad to meet any other request that we might make.

I was not well when I left Calcutta for Bombay on 3 August. I was suffering from influenza even during the meeting of the A.I.C.C. and this fact was known to the Government. The Inspector-General was a physician and wanted to examine me. I did not, however, agree.

We were completely cut off from the world and did not know what was happening outside. We felt that we must draw out a program of activities in order to maintain our health and spirits. As I have said, the rooms were arranged round a quadrangle. I occupied the first room in one line. The next was occupied by Jawaharlal and the third by Asaf Ali and Dr. Syed Mahmud. The last room of this line was our dining room. We used to meet for breakfast at eight in the morning and for our midday meal at eleven. Afterwards we met in my room and discussed various topics for a couple of hours. Then we had a little rest and met again for tea at four. After tea we took some exercise in the quadrangle. Dinner was served at eight and we used to carry on our discussions till ten. Then we retired to our rooms.

The quadrangle was quite bare when we came. Jawaharlal proposed that we should prepare a flower garden as this would keep us occupied and also beautify the place. We welcomed the idea and asked the superintendent to write to Poona for seeds. We then prepared the ground for flower beds. Jawaharlal took the leading role in this. We planted some thirty or forty kinds of seeds, watered them every day and cleaned the beds. As the plants began to sprout, we watched their growth with fascinated interest. When the flowers started to bloom, the compound became a place of beauty and joy.

After we had been in jail for about five days, an officer appeared who, we learnt, had been appointed Superintendent of the Jail to look after us. He stayed in the town, came every morning at 8:00 A.M. and left in the evening. We did not know his name and thought we must find a name for him. I remembered that, when Chand Bibi was detained in this very jail, she had an Abyssinian jailor called Cheeta Khan. I suggested that we should give the same name to our superintendent. My colleagues readily agreed. The name became so popular that very soon everybody started calling him Cheeta Khan. I was surprised when three or four days later the jailor came and told us that Cheeta Khan had left early that day.

Cheeta Khan, as I shall call him, had been in Port Blair when the Japanese attacked and occupied the Andaman Islands.

On 25 August, I wrote a letter to the Viceroy. I said that I did not complain that the Government thought it necessary to arrest my colleagues and me. I had, however, a complaint about the treatment meted to us. Even convicted criminals are allowed to correspond with their near relations. In our case this right had been denied. I wrote that I would wait for two weeks and, if we had no satisfactory reply from the Government, my colleagues and I would decide what should be our course of action.

On 10 September, Cheeta Khan came and said that he had received orders that we could correspond once a week with our relations. We were also to be supplied with one newspaper a day. A copy of the *Times of India* was placed on my table and from then on we received it regularly. That night I read the paper for a long time. We had been without any news for over a month. Now at last we came to know of the events in the country after our arrest and about the progress of the war.

Next day I asked Cheeta Khan to send me the back numbers of the newspaper. Now that Government had agreed to supply us with newspapers regularly, there could be no objection to my proposal. Cheeta Khan agreed with me and after two or three days sent me a complete file of the *Times of India* from the date of my arrest.

As I read the reports, I realized that my reading of the situation that there would be disturbances in the country after our arrest had proved correct. Bengal, Bihar, U.P. and Bombay had taken the lead in the struggle against the Government. Communications had been disrupted and factories closed down. Police stations were raided and burnt. Railway stations had been attacked and in some cases destroyed. Military lorries had also been burnt in large numbers. Factories had closed down and production of war materials suspended or reduced. In a word, the country had reacted violently to the leonine violence of the Government. The movement was not confined to nonviolent resistance. This was what I had anticipated and to some extent even advised and discussed with our workers.

The remaining months of 1942 passed without any major incident.

Early in 1943, there was again a change in the atmosphere. In February we read in the newspapers that Gandhiji had written to the Viceroy that he would undertake a fast for twenty-one days. He described it as a fast for self-purification. I was convinced that Gandhiji was prompted to take this step for two main reasons. As I have said earlier, he had not expected that Government would arrest the Congress leaders so suddenly. He had also hoped that he would get time to develop the movement on nonviolent lines according to his own ideas. Both his hopes had been shattered. He accepted the responsibility for what had happened and, as was usual with him, he was planning to undergo the fast as an expiation for the situation. I could not see any sense in his fast on any other hypothesis.

The Government, however, looked at his action from an entirely different point of view. They thought that he could not at his age and in the existing state of his health stand a fast for twenty-one days. To undertake the fast was in their view to court certain death. The Government thought that this was Gandhiji's intention and he wanted the Government to be held responsible for his death. Later we learnt that the Government made all necessary arrangements on this basis. Convinced that he would not survive the fast, they even brought sandalwood for his cremation. Their reaction was that, if Gandhiji wanted to place the responsibility of his death on the Government, the Government would not change their policy on that account. His last rites would be performed within the Aga Khan Palace where he was held and his ashes delivered to his sons.

Dr. B. C. Roy [1] wrote to the Government that he wanted to act as Gandhiji's physician during the period of his fast. To this the Government raised no objection. At one stage during the fast it seemed that Government's calculations were going to prove correct. Even his physicians gave up hope. Gandhiji, however, upset all the calculations of the Government and his physicians. The extraordinary capacity for suffering he had shown on other occasions was displayed in an amazing degree. His stamina overcame the challenge of death and after twenty-one days he broke his fast.

After the excitement of Gandhiji's fast, we again settled down to our daily routine. During the period of his fast, we had felt acutely our utter helplessness in captivity. This came to me with added poignancy in the course of the next year.

For several years my wife had been unwell. When I was in Naini jail in 1941, her condition had become very serious. When I was released, I consulted doctors and they advised a change. She went to Ranchi and returned only in July 1942. She was then somewhat better but, when I started for Bombay in the first week of August, her health was again causing anxiety. The news of my arrest on 9 August must have come as a great shock to her and her health, which was already frail, took a turn for the worse. One of my greatest worries during imprisonment was the reports of her deteriorating health. Early in 1944 I received news from home that she was again seriously ill. Later came more alarming news. Her physicians were worried about her and on their own initiative wrote to the Government that I should be allowed to see her once as there was little hope for her survival. The Government ignored this letter

[1] Prominent physician and Congressman, later for many years Chief Minister of the Bengal state.

from the physicians. I also wrote to the Viceroy but our correspondence was inconclusive.

One day in April Cheeta Khan came in the middle of the day. This was most unusual. He said nothing and handed me a telegram. It was in cypher but there was an English transcript. It was from Calcutta and said that my wife was dead. I wrote to the Viceroy that the Government of India could easily have arranged for my transfer to Calcutta on a temporary basis so that I could have seen my wife before she died. To this letter I received no reply.

After three months, fate had another shock in store for me. My sister, Abru Begum, who lived in Bhopal fell ill. In about two weeks time I heard that she also was dead.

About this time we suddenly read in the papers that Gandhiji was released. I am inclined to think that he did not himself realize the reasons for this. He seemed to have thought that he owed his freedom to a change in British policy. Later events showed that he was again wrong. His health had been shattered by the fast he had undertaken. Since then he had suffered from one ailment after another. The Civil Surgeon of Poona examined him and reported that he was not likely to survive for long. The fast had been beyond his capacity and the Civil Surgeon felt that his days were numbered. When the Viceroy received this report, he decided to release him so that the Government would not be held responsible for his death. Besides, the political situation had changed so much that the British did not anticipate any danger from him. The crisis of the war was over. Allied victory was now only a question of time. The Government also felt that with all the leaders of the Congress in jail, Gandhiji alone could do little. On the contrary his presence might act as a check on elements which were trying to adopt violent means.

For some time after his release, Gandhiji was too ill to take any effective step. He was for some months under treatment but, as soon as he felt a little better, he initiated a number of political moves. Two of them deserve special mention. Gandhiji made a fresh attempt for an understanding with the Moslem League and arranged to meet Mr. Jinnah. His second move was an attempt to

open fresh negotiation with the Government. Contrary to his previous declarations, he now issued a statement to the *News Chronicle*
of London that, if India were declared free, she would voluntarily
side with the British and give full support to the war effort. I was
completely taken aback when I read his statements and knew that
both these actions were doomed to failure.

I think Gandhiji's approach to Mr. Jinnah on this occasion was
a great political blunder. It gave a new and added importance to
Mr. Jinnah which he later exploited to the full. Gandhiji had in
fact adopted a peculiar attitude to Jinnah from the very beginning.
Mr. Jinnah had lost much of his political importance after he left
the Congress in the twenties. It was largely due to Gandhiji's acts
of commission and omission that Mr. Jinnah regained his importance in Indian political life. In fact, it is doubtful if Mr. Jinnah
could ever have achieved supremacy but for Gandhiji's attitude.
Large sections of Indian Moslems were doubtful about Mr. Jinnah
and his policy, but, when they found that Gandhiji was continually
running after him and entreating him, many of them developed
a new respect for Mr. Jinnah. They also thought that he was perhaps
the best man for getting advantageous terms in the communal
settlement.

I may mention here that it was Gandhiji who first gave currency
to the title "Qaid-i-Azam," or "great leader," as applied to Mr.
Jinnah. Gandhiji had in his camp a simple but well-intentioned
woman called Miss Amtus Salam. She had seen in some Urdu
papers a reference to Mr. Jinnah as Qaid-i-Azam. When Gandhiji
was writing to Mr. Jinnah asking for an interview, she told him that
Urdu papers called Mr. Jinnah Qaid-i-Azam and he should use the
same form of address. Without pausing to consider the implications
of his action Gandhiji addressed Mr. Jinnah as Qaid-i-Azam. This
letter was soon after published in the press. When Indian Moslems
saw that Gandhiji also addressed Mr. Jinnah as Qaid-i-Azam, they
felt that he must really be so. When in July 1944, I read the report
that Gandhiji was corresponding with Mr. Jinnah and going to
Bombay to meet him, I told my colleagues that Gandhiji was

making a great mistake. His action would not help to solve, but on the contrary aggravate, the Indian political situation. Later events proved that my apprehensions were correct. Mr. Jinnah exploited the situation fully and built up his own position but did not say or do anything which could in any way help the cause of Indian freedom.

Gandhiji's second step in approaching the Government was also ill-timed. It will be recalled that when hostilities began, I had tried hard to persuade Congress to take a realistic and positive attitude towards the war. Gandhiji at that time had taken the stand that political independence of India was no doubt important but adherence to nonviolence was even more important. His declared policy was that if the only way of achieving Indian independence was to participate in the war, he for one would not adopt it. Now he said that Congress would cooperate with the British if India were declared free. This was a complete reversal of his earlier views and caused misunderstanding in India and abroad. The Indians were confused, while the impression created in Britain was still more unhappy. Many Englishmen thought that Gandhiji had refrained from helping the British when the issue of war was in doubt. In this, however, they were wrong, for the issue of the war had no influence on Gandhiji's views. They therefore interpreted his present offer of support as an attempt to gain British sympathy now that the victory of the Allies was assured. In consequence they did not pay the attention to his offer which he had expected. Besides, the British were no longer so much in need of Indian support as they had been in the earlier days of the war. This also contributed to their indifference to Gandhiji's move.

Now when I am writing in 1957 and looking at events in retrospect, I cannot refrain from saying that there was an astonishing transformation in the attitude of some of his closest followers on the question of violence versus nonviolence. Sardar Patel, Dr. Rajendra Prasad, Acharya Kripalani and Dr. Profulla Ghosh had wanted to resign from the Working Committee when the Congress passed a resolution that it would support the war effort if the British declared India free. They then wrote to me that for them non-violence was a creed and even more important than Indian independence. When, however, India did become free in 1947, not one of them said that the Indian army should be disbanded. On the contrary, they insisted that the Indian army should be partitioned and brought under the immediate control of the Government of India. This was contrary to the proposal made by the Commander-in-Chief of the time. The Commander-in-Chief had suggested that for three years there should be a joint army and a joint command but they would not agree. If nonviolence were really their creed, how was it possible for them to take responsibility in a Government which spent over a hundred crores [2] a year on the army? In fact, some of them wanted to increase and not diminish the expenditure on armed forces and today the expenditure is some two hundred crores.

I have always had the feeling that these colleagues and friends did not exercise their own minds on most political issues. They were out-and-out followers of Gandhiji. Whenever a question arose they waited to see how he would react. I was not and I am not behind any of them in my regard and admiration for Gandhiji but I could not for a moment accept the position that we should follow him blindly. It is strange that the issue on which these friends wanted to resign from the Working Committee in 1940 completely escaped their notice after India became free. They cannot for a moment think of running the Government of India without an army and a large defence establishment. Nor have they ruled out war as an instrument of policy. Jawaharlal was the only member of the Working Committee who fully shared my views. I believe that the logic of events has supported his stand and mine.

In June 1944, we read reports about "D" Day. This was the turning point of the war. The Allied victory was now certain and in sight. The world also realized that the greatest personality thrown up during the war was President Roosevelt. It seemed that his picture of the future was being steadily justified. In both Africa

[2] A crore equals ten million; in this case, rupees.

and Asia, the Allied forces had triumphed and were now marching on Hitler's European citadel. This was no surprise to me. I had long held that, as in World War I, this time also Germany had committed the blunder of fighting on two fronts. In fact the day Hitler decided to attack the U.S.S.R., he sowed the seed of his downfall. There was now no escape from ruin for him or his people.

An unexpected incident took place in our camp about this time. Cheeta Khan came one day and said that he had received orders for Dr. Syed Mahmud's release. We were all surprised for we could not understand why he was singled out for such treatment.

Some months ago, there had been the risk of a cholera epidemic in Ahmednagar. Cheeta Khan advised us to be inoculated against the disease. Five of us—Jawaharlal, Pattabhi Sitaramayya, Asaf Ali, Dr. Syed Mahmud and I—acted according to his advice. Four others—Sardar Patel, Acharya Kripalani, Shankar Rao Deo and Dr. Profulla Ghosh—refused on grounds of conscience.[3] I had a touch of fever as a reaction but it seemed Dr. Mahmud had an allergy to the inoculation. He had unusually high and persistent fever for almost a fortnight. We were all worried about him and Jawaharlal with his customary friendliness acted as his nurse and mentor. Finally the fever left him but he continued to bleed from his gums. He was under Cheeta Khan's treatment and had almost recovered when the order for his release came. His illness could not, therefore, be sufficient ground for his release. We thought that perhaps it meant a change in the Government's policy. They were now prepared to act more leniently and had released Dr. Syed Mahmud on the grounds of health. I later came to know the real reason, but, after the lapse of so many years, I do not think it necessary to go into the details of this unhappy incident.

Though we did not know it for certain, we felt that the days of our imprisonment were also drawing to a close. Some time in the latter half of 1944, the Government of India came to the conclusion that it was no longer necessary to detain us in Ahmednagar. We had been taken there for several reasons. The Government had

---

[3] They were opposed, in principle, to inoculations of any kind.

thought that our detention there would remain a secret. They also thought that if we were kept in a civil jail, we might be able to establish contact with the world outside. Detention under military control would prevent this. In Ahmednagar camp jail, there were only European army men and they would surely prevent any communication with the outside world. We had evidence of the Government's anxiety to block physical contacts with the world outside as soon as we arrived at Ahmednagar. The barracks in which we were kept had skylights through which one could see the compound of the Fort. These were completely blocked before we were brought there. The plaster was so new that it was still damp when we arrived. During our three and a half years' detention in Ahmednagar we hardly ever saw an Indian from outside. Once or twice some small repairs had to be undertaken to the buildings. Even for this no Indian labor was used. We were thus completely cut off from the world.

The Government had succeeded in preventing any contacts with the outside world but their first objective had failed. The public knew within a week of our arrival that we were all held in Ahmednagar Fort jail. By now the need for secrecy had also gone. British victory was now in sight. The Government of India therefore felt that it was no longer necessary to keep us in this military prison and we could safely be transferred to the civil jails in our own provinces.

Sardar Patel and Shankar Rao Deo were the first to move and went to Poona jail. Asaf Ali was sent to Batala, where political prisoners from Delhi were generally held. Jawaharlal was taken first to Naini near Allahabad and then to Almora. As he was leaving, Jawaharlal said that perhaps the time of our release was approaching. He requested me that I should not call a meeting of the Working Committee or the A.I.C.C. immediately on release. He said he wanted a little time for rest and recreation, and also in order to finish a book on India which he was writing.

I told Jawaharlal that this was also what I would like to do. I, too, wanted a little time for rest and recuperation. I did not then know that we should be freed in circumstances which would demand immediate and hectic political action and that no question of rest would arise for perhaps the remainder of our lives.

When the time for my transfer came, Cheeta Khan said that, since I was not well, Calcutta with its damp climate would not be a suitable place for me. He hinted that I should be sent to a drier place within Bengal. One afternoon he asked me to get ready. After my things had been placed in the car, he drove me, not to the Ahmednagar station, but to a village station several miles away. The reason was that, if I travelled from Ahmednagar, the fact would immediately be known. The Government did not want any publicity about my movements.

Most of the time I spent in the Ahmednagar jail was passed under conditions of great mental strain. This had a very adverse effect on my health. When I was arrested, my weight was 170 pounds. When I was transferred from Ahmednagar I was reduced to 130 pounds. I had no appetite and could hardly eat.

A C.I.D. Inspector from Bengal had come with four constables to escort me. When we reached the station, Cheeta Khan handed me over to their charge. We travelled from Ahmednagar to Asansol via Kalyani. At Asansol, I was taken to the retiring room, where special arrangements had been made for me. In spite of Government's attempt to keep the whole matter secret, the press had somehow got hold of the news. I found in Asansol some press reporters from Calcutta and some friends from Allahabad. A crowd of local people had also collected.

The Superintendent of Police, Asansol, received me at the station and made a personal appeal. He said that if I wanted to meet the public, he could not stop me but, if I did so, the Government would come down heavily on him. He would therefore be very grateful if I agreed to go upstairs to a room and avoided the public. I assured him that I did not want to harm him or make him the subject of the Government's displeasure. Accordingly I went with him to an upstairs room.

The Superintendent of Police was a connection of the Nawab of Dacca. Both he and his wife attended me and his wife insisted that I should sign an autograph book. They did everything to make me comfortable.

I now learnt that I was being taken to Bankura. The train came to the platform at about 4:00 P.M. and soon after I was brought to my compartment. By now a huge crowd had collected on the platform. Apart from the local people, many had come from Calcutta, Allahabad and Lucknow. The Superintendent of Police and his Inspector seemed to be very anxious that I should not meet anybody. The sun was very hot and they had brought an umbrella for me. The Inspector held it but, in his anxiety to hide me from the crowd, he brought it down lower and lower till it rested almost on my head. His object was that the people should not see my face. He thought that in this way they could take me to the compartment without attracting notice.

I had no special desire to meet anyone, but, when I saw that people had come from Calcutta, Allahabad and Lucknow only to see me, I thought it was very unfair that they should not get even a glimpse. I therefore took the umbrella from the Inspector and closed it. The people now ran towards me, but I asked them to stop. It was obviously impossible for me to greet everyone individually, but I spoke to them generally and laughingly said, "The Superintendent of Police and the Inspector are getting more and more worried every moment and I do not want them to get a headache on this hot day."

After waving to the people, I got into my compartment but the crowd surged all round. Apart from the people on the platform, quite a large number crossed the line and came to my compartment from the other side. Soon the train left and by seven we reached Bankura. The Superintendent of Police, Bankura, and other officers received me and escorted me to a two-storeyed bungalow outside the town.

It was the beginning of April and the days were getting warm.

When, however, I sat on the verandah of the first floor, I felt the
pleasant evening breeze play on my face. Mornings and evenings
were not too bad, but during the day it grew very hot. I had an
electric fan and ice was also available but it was so hot at midday
that they were of little use. The Collector used to visit me once a
week. One day he said that he had already written to the Government that I could not stay in Bankura any longer. He was waiting
for a reply and would send me to a cooler place as soon as this was
received.

A good cook is always difficult to find. In Bankura also there was
some difficulty in the beginning, but soon a good cook was engaged.
I liked his work so much that after my release, I brought him with
me to Calcutta.

I have already mentioned that when I entered Ahmednagar Fort,
my radio set was taken away from me. After a few days, Cheeta
Khan had asked me if he could use it. I gladly gave him permission,
but I did not see that radio again till I left Ahmednagar. When I
was being transferred to Bengal, the radio set was placed among my
luggage. When I tried to use it, I found it had got out of order. The
District Magistrate of Bankura supplied me with another set and
after so long a time I could hear directly the news from other
countries.

Towards the end of April, I learnt from press reports that Asaf
Ali was very seriously ill in Batala jail. He was unconscious for a
long period and there were apprehensions for his life. The Government decided to release him and return him to Delhi.

In May 1945, Lord Wavell [who had been appointed Viceroy]
went to London to have further discussions on the Indian political
situation. Towards the end of May, he returned to India. One evening in June, I was listening to the Delhi broadcast when I heard
that the Viceroy had declared that, in accordance with earlier
British assurances, fresh steps would be taken to solve the Indian
political problem. A conference would be held at Simla to which
leaders of the Congress, the Moslem League and other political

parties were to be invited. The President and members of the Working Committee would be released so that Congress could participate in that conference.

The next day I heard that orders had been passed for my and my colleagues' release. I heard this news at about 9:00 P.M. The District Magistrate also heard the broadcast and sent me a message at 10 P.M. that, although he had heard the news, he had not received any official order. He would inform me as soon as this was received. Accordingly at midnight, the jailor came and informed me that orders of release had come. No action could be taken at this late hour and the District Magistrate came to see me early next morning. He read out the order of release and informed me that the Calcutta Express left Bankura at 5:00 P.M. A first class coupé was being reserved for me on this train.

Within a few hours, press correspondents from Calcutta arrived to meet me. Local people also came in their thousands. At 3:30 that afternoon the local Congress Committee organized a meeting which I attended and addressed briefly. I left for Calcutta by the express and reached Howrah next morning.

The platform and station at Howrah were a welter of humanity. It was with the greatest difficulty that I could get out of my compartment and enter my car. The President of the Bengal Congress, Mrs. Labanya Prabha Datta, and several other local leaders were in the car with me. Just as we were about to move, I noticed that there was a band playing in front of my car. I asked Mrs. Datta why they had brought a band. She replied that it was to celebrate my release. I did not like this and told her that this was no occasion for festivities. It is true that I was released, but thousands of my friends and colleagues were still in jail.

The band was stopped and removed at my request. As the car was crossing the Howrah bridge, my mind moved back to days of the past. I remembered the day when three years ago I started for Bombay to attend the meetings of the Working Committee and the A.I.C.C. My wife had come up to the gate of my house to bid me farewell. I was now returning after three years but she was in her grave and my home was empty. I remembered the lines of Wordsworth:

> But she is in her grave, and, oh,
> The difference to me!

I told my companions to turn the car, for I wished to visit her grave before I went home. My car was full of garlands; I took one and placed it on her grave and silently read the *Fateha*.[4]

[4] The first chapter of the Koran, recited as a funeral prayer.

CHAPTER 10

The Simla Conference

FROM the very beginning of the war, American public opinion had recognized that India's full cooperation in the war effort would not be available without a solution of the Indian political problem. They, therefore, pressed the British Government to grant India her freedom. After the Japanese attack on Pearl Harbor, the U.S.A. became directly involved in the war. President Roosevelt repeatedly raised the issue with Churchill, and perhaps the British felt that something must be done to meet American demands. When the Cripps Mission came, the Overseas Service of the B.B.C. broadcast again and again that India now had an opportunity of winning her freedom and deciding about the war freely. A personal representative of President Roosevelt [1] had also come to India and brought me a letter from him. In his letter, the President had expressed the hope that India would accept the Cripps offer and join the war on the side of the democracies. The Cripps Mission, however, failed and the situation remained as before.

When we were arrested in August 1942, this created an unfavorable reaction against the British in China and the U.S.A. We did not know it then but later learnt that the people had expressed strong disapproval of the British action. In Washington, the Senate and the House of Representatives discussed the matter and very strong speeches were made.

As the war situation improved in Europe, the Americans renewed their pressure for the solution of the Indian political problem. This

---

[1] Colonel Louis A. Johnson, later Secretary of Defense.

may have been one reason why Lord Wavell went to London in May 1945 to discuss with the Secretary of State the next step in India. It was then decided to convene a round-table conference. The war in Europe was practically over in April, but the war in Asia showed no sign of an early termination. Japan was still in possession of vast territories and her homeland was practically untouched. The greater weight of American arms had till now been used in the European theatre of war with the result that there was as yet hardly any sign of Japanese defeat. For the United States, the defeat of Japan was, however, even more important than the defeat of Germany. That is why President Roosevelt made Marshal Stalin promise that Russia would attack Japan when war came to an end in Europe. The Americans also realized that a Japanese defeat would become much easier if the full support of India could be secured. Japan was in occupation of Burma, Singapore and Indonesia. In all these areas, India could offer the greatest help. Though Hitler had been crushed in Europe, Indian cooperation was necessary for the early defeat of Japan. This was one main reason why American pressure for securing Indian support was so persistent.

Calcutta was at this time one of the biggest centres of the American army in the East. As such, it was full of American press correspondents and Army officers. They were anxious to meet me after my release and I received some of them the day after I reached Calcutta. Without beating about the bush, they came straight to the point. They asked me what would be the Congress reaction to the offer brought by the Viceroy. I replied that I was not in a position to give a definite reply till I knew the details of the offer. So long as India was under the political domination of the British, it was self-evident that she could not feel any enthusiasm for the war. How could a man who was bound hand and foot feel enthusiasm to fight the enemy of those who tied him?

They countered by asking whether the independence of India had not been guaranteed by the Atlantic Charter.

I retorted that I had not seen the charter and did not know where and what it was.

I added that they must be referring to the well-known statement issued by President Roosevelt after his discussions with Mr. Churchill. The President had said that, after the war, all nations would be given the opportunity to decide their future according to the principle of self-determination. When Mr. Churchill was asked in Parliament whether the future of India would be decided on the basis of this statement, he had emphatically and categorically said "No." He had declared not once but three times that never would the so-called charter be applied to India and made it clear that the President's statement had no application to India. When Mr. Roosevelt's attention was drawn to Mr. Churchill's reply, the President admitted that their discussion had been oral and that there was no formal record. It would, therefore, be wrong to call it a charter.

The American correspondents were not unaware of these facts. They therefore only smiled when I asked them where and what the charter was. There was one woman among the correspondents. She asked me if my rhetorical question about the existence of the charter referred to the President's admission that there was no written record of his understanding with Mr. Churchill.

I said, "Of course this is what I have in mind."

The last question the correspondents asked was whether I would support conscription for India if the Wavell offer was accepted by the Congress.

I replied that if India were assured of her freedom she would join the war voluntarily. Our first duty then would be to mobilize total national effort and we would support conscription.

I reminded the correspondents of a statement I had made as early as 1940 as the President of the Indian National Congress. I had declared that, if India's political problem were solved, she would not only join the war of her own free will but would also adopt conscription and send every able-bodied young man to the war front. I had then also said that our offer was not merely to live but also to die for democracy. It was a pity, I added, that the British did not give us even the opportunity of dying with honor and my offer was not accepted.

On 14 June 1945, Mr. L. S. Amery, Secretary of State for India, made a statement in the House of Commons in which he declared that full scope would be given to India to decide about the war as a free nation. Asked further whether the leaders of the Indian National Congress would be allowed to run the Government, Mr. Amery said that he was asking the representatives of the Congress and the Moslem League to form the Government. The Congress would thus have full freedom to choose any representatives they liked, including Maulana Azad and Pandit Nehru.

This statement created the general impression in India that at last the Indian political problem was about to be solved. The people felt that there was no reason now why Congress should not accept the offer. I started receiving hundreds of telegrams and letters every day pressing me that Congress should accept the offer. When I saw this atmosphere in the country I sent a brief statement to the press. I pointed out that Congress had never avoided responsibility but always welcomed it. If India were offered the opportunity of guiding her own political and administrative destiny, I would make every effort to see that the challenge was accepted. I declared in categorical terms that our approach was constructive and not destructive.

A day after my release, I received in Calcutta the Viceroy's invitation to the round-table conference which was to be held at Simla on 25 June. I replied that I had called a meeting of the Working Committee to meet at Bombay on 21 June. The Working Committee would consider his letter and nominate its representatives. I also wrote to him that I would like to meet him before the Conference and asked if he had any objection to the release of the correspondence I had carried on with him from the Ahmednagar Fort jail.

My health was very poor at this time. I had lost more than forty pounds and could hardly eat. I was also suffering from all-round general weakness and felt completely exhausted. Doctors advised me that I should ask the Viceroy to postpone the Conference for at least two weeks. This would give me an opportunity for treatment and recuperation. I did not, however, consider it proper that I should

Meeting of the Congress Working Committee, Wardha, February 1942.

Meerut Congress 1946, Kripalani, Patel, Azad, Ghaffar Khan.

PLATE IV   Panditji, Badshah Khan, Sardar Patel, the Maulana, and the Mahatma. A.I.C.C. meeting, Delhi 1947.

ask for the postponement of such a momentous meeting on grounds
of personal health.

I asked Humayun Kabir, a leading member of the Bengal Legislative Council, to act as my secretary during the Simla Conference.
Thus began an association which has continued to this day. I sent
him ahead to Bombay with a message for Jawaharlal. I asked
Jawaharlal that he and I should meet first and decide on our line of
action before the formal meeting of the Working Committee.
Jawaharlal agreed with my suggestion and said that this was the
course of action he himself had in mind.

I reached Bombay on 21 June. As usual I stayed with Bhulabhai
Desai. It was the same room from which I was arrested on the morning of 9 August 1942. When I sat on the verandah and talked to
friends I could hardly believe that three years had passed. I felt as
if it was only yesterday that I was talking to friends and that the
incidents since 9 August had never taken place. The familiar sur-
roundings and old friends were the same. The same Arabian Sea
stretched before me to the far horizon.

Gandhiji was staying in Birla House according to his usual custom
and the meeting of the Working Committee was held there. I reported to the Committee the invitation I had received to attend the
Simla Conference. The Committee considered the letter and decided that I should be authorized to represent the Congress at the
round table. This was conveyed to the Viceroy who made arrangements for our journey from Bombay. He placed at my disposal an
aeroplane which flew me to Ambala. From there I drove up to Simla.
I may add that before I left Bombay, I received from the Viceroy a
reply to my letter from Calcutta. He gladly agreed to meet me
before the Conference, but regarding the release of the correspondence he said that since I was coming to Simla he would like to
discuss the matter with me when we met.

It was a very hot day and when I arrived at Delhi I was already
exhausted. The drive from Ambala to Kalka proved even more
trying. All along the way I had to meet immense crowds. They
surrounded the car, got up on the running boards and even climbed

on the roof. It was with the greatest difficulty that we could move at all. It was as if the people had gone mad and they made way for the car only when we appealed again and again that they should not delay us but let us go. Finally at about 10:00 P.M., I reached Simla. I drove to the Savoy Hotel where rooms had been reserved for me. I did not, however, stay in the Savoy Hotel for long. When Lord Wavell saw the state of my health he felt that a hotel was not the proper place for me. He therefore placed at my disposal one of the houses attached to the Viceregal Estate and arranged that staff from the Viceregal establishment should look after me. I was touched by this courteous gesture and I may add that I always found Lord Wavell a man of innate refinement and consideration for others.

The next morning I met the Viceroy at ten o'clock. He received me courteously and described briefly the proposals he had brought on behalf of the British Government. He said that no far-reaching constitutional changes would be carried out for the duration of the war, but the Viceroy's Executive Council would be completely Indian and he would endeavor to set up a convention that the Viceroy would always act on the advice of the Council. He appealed to me to trust the Government. It was his sincere desire that the problem of India must be solved after the war was over. He pointed out that the war was approaching its end. It would therefore be to India's advantage to accept the offer and cooperate with the British in bringing the war to a victorious close. He then referred to the Moslem League and said that it was necessary that there should be an understanding between the Congress and the League.

I told him clearly that an agreement with the League seemed very doubtful. Those who were in control of the League seemed to be under the impression that they had the support of the Government and they would not therefore accept any reasonable terms.

The Viceroy emphatically said that there was no question of the Government supporting the League. If the leaders of the Moslem League had any such ideas, they were completely in the wrong. He assured me that the Government was and would remain neutral.

I then raised the question of my correspondence with him from Ahmednagar Fort jail and expressed the hope that he would have no objection to its publication.

The Viceroy said that he would not object if I was really keen but to him it seemed that publication just now would be unfortunate. He pointed out that we were now meeting in an effort to solve the Indian problem in a new spirit and desired that people should forget the bitterness of the past. If old memories were revived at such a time, the atmosphere would change and, instead of an attitude of friendship and amity, there would be a spirit of distrust and anger. He appealed to me that I should not press for the publication of the correspondence and said that he would appreciate it very much if I accepted his suggestion.

I saw that the Viceroy was sincere and genuinely desired a change in the atmosphere. I told him that I shared his desire that we should create a new atmosphere and discuss our problem in a new spirit of friendship. I would do nothing which would prejudice such a development and therefore agreed to his suggestion.

The Viceroy repeated twice that he was grateful to me for this gesture.

The Viceroy then described to me the details of his proposal. My first reaction was that it was not different in substance from the Cripps offer. There was, however, one material difference in the circumstances. The Cripps offer was made when the British were in dire need of Indian cooperation. Today the war was over in Europe and the Allies had triumphed over Hitler. In spite of this, the British Government had repeated their earlier offer in an attempt to create a new political atmosphere in India.

I told the Viceroy that the Indian National Congress had authorized me to act on its behalf but all the same I would like to consult my colleagues before I gave a definite reply. I had therefore called the Working Committee to meet in Simla to consider the proposal. I would in this way be able to place the decision of the Congress before the Conference. I assured Lord Wavell that my endeavor would be to find a solution and not create difficulties.

I was impressed by the frankness and sincerity of the Viceroy as he described the proposals to me. I saw that his attitude was not that of a politician but of a soldier. He spoke frankly and directly and came to the point without any attempt at beating about the bush. It struck me that his approach was very different from that of Sir Stafford Cripps. Cripps had tried to present his proposals in as favorable a light as possible. He had highlighted the strong points and tried to slur over the difficulties. Lord Wavell made no attempt at embellishment and he certainly was not trying to make an impression. He put it quite bluntly that the war was still on and that Japan was a formidable enemy. In such a situation the British Government were not prepared to take any far-reaching steps. Such developments must wait till the end of the war, but he felt that the foundation for far-reaching changes could now be laid. The Executive Council would be exclusively Indian. The top administration of the country would thus come into Indian hands. Once this happened, a completely new situation would develop and further progress after the war would be assured.

My interview with Lord Wavell created a new atmosphere in Simla. He was giving a state banquet that night and I heard that during the dinner he spoke about me in high terms. He also said that whatever their political opinion or their differences with the Government, Congress leaders were gentlemen. This remark of the Viceroy spread all over Simla and created a stir in both official and nonofficial circles. Many who till then had been cold to the Congress and hardly recognized my existence suddenly developed warm feelings for us. They brought me many presents and tried to impress on me that in their heart of hearts they had always admired the Congress and sided with it.

On the afternoon of the 24th, the Working Committee met in the house of Sardar Harnam Singh where Gandhiji was staying. I gave a brief report of my interview with the Viceroy and expressed the opinion that, though this offer was not different from that of Cripps, we should accept it. In support of my position, I referred to the changed circumstances. The war in Europe was now over and even

Japan could not last very long. Once the war was over, the British would have no special reason to seek our cooperation. It was therefore not desirable for us to reject Lord Wavell's offer. We should participate in the Conference with a view to accept if the terms were at all suitable.

There was a long discussion but in the end the Working Committee decided that we should stress the following points at the Conference:

(1) We must have a clear statement about the relation of the Executive Council to the Viceroy. If the Council arrived at a unanimous conclusion, would its decision be binding on the Viceroy or would the Viceroy have a veto even in such cases?

(2) The position of the army must be defined. There was at the time a wall dividing the army and the people. This must be changed so that Indian leaders had an opportunity of coming into touch with the army.

(3) The British Government had pushed India into the war without consulting Indian opinion. The Congress had refused to accept this position. If there was a settlement and a new Executive Council formed, it must have the right to refer the question of India's further participation in the war to the Indian Legislative Assembly. India would participate in the war against Japan not as a result of a British decision but by a vote of her own representatives.

Gandhiji, who was present throughout the meeting of the Working Committee, was a party to this decision. He did not on this occasion bring up the point that participation in the war meant that Congress was giving up nonviolence. In other words, he did not for a moment raise the question of violence or nonviolence. Those members of the Working Committee, who had earlier resigned on this issue, remained equally silent.

In accordance with the Viceroy's declaration, the Conference was attended by the presidents of the Indian National Congress and the Moslem League as well as representatives of the Scheduled Castes [or the Untouchables. Gandhi called them the "Harijans," which means "Children of God."] and the Sikhs. The leader of the Congress party and the deputy leader of the Moslem League in the Central Assembly, the leaders of the Congress party and the Moslem League in the Council of State, and the leaders of the Nationalist party and the European Group in the Assembly were also invited. The other participants were those who then held office as premiers in provincial governments or had recently held that office. The Hindu Mahasabha tried to get an invitation but the Viceroy did not accept its claim.

We were asked to come a little before the actual time of the Conference. The Viceroy received us on the lawns of the Viceregal Lodge, where we were formally introduced to him. I was very weak at the time and found it difficult to remain standing for more than a few minutes. I mentioned this to Sir Evan Jenkins, the private secretary to the Viceroy, who took me to a corner where a sofa was placed. After I had been sitting there a few minutes, he came back with a lady who was introduced to me as a proficient Arabic scholar. Perhaps he thought that I was sitting alone and should have company. And what better company could I have than an orientalist? I tried to speak to her in Arabic but found that the poor lady's knowledge of Arabic did not extend beyond *Nam* (Yes) and *La* (No). I I then asked her in English why the private secretary thought her to be a fluent Arabic speaker. She said that she had been in Baghdad for some months and, at the dinner party last night, she had told some of the invitees that the Arab used the expression "Ajib, Ajib" ["Extraordinary, Extraordinary"] whenever he was surprised. She laughingly added that this had obviously impressed the guests and given them the impression that she was an Arabic scholar.

After a few minutes Lord Wavell came up and said that it was time to go to the Conference room. The seats were arranged with the Viceroy in the centre. The Congress, as the principal opposition party, sat to the left of the Viceroy. The League was on his right, perhaps an unconscious admission that it was a supporter of the Government.

Lord Wavell made a brief opening speech after which I placed before the Conference the point of view of the Congress Working Committee. The Viceroy's reply on all the three points raised by me was favorable. The discussion continued the whole day with only a break for lunch.

The Conference was private and the press was not invited. After the first sitting, I told Lord Wavell that there would be wild speculation about our discussions unless something was officially given to the press. It would therefore be desirable to issue a press release but it must be something on which the parties could agree. He said that, after every sitting, an official statement would be prepared and approved by the Conference before release. Accordingly I received a draft that evening and sent it back with one or two minor amendments. These were incorporated before the statement was issued to the press. The same procedure was followed throughout the Conference.

Soon after the Conference began, the differences between the Congress and the Moslem League came out into the open. By the second day, the Conference had agreed on certain main principles like representation for minorities, wholehearted support for the war effort and continuance of the reconstituted Executive Council under the Government of India Act till the end of the war. Differences, however, arose about the composition of the Executive Council. Mr. Jinnah's demand was that Congress could nominate all the Hindu members but all the Moslem members must be nominees of the League. I pointed out that Congress could never accept such a demand. It had approached all political problems from a national point of view and recognized no distinction between Hindus and Moslems on political issues. It could not in any circumstances agree to be an organization of Hindus alone. I therefore insisted that the Congress should have the freedom to nominate any Indian it liked regardless of whether he was a Hindu, a Moslem, a Christian, a Parsee or a Sikh. Congress should participate on the basis of Indian nationhood or not participate at all. So far as the Moslem League was concerned, it was for the League to decide who should be its nominees.

The Conference reassembled on the morning of 26 June but dispersed before lunch so that the delegates could confer among themselves. Mr. Jinnah had expressed a wish to have an informal discussion with the Congress. I nominated for the purpose Pandit

Govind Ballabh Pant, who, I thought, would be the right person to negotiate with Mr. Jinnah. Their discussions continued for several days but in the end proved abortive. Khizir Hayat Khan, who was attending the Conference as the Premier of the Punjab, met me several times during this period. I was glad to find that he had taken up a very reasonable attitude on all questions and was helpful and cooperative in solving problems as they arose.

The Simla Conference marks a turning point in Indian political history. This was the first time that negotiations failed, not on the basic political issue between India and Britain, but on the communal issue dividing different Indian groups. A retrospect into the history of the Moslem League is necessary in order to understand this change. Three phases can be clearly distinguished in the attitude of the Moslem League towards political problems.

The Moslem League was established in 1906 in Dacca after the session of the Moslem Educational Conference during Christmas. It owed its origin to the efforts to Nawab Mushtaq Husain. I was present at the session and remember the two reasons advanced for the establishment of the League. It was said that one would be to strengthen and develop a feeling of loyalty to the British Government among the Moslems of India. The second was to advance the claims of the Moslems against Hindus and other communities in respect of service under the Crown, thus safeguarding Moslem interests and rights. The leaders of the League were therefore naturally opposed to the demand for political independence raised by the Congress. They felt that if the Moslems joined in any such demand, the British would not support their claims for special treatment in elective bodies and services. In fact they described the Congress as a disloyal organization of rebels and distrusted even moderate political leaders such as Gokhale or Sir Ferozesah Mehta. During this phase, the British Government always used the Moslem League as a counter to the demands of the Congress.

The Moslem League entered into the second phase of its activities when it found that the Government was compelled to introduce various reforms as a result of Congress pressure. It was somewhat disturbed when it saw the Congress achieving its object step by step. The League still remained aloof from the political struggle, but as soon as any advance was made it put in a claim on behalf of the Moslem community. This program of the Moslem League suited the Government well. In fact, there are reasons to think that the League was acting according to the wishes of the British. During the Morley-Minto Reforms, as well as during the Montford scheme of provincial autonomy, this was the attitude adopted by the League.

Then came the third phase in the League's program during World War II. Congress had gained immensely in prestige and strength. It was now clear that the British Government would have to recognize Indian freedom. Mr. Jinnah had now become the leader of the Moslem League and felt that he must take advantage of every difference between the Congress and the Government. Whenever there were discussions between the Congress and the Government for the transfer of power, Mr. Jinnah would begin by remaining silent. If the negotiations failed, he issued a milk-and-water statement condemning both parties and saying that, since there was no settlement, there was no need for the Moslem League to express any opinion on the British offer. This is what he did during the August offer in 1940 and the Cripps proposals of 1942. The Simla Conference presented him with a situation that he had never faced before.

As I have said earlier, all discussions between the Congress and the Government had till now failed on political issues. The British were not willing to transfer power and the Congress was not ready to accept any solution which did not ensure Indian freedom. Discussions had therefore failed on political issues and never reached the communal question. In the Simla Conference, I was able to persuade the Congress Working Committee to accept Lord Wavell's offer. Now that the political issue between India and Britain seemed on the point of solution, the Conference broke down over the question of communal representation in the new Executive Council.

I have already explained that the Congress had taken a national stand on this question, while the Moslem League demanded that the

Congress should give up its national character and function as a communal organization. Mr. Jinnah took the strange stand that the Congress could nominate only Hindu members of the Executive Council. I asked the Conference what right Mr. Jinnah or the Moslem League had to dictate whom the Congress should nominate. If the Congress put forth the names of Moslems, Parsees, Sikhs or Christians, this would reduce the number of Hindu representatives, but how did this concern the Moslem League? I asked Lord Wavell to say in categorical terms whether the stand of the Moslem League could be regarded as reasonable.

Lord Wavell said in reply that he could not accept the stand of the Moslem League as reasonable. At the same time he said that this was a matter which should be decided between the Congress and the Moslem League and it would not be proper for either the Government or for himself as an individual to force a decision on either party.

This difference regarding the composition of the Council came out into the open after agreement had been reached on the political issue. When the general pattern had been accepted, the time came for the parties to suggest the names of their representatives. Naturally the first name in the Congress list was that of the Congress President. We included also the names of Jawaharlal and Sardar Patel. Regarding the other two names, there was a good deal of discussion among us before we could come to an agreement. I was keen to include one Parsee and one Indian Christian.

A word of explanation is necessary as to why I pressed for the inclusion of these representatives of minorities. When we were arrested in August 1942, the British Government had tried hard to work up some of the minorities against the Congress. One of the minorities approached were the Parsees. They are a very small community but occupy an important position in national life because of their education, wealth and ability. I felt that an injustice had been done to a member of this community when Nariman was passed over at the time of the formation of the first Congress Ministry of Bombay. The Parsees had also been affected by one of the decisions which

Congress had taken in 1937. When prohibition was introduced in
Bombay, the law affected the Parsee businessmen more than men
of any other community. They had almost a monopoly of the wine
trade and prohibition made them lose business worth crores. The
Government perhaps thought that the Parsees would be against the
Congress because of these incidents, but as a community they refused to play the British game. A statement signed by almost all
important and reputed leaders of the community declared in categorical terms that they were and would remain with the Congress
on the question of Indian freedom.

When I read the statement in Ahmednagar Fort jail, I was greatly
impressed and told my colleagues that the Parsees had served India
well in issuing this statement. I also suggested that we must give
proper recognition to this gesture. Though the Parsees were a very
small community, I felt that they must find a place in the first free
Government of India. When therefore we were drawing up the list
of Congress nominees for the Executive Council, I insisted that there
should be a Parsee name in the list submitted by the Congress.
Gandhiji liked my idea but felt that, since the Congress could nominate only five persons, it would not be possible to include a Parsee.
It was, however, agreed that in a future government every effort
must be made to accommodate a Parsee. To this I could not agree.
I said that the future was uncertain. Now that we had an opportunity
to nominate persons of our own choice, we must include a Parsee in
our list. After two days' discussion, my view ultimately prevailed.

I also insisted on the inclusion of an Indian Christian in the
Congress list. I knew that a representative of the community could
not come from any other source. Sikhs and Scheduled Castes would
be represented in any case, but no Christian would find a place in
the Government unless Congress sponsored him. I also remembered
that the Indian Christian community had always stood by the Congress and adopted a national approach on all our political problems.

The upshot was that the list submitted by the Congress contained
only two Hindu names. This proved, if proof were needed, that
Congress was a truly national organization. It could have been

said that the Hindus, who constituted the majority community of
India, would object to such a proposal, but be it said to their credit
that the Hindus of India stood solidly behind the Congress and did
not waver even when they found that in the Congress list of five,
three men were drawn from the Moslems, the Christians and the
Parsees. Later, the Hindu Mahasabha tried to make political capital
out of this decision of the Congress, but everyone knows how miserably the Mahasabha failed. It is a strange irony of fate that, like the
Mahasabha, the Moslem League also opposed the inclusion by the
Congress of a Moslem name in its list.

Looking back on events after a period of ten years, I still cannot
help feeling surprised at the strange situation which developed as
a result of the attitude of the Moslem League. The provisional list
which Lord Wavell had himself prepared included four names in
addition to the five names each of the Congress and the Moslem
League. One of these was a representative of the Sikhs, two of the
Scheduled Castes and the fourth was Khizir Hayat Khan, then
Premier of the Punjab. Jinnah reacted violently against the suggestion that there should be two Moslems in the Executive Council who
were not his nominees. Khizir Hayat Khan came to see me and I
assured him that the Congress would not object to his inclusion. I
repeated this to Lord Wavell. If therefore the Conference had not
broken down because of Jinnah's opposition, the result would have
been that the Moslems, who constituted only about 25 per cent of
the total population of India, would have had seven representatives
in a Council of fourteen. This is evidence of the generosity of the
Congress and also throws a lurid light on the stupidity of the Moslem
League. The League was supposed to be the guardian of Moslem
interests and yet it was because of its opposition that the Moslems of
India were denied a substantial share in the Government of undivided India. The intransigent attitude of the Moslem League
finally led to the breakdown of the Conference.[2]

After the Conference was over, I issued a statement and held a
press conference in which I explained the difficulties in the way of

[2] Wavell made a statement to the same effect.

Congress participation in the Simla Conference. The proposals were presented to us suddenly. On 15 June 1945 my colleagues and I were released and we had to take a decision straightaway on the invitation. We realized that vast changes had taken place in the international sphere and that these had undoubtedly had repercussions on the Indian problem. The inevitable result of these changes was to bring to the forefront the question of Indian freedom and that of the freedom of other Asian countries. In spite of all these difficulties, the Working Committee had decided to participate in the Conference.

I told the press that at all stages during the Conference I had emphasized the national character of the Congress. I had also made it plain to the Viceroy that the Congress Working Committee wished to cooperate in every reasonable way in helping to resolve the present political deadlock.

I pointed out that if the Simla Conference had succeeded, the war against Japan would have become not only Britain's but India's war against Japan. India was directly concerned with the question of liberating countries in Southeast Asia. It would therefore be the duty of the new Government of India to carry on the war against Japan till all these countries were liberated. The new Indian Government could not, however, be a party to any proposal for restoring the domination of former European imperialist powers. We would not permit the use of a single Indian soldier or the expenditure of a single pie for restoring the prewar colonial régimes in Southeast Asian countries.

I also told the press that, after the fundamental issue of the transfer of power to Indian hands had been settled, the Conference began to consider the strength and composition of the new Executive Council. The Conference was adjourned to enable private and informal talks to take place among the parties but these conversations led to no result. In the course of these informal talks the position taken up by Mr. Jinnah was that the Moslem League alone should nominate Moslem members in the new Executive Council, and that Congress would have no right to nominate any Moslem. The Congress found that such a position would be inconsistent with its basic national character. It was not merely a question of seats, but one affecting a fundamental principle. We were prepared to accommodate the Moslem League to the farthest possible extent, but Mr. Jinnah took up an uncompromising attitude. He refused to submit even a list of names unless his point of view was accepted. The Viceroy had told me that he did his best, but failed to persuade Mr. Jinnah, who insisted that the Moslem nominees should all be nominated by the League Working Committee. The Viceroy was unable to agree to this and felt that it was not profitable to proceed with the proposal at present.

I may here quote from the statement I had then issued:

Two points arise out of the present situation. The first is that the attitude of the Muslim League has been responsible for the failure of the Conference. The second point which emerges from the refusal of the Muslim League is that it is for Lord Wavell to decide whether to go forward or not. His Excellency has decided not to proceed for the present. In this connection I must repeat what I said at the Conference. The British Government cannot absolve themselves of the responsibility for the communal problem here. Whether it is today or tomorrow, they must take up a firm stand on a just and fair basis. There is no other alternative but to do so. And once a decision is taken, we must move forward. Those who are prepared to go forward must be allowed to go forward and those who wish to be left out should be left out. Without determination, nothing can be done. Wavering minds and faltering steps will never carry us forward in the path of progress. We must think before we take a step, but once we decide, hesitation is not a virtue but a sign of definite weakness.

I told the representatives of the press that I had no regrets whatsoever for the Congress stand in this conference. We had gone as far as we could to meet the wishes of Mr. Jinnah, but we could not accept his claim that the Moslem League was the sole representative and authoritative organization of the Moslems of India. In the provinces where Moslems were in a majority, there was no League Ministry. There was a Congress Ministry in the Frontier Province. In Bengal, there was Governor's rule, while in the Punjab it was a Unionist Ministry. In Sind, Sir Ghulam Hussain depended on

Congress support and the same position held in Assam. It could not therefore be claimed that the Moslem League represented all the Moslems. There was in fact a large bloc of Moslems who had nothing to do with the League.

Before I conclude this chapter, I would like to refer to one of the consequences of the "Quit India" Movement. During this period, some new personalities appeared on the Indian scene. They were thrown up by the demands of the new situation. Among them was Mrs. Asaf Ali. I have already mentioned that, on the morning of 9 August 1942, she told me on the Bombay railway platform that she would not remain idle. After our arrest, she toured all over the country and sought to organize resistance to the British war effort. She was not worried about the distinction between violence and non-violence but adopted any method she found useful. After some time, the Government began to take notice of her activities and attempts were made to arrest her. She, however, went underground and was able to evade arrest. In this she was helped by a large number of Indians many of whom were Government officers or industrialists who were normally regarded as loyal supporters of the Government. Some businessmen of Bombay and Calcutta helped her. She even stayed in the homes of officers of the Indian Civil Service and the Indian Army. She was able to raise the funds she needed and remained active throughout the whole period of our detention.

When I was released in 1945, she came to see me secretly in Calcutta. I spoke to Lord Wavell about her, who said that he would not arrest her for her past activities but what about the future? I told Lord Wavell that the political situation had changed and there was little likelihood of her continuing with subversive activities. When I was satisfied that she would not be arrested, I asked her to come out and this she did in the latter half of 1945.

Her activities had become so well-known that the Viceroy cited her case in a speech in which he questioned the *bona fides* of the Congress regarding nonviolence. He said that, when the wife of a member of the Working Committee was engaged in violent activities, it was difficult for the Government to believe in Congress declara-

tions concerning nonviolence. When we learnt about these developments in Ahmednagar Fort jail, I found that Asaf Ali was worrying
not about his own imprisonment but about the dangers which his
wife was facing. I tried to reassure him by saying that he should
not worry, but be proud that she was exhibiting such courage and
initiative in a noble cause.

CHAPTER 11

General Elections

AFTER the Simla Conference the doctors strongly advised me to go to Kashmir for a change. My health was still weak and it was with difficulty that I could carry on even the normal duties of the Congress President. Jawaharlal also needed a change and he, too, decided to go to Kashmir. I spent the months of July and August in Gulmarg. It was while I was there that I learnt that the Labour party had won an unprecedented victory in the British General Elections. I immediately sent a telegram of congratulations to Mr. Attlee and Sir Stafford Cripps. I expressed the hope that now that Labour had come to power, it would fulfil the pledges it had always given to India during the years it was in opposition. In his reply Attlee said that the Labour party would do its best to arrive at a right solution of the Indian problem. Cripps cabled that it was his hope that India would not be disappointed. I may add that Gandhiji and Jawaharlal did not like this exchange of telegrams. They were both skeptical about the Labour attitude to India. I was, however, convinced that the Labour party would approach the Indian problem from a fresh angle and I was optimistic about the outcome.

Shortly after this, the Viceroy declared that General Elections should be held in India in the coming winter. This made it necessary to call a meeting of the Working Committee and the A.I.C.C. It was necessary for the Congress to decide what attitude to adopt as a result of the failure of the Simla Conference. There were those who were in favor of starting a new movement. Others held that, even if no movement was launched, the Congress should boycott

139

the elections. I was of the view that there was no justification for either of these suggestions. If the Simla Conference had failed it was not the fault of the British. The cause of the failure was communal, not political.

I was still at Gulmarg when there was a new and unprecedented development in world history. The Americans dropped atom bombs on Hiroshima and Nagasaki. Before these bombs were used, it was the general estimate that it would take at least two years to break down Japanese resistance. After Hiroshima and Nagasaki, the situation was completely transformed. The Japanese had no answer to this new and frightful weapon of destruction and were compelled to accept unconditional surrender. The war in Europe was already over. Within a few weeks, the American army had landed on Japanese soil and occupied Tokyo. General MacArthur became the virtual ruler of Japan.

I am still convinced that there was no justification for the use of atom bombs on Japan without previous warning. It was a weapon which completely destroyed not only military forces but the civil population and harmed even unborn generations. In fact, it threatened the destruction of man. When, in World War I, the Germans had used poison gas against the Allies, world opinion condemned them in unqualified terms. If the Germans had then been guilty of inhumanity, how could one absolve the Americans of the same charge? I felt that the use of the atom bombs exceeded the limits of permissible destruction and did not redound to the prestige or heroism of the Allies. I also noted with regret that the Allies hailed this event as a magnificent victory and there was hardly one word of protest.

My health was still weak. July and August are not the proper season for Kashmir and I had not benefited much by my stay there, but September brought a most pleasant change and I began to improve rapidly. My appetite returned and I was able to take exercise. If I could have stayed for another month, I feel sure that my health would have been fully restored. Circumstances, however, demanded that I should leave Kashmir. The Working Committee and the

A.I.C.C. needed my presence. When I came down to the plains, the temporary improvement in my health disappeared.

There was at that time no air service to Kashmir. One had to go by the long and circuitous motor route. The Americans, however, were flying large numbers of army officers to Kashmir for rest and recreation. Every two weeks a fresh batch was sent by aeroplane to Srinagar. Some of these officers came to meet me. When they heard I had to return to Delhi, they offered to fly me down in the special plane of the American Commander. On 10 September, I reached Delhi by their plane and started for Poona. The Working Committee met at Poona on 14 September and after a few days adjourned to Bombay. Both in the Working Committee and the A.I.C.C., there were heated discussions about our new line of policy. A majority, including Gandhiji, held that we must devote ourselves to exclusively constructive work. They believed that there was not much hope on the political plane.

I argued that there was a great change in Britain as the result of the formation of the Labour Government. The Labour party had always been friendly to India. In view of this, it was desirable that we should give it an opportunity of proving its *bona fides*. My firm conviction was that we should not start a new movement but participate in the General Elections. I also pointed out that the Simla Conference had been a serious attempt to solve the Indian problem. Though it had failed, we must appreciate the spirit displayed by Lord Wavell and, now that Labour was in power, await further developments. After a good deal of discussion, my views finally prevailed.

I now thought it necessary to take up the question of political prisoners. The Government of India had released the members of the Working Committee, but thousands of ordinary members of the Congress were still in jail. At the time of the Simla Conference, it was not clear to me what our next step should be. I did not therefore raise the question of a general amnesty for all political prisoners at the Conference.

After the Conference two events transformed the entire scene. The first was the sweeping victory of Labour in Britain and the second was the dropping of the atom bomb and the end of the war. The political picture, both national and international, had now become much clearer. I was convinced that we should follow a dual policy. On the one hand, we must keep the spirit of struggle alive among the Indian people and, on the other, we must refrain from any precipitate step.

Events developed as I had anticipated. Some time after the end of the war, Lord Wavell declared that General Elections would be held in India. As soon as I heard this announcement, I knew that the time had come to raise the question of the release of the political prisoners. Once General Elections had been announced, there could be no justification for keeping them in jail. I wrote to Lord Wavell from Gulmarg and said that I had not raised the question of the political prisoners in Simla as the time was not opportune. Now the situation had changed. Since the war was over and General Elections had been announced, there should be a general amnesty. This was necessary in the interests both of the Indian people and of the Government. So far as the prisoners themselves were concerned, they had been in jail for years and would be prepared to stay there for some more months. Continued detention would not harm them but it would reduce the prospects of a settlement. If the Government desired to create a new political atmosphere, they would have to release all political prisoners.

Lord Wavell replied by telegram. He said that he agreed with my views and was issuing orders for the release of the political prisoners. He did not, however, issue orders for a general amnesty. The result was that while the majority of Congress prisoners came out, a small group of leftist workers of the Congress were still detained. They included Jai Prakash Narain,[1] Ramanandan Mishra and several others.

I was not satisfied with the outcome of my intervention. I saw

[1] The leader of the Socialist party who later abjured violence, became a Gandhian, and collaborated with Vinoba Bhave in the Bhooden (land gift) and Gramdan (voluntary village cooperative) movements. Nehru said to me in 1946, "Jai Prakash is a future Prime Minister of India."

no reason why a small group of leftists should be detained when all the others were being released. The Government of India had suspicions against them, but there was no proof that they had behaved differently from the other Congress workers who had taken part in the "Quit India" Movement. After the A.I.C.C. met in Bombay in September, I wrote a long and detailed letter to Lord Wavell. I said that the effect on the country would be very unfortunate if this handful of political prisoners was not released. If Lord Wavell wanted to create a proper atmosphere in the country he should agree to a general amnesty. Lord Wavell finally agreed and they were all released.

The A.I.C.C. had decided that an election manifesto should be prepared by the Working Committee and placed before the A.I.C.C. for its consideration and adoption. It also authorized the Working Committee to issue a preliminary manifesto on behalf of the Central Election Committee. It was not possible to hold another meeting of the A.I.C.C. to consider the fuller manifesto in view of the imminence of the General Elections. The Working Committee therefore issued the following manifesto on its own authority:

For sixty years the National Congress has laboured for the freedom of India. During this long span of years its history has been the history of the Indian people, straining at the leash that has held them in bondage, ever trying to unloose themselves from it. From small beginnings it has progressively grown and spread in this vast country, carrying the message of freedom to the masses of our people in the towns as well as the remotest villages. From these masses it has gained power and strength and developed into a mighty organization, the living and vibrant symbol of India's will to freedom and independence. From generation to generation it has dedicated itself to this sacred cause, and in its name and under its banner innumerable countrymen and countrywomen of ours have laid down their lives and undergone suffering in order to redeem the pledge they had taken. By service and sacrifice it has enshrined itself in the hearts of our people; by its refusal to submit to any dishonour to our nation it has built up a powerful movement of resistance to foreign rule.

The career of the Congress has been one of both constructive effort for the good of the people and of unceasing struggle to gain freedom. In this struggle it has faced numerous crises and come repeatedly into direct conflict with the armed might of a great Empire. Following peaceful methods, it has not only survived these conflicts but has gained new strength from them. After the recent three years of an unprecedented mass upheaval and its cruel and ruthless suppression, the Congress has risen stronger than ever and more loved by the people by whom it has stood through storm and stress.

The Congress has stood for equal rights and opportunities for every citizen of India, man or woman. It has stood for the unity of all communities and religious groups and for tolerance and goodwill between them. It has stood for full opportunities for the people as a whole to grow and develop according to their own wishes and genius; it has also stood for the freedom of each group and territorial area within the nation to develop its own life and culture within the larger framework, and for this purpose such territorial areas or provinces should be constituted, as far as possible, on a linguistic and cultural basis. It has stood for the rights of all those who suffer from social tyranny and injustice and for the removal for them of all barriers to equality.

The Congress has envisaged a free, democratic State with the fundamental rights and civil liberties of all its citizens guaranteed in the constitution. This constitution, in its view, should be a federal one with a great deal of autonomy for its constituent units and its legislative organs elected under universal adult franchise.

A hundred and fifty years and more of foreign rule have arrested the growth of the country and produced numerous vital problems that demand immediate solution. Intensive exploitation of the country and the people during this period has reduced the masses to the depths of misery and starvation. The country has not only been politically kept under subjection and humiliated, but has also suffered economic, social, cultural and spiritual degradation. During the years of war, and even now, this process of exploitation by irresponsible authority and complete ignoring of Indian interests and views has reached a new height, an incompetence in the administration, leading to terrible famine and widespread misery among our people. There is no way to solve any of these urgent problems except through freedom and independence. The content of political freedom must be both economic and social.

The most vital and urgent of India's problems is how to remove the curse of poverty and raise the standards of the masses. It is to the well-being and progress of these masses that the Congress has directed its special attention and its constructive activities. It is by their well-being and advancement that it has judged every proposal and every change and it has declared that anything that comes in the way of the good of the masses of our country must be removed. Industry and agriculture, the social services and public utilities must be encouraged, modernised and rapidly extended in order to add to the wealth of the country and give it the capacity for self-growth, without dependence on others. But all this must be done with the primary object, and paramount duty of benefiting the masses of our people and raising their economic, cultural and spiritual level, removing unemployment, and adding to the dignity of the individual. For this purpose it will be necessary to plan and co-ordinate social advance in all its many fields, to prevent the concentration of wealth and power in the hands of individuals and groups, to prevent vested interests inimical to society from growing and to have social control of the mineral resources, means of transport and the principal methods of production and distribution in land, industry and in other departments of national activity, so that free India may develop into a co-operative commonwealth.

In international affairs, the Congress stands for the establishment of a world federation of free nations. Till such time as such a federation takes shape, India must develop friendly relations with all nations, and particularly with her neighbours on the east and the west and north. In the Far East, in South-East Asia and in Western Asia, India has had trade and cultural relations for thousands of years and it is inevitable that with freedom she should renew and develop these relations. Reasons of security and future trends of trade also demand these closer contacts with these regions. India, which has conducted her own struggle for freedom on a non-violent basis, will always throw her weight on the side of world peace and co-operation. She will also champion the freedom of all other subject nations and peoples, for only on the basis of this freedom and the elimination of imperialism everywhere can world peace be established.

On 8 August 1942, the All-India Congress Committee passed a resolution, since then famous in India's story. By its demands and challenge the Congress stands today. It is on the basis of this resolution and with its battle-cry that the Congress faces the elections for the Central and Provincial Assemblies.

The Central Legislative Assembly is a body with no power or authority and is practically an advisory body whose advice has been constantly flouted and ignored. It is completely out of date and is based on a very restricted franchise. The electoral registers for it are full of errors and omissions and no opportunities for correcting or adding to them have been given. Large numbers of our countrymen are still in prison and many others who have been released are disqualified from standing for election. Obstructions in the way of holding public meetings still continue in many places. Yet, with all these and other handicaps and drawbacks, the Congress has decided to contest the elections to show that the inevitable result of elections, however restricted, must be to demonstrate the overwhelming solidarity of the opinion of the voters on the issue of independence. Therefore, in this election, petty issues do not count, nor do individuals, nor sectarian cries—only one thing counts; the freedom and independence of our Motherland, from which all other freedoms will flow to our people.

So the Congress appeals to the voters for the Central Assembly all over the country to support the Congress candidates in every way at the forthcoming elections, and to stand by the Congress at this critical juncture, which is so pregnant with future possibilities. Many a time the people of India have taken the pledge of independence; that pledge has yet to be redeemed, and the well-beloved cause for which it stands and which has summoned us so often, still beckons to us. But the time is coming when we shall redeem it in full, not by the election but by what comes after it. Meanwhile, this election is a small test for us, a preparation for the greater things to come. Let all those who care and long for freedom and the independence of India meet this test with strength and confidence, and march together to the free India of our dreams.

As was generally expected, Congress achieved an absolute majority in all the provinces except Bengal, the Punjab and Sind. In these three provinces, the position was complex. In Bengal the Moslem League was the largest single party and captured almost half the seats. In the Punjab, the Unionist party and the League were balanced in almost equal numbers. In Sind also, the Moslem League won a large number of seats but could not achieve a majority. In these three provinces the Moslem population was in the majority and the Moslem League had carried on propaganda to arouse religious fanaticism and communal passions. This clouded the political issues so much that Moslems who stood on Congress or any other ticket had great difficulty in even securing a hearing from the people. In the North West Frontier Province, where the Moslem majority was the largest, all the efforts of the League failed and the Congress was able to form the Government.

It would be appropriate at this stage to review once again the political situation in India. When the Second World War broke out, the communists were at a loss because Hitler and Stalin had entered into a nonaggression past. Till the Nazi-Soviet agreement, the communists had been in the forefront in attacking Hitler and condemning the Nazi philosophy of life. Indian communists knew in their heart of hearts that Stalin had committed a great blunder in entering into this pact, but, like communists in other parts of the world, they lacked the courage to say so. They therefore described the understanding as an attempt to limit the extent of the war which was described as an imperialist war. Being almost helpless they sought to justify their position by describing Hitler as the lesser evil. In view of this they could not offer any help to the British and in fact strongly supported Indian neutrality between the two camps. When, however, Hitler attacked Russia, the communists turned a complete somersault. They declared the war to be a people's war and went all out in support of the British. In India they openly joined the war propaganda and did everything to help the British war effort. Mr. M. N. Roy accepted funds from the Government openly and carried on propaganda in favor of the war. The communists also received Government assistance in various ways. The ban on the Communist party was removed and members of the party helped to carry on war propaganda.

The Congress on the other hand had launched the "Quit India" Movement. Congressmen had been arrested in large numbers while the communists who had previously been under arrest or in hiding could now work openly in favor of their party. Even when Congressmen were released after the Simla Conference, they were not clear as to their line of action and waited for a decision by the Congress.

A most remarkable change had in the meantime come about in all the public services. During the war the Defence Forces had recruited a large proportion of young men who came from different provinces and different social classes. The earlier British practice of recruiting only from certain selected groups had been abandoned under the pressure of war needs. The young men who had now joined the Armed Forces had accepted the British at their word that after the war India would be free. This belief had moved them to make great efforts during the period of hostilities. Now that hostilities were over, they expected that India would become free.

All the three branches of the Armed Forces—the Navy, the Army and the Air Force—were inspired by a new spirit of patriotism. They were in fact so full of enthusiasm that they could not conceal their feelings whenever they saw any of the Congress leaders. Wherever I went during this period, the young men of the Defence Forces came out to welcome me and express their sympathy and admiration without any regard for the reaction of their European officers. When I went to Karachi a group of naval officers came to see me. They expressed their admiration for the Congress policy and assured me that, if Congress issued the necessary orders, they would come over to us. If there was a conflict between Congress and the Government, they would side with the Congress and not with the Government. Hundreds of naval officers in Bombay expressed the same feelings.

These sentiments were widespread, not only among officers but also among the ranks. I flew to Lahore in connection with the formation of the provincial Ministry. A Gurkha regiment [from Nepal] which was stationed in Lahore had its quarters near the aerodrome. When the soldiers heard that I was coming, they lined up in hundreds and said that they wanted to have my *darshan*.[2] Even policemen exhibited the same feelings. In the history of the Indian political struggle, the police had always been the stanchest supporters of the Government. They had in fact little sympathy with political workers and often acted harshly towards them. They had also undergone a transformation of sentiment and were not behind any other group in their feeling of loyalty to the Congress.

Once when I was passing along Lal Bazar in Calcutta, my car was held up in a traffic jam. Some police constables recognized me and reported to their barracks, which were near by. In a few minutes a large gathering of constables and head constables surrounded my car. They saluted me and some touched my feet. They all expressed

[2] The grace or spiritual benefit that comes from being in the presence of a beloved religious or political person.

their regard for Congress and said that they would act according to our orders. I remember another incident clearly. The Governor of Bengal had expressed a wish to meet me. When I went to Government House, the constables on duty surrounded my car and as I came out each man came up individually and saluted me. They all assured me that they would act according to my orders. Since I had gone to Government House at the invitation of the Governor, I did not think it proper that there should be any slogans. However, the constables would not keep quiet, but shouted slogans in my honor. This was clear evidence that their sympathies were with Congress and that they were no longer afraid of expressing them openly. If the Government wished to punish them for their sympathy with the Congress, they were even ready for it.

These developments were naturally reported to the authorities. Government received detailed reports and passed them on to the Secretary of State for India. The British realized that, for the first time in Indian history, the entire people was aflame with the desire for independence. Political freedom was no longer the objective of the Congress alone but of all sections of the people. Still more important was the fact that all sections of the services—civil and military— were moved by the same impulses. There was no longer anything secret about this upsurge for freedom. Men and officers of the Defence Forces declared openly that they had poured out their blood in the war on the assurance that India would be free after the cessation of hostilities. They demanded that this assurance must now be honored.

After the General Elections were over, the question of forming the new Government arose in each province. It became necessary for me to visit the provincial capitals and supervise the formation of the Ministries. The time at my disposal was very short but air transport helped to solve the problem. During the war, all air services had been brought under the control of the Government. They also controlled the allotment of seats. Lord Wavell issued instructions that I should be given every facility and this made it possible for me to visit all the provincial capitals.

When I came to Bihar for the formation of the Government, I found the situation complicated by the rivalries of different groups within the Congress. To these were added the personal problems of important Congressmen. There was the acute and long-standing rivalry between Dr. Srikrishna Sinha and Dr. Anugraha Narayan Sinha. There was also the question of Dr. Syed Mahmud, as some Congressmen had turned against him after his release from Ahmednagar Fort jail. In the end, all the three were included in the Cabinet and I was glad that this was done with the support of every important Congress leader of Bihar, including Dr. Rajendra Prasad.

I had made up my mind that we should adopt a generous attitude towards the Moslem League in the matter of the formation of the Ministries. Wherever members were returned to the Assembly on the League ticket, I sent for them and invited them to cooperate in the formation of the provincial Ministries. I did this both in the provinces where Congress had an absolute majority and in those where it was the largest single party. I knew that in many provinces, particularly in Bihar, Assam and the Punjab, members of the Moslem League would have been glad to come in, but Mr. Jinnah's policy was to prevent them from cooperating with the Congress.

The position was specially difficult in the Punjab. It was a Moslem majority province but no party had a clear majority. The Moslem members were divided between the Unionist party and the Moslem League. I held discussions with both groups. As I have said, under instructions from Mr. Jinnah, the League declined my invitation. However, I was able to carry out negotiations in such a way as to give the Unionist party the opportunity of forming the Ministry with the support of Congress. The Governor was personally inclined towards the Moslem League but he found that he had no option but to invite Khizir Hayat Khan, the leader of the Unionist party, to form the Government.

This was the first time Congress had come into the Government in the Punjab. This was a development which had till then been regarded as almost impossible. Political circles throughout the country declared that I had shown great skill and statesmanship in the negotiations which had led to the formation of the Punjab Ministry. Independent members throughout the country congratulated me in unqualified terms. The *National Herald,* which is the organ of the U.P. Congress, congratulated me on the manner in which I had solved the complex and difficult problem of the Punjab and went so far as to say that my handling of the situation was one of the clearest examples of statesmanship and skill in negotiation exhibited by any Congress leader.

I was pleased by this response in the country but there was one development, fortunately temporary, which saddened me. From the very beginning of my activities in the Congress, Jawaharlal and I have been the best of friends. We have always seen eye to eye and leaned on one another for support. The question of any rivalry or jealousy between us had never arisen and I thought would never arise. In fact my friendship with the family dated from the days of Pandit Motilal Nehru. In the beginning I had looked on Jawaharlal as a brother's son and he had regarded me as his father's friend.

Jawaharlal is by nature warmhearted and generous, and personal jealousies never enter his mind. However, there were some among his relations and friends who did not like his cordial relations with me and sought to create difficulties and jealousies between us. Jawaharlal has a weakness for theoretical considerations and they took advantage of this to turn him against me. They spoke to him and said that the alliance of Congress with the Unionist party was in principle wrong. They argued that the Moslem League was a mass organization and that the Congress should have formed a coalition with the Moslem League and not with the Unionists in the Punjab. This was the line which the communists had adopted openly. Jawaharlal was partially influenced by their views and may have thought that I was sacrificing leftist principles in forming a coalition with the Unionist party.

Those who wanted to create a division between Jawaharlal and myself also kept on telling him that the praise showered on me was a reflection on all other Congress leaders. They knew his generous nature and therefore spoke more about the others than him, but they insisted that if his own paper, the *National Herald*, continued to speak so highly of me, the result would be that I should soon achieve an unrivalled position in the Congress organization and this would not be good for democracy within the Congress.

I do not think that personal considerations had any effect on Jawaharlal's mind, but he may have been influenced by the ideological sophistries. In any case, during the meeting of the Congress Working Committee at Bombay, I found that, for the first time since we had worked together in the Congress, he opposed my line of action on almost every item. Jawaharlal took the line that the policy I had adopted in the Punjab was not correct. He even said that I had brought down the prestige of the Congress. I was both surprised and sorry to hear this. What I had done in the Punjab was to put Congress into the Government despite the fact that the Governor had been working for the installation of a Moslem League Ministry. Through my endeavors, the Moslem League had been isolated and Congress, though it was a minority, had become the decisive factor in Punjab affairs. Khizir Hayat Khan was the Chief Minister through Congress support and he had naturally come under its influence.

Jawaharlal held that the participation of Congress in the Government without its being the majority party was not right. This would force the Congress to compromise and perhaps make it resile from its principles. I denied that there was any risk of the Congress giving up its principles but at the same time made it clear that, if the Working Committee did not approve of my decision in Lahore, it could adopt any new policy it liked. Congress had not given any guarantee of remaining in office and could come out whenever it chose.

Gandhiji came out strongly in support of my views. He said that though Congress was in a minority in the Punjab, it had secured a decisive voice in the formation and working of the Ministry through negotiation. He held that there could be no better solution from the Congress point of view and he was against any change in the decision I had taken. When Gandhiji expressed himself in categorical terms, all other members of the Working Committee supported me and Jawaharlal had to acquiesce.

It is possible that Jawaharlal felt that the matter had gone too far and had perhaps hurt my feelings. As was my usual practice, I was staying with Bhulabhai Desai. Jawaharlal came to me early next morning and with great affection and sincerity assured me that his criticism did not for a moment indicate any lack of confidence in my leadership. He admitted frankly that his reading had been wrong and he desired that we should forget the whole episode. This was exactly what I had expected of him. His nature is such that, if he is moved by an idea, he expresses it without any mental reservation, but, if he finds later that he has been wrong, he never hesitates to admit his mistake. I was pleased by this frank talk. He and I have always been the best of friends and it had hurt me that there should be any difference between us.

I have said earlier that some officers of the Indian Navy had met me in Karachi. Among other things they had complained about racial discrimination and said that their protests and representations against such discrimination had been of no avail. Their discontent went on mounting and one day in Delhi I suddenly read in the newspapers that they had resorted to direct action. They had given notice to the Government that, unless their demands were met by a particular date, they would resign in a body. This date had now passed and they held a mass meeting in Bombay in pursuance of their earlier decision. The news electrified the country and a vast majority of the people at once sided with them. The Government was also greatly disturbed. They called out British troops and placed all ships of the Indian Navy in charge of British officers and men.

It was clear to me that this was not an appropriate time for any mass movement or direct action. We had now to watch the course of events and carry on negotiations with the British Government. I therefore felt that this move on the part of the officers of the Indian Navy was wrong. If they suffered from racial discrimination, this was not an evil peculiar to them but one common to all sections of the Army and the Air Force. They were justified in protesting against the discrimination but recourse to direct action at the present time seemed to me unwise.

Mrs. Asaf Ali took up the cause of the naval officers and became their ardent supporter. She came to Delhi to win my support. I told her that the officers had not acted wisely and my advice to them was that they must go back to work unconditionally. The Bombay Congress telephoned to me for my advice and I sent them a telegram to the same effect. Sardar Vallabhbhai Patel was then in Bombay and he also consulted me. I told him that the steps taken by the naval officers were wrong and they should go back to work. Sardar Patel asked what they should do in case the Government did not give them the opportunity to return to their work. I replied that it was my reading of the situation that the Government would agree to let them return. In case the Government raised any difficulty, we should take such action as might be proper.

I was due to leave for Peshawar the next day in connection with the formation of the Ministry there. However, I postponed my visit and asked for an immediate interview with the Commander-in-Chief. Lord Auchinleck met me in Parliament House at 10:00 A.M. next morning. I put for his consideration two points:

(1) Congress has not approved of the action of the naval officers and has advised them to go back to work unconditionally. Congress is, however, anxious that there should be no victimization. If the Government adopted any vindictive measures, Congress would take up the cause of these officers.

(2) The racial discrimination and other grievances of the naval officers must be examined and removed.

Lord Auchinleck spoke in a most friendly spirit. In fact, his tone was more cordial than I had expected. He said that there would be no victimization if the officers returned to duty unconditionally. So far as discrimination was concerned, his entire effort would be to remove it completely. His replies satisfied me and I immediately issued a statement calling upon the officers to return to duty and assuring them that there would be no victimization.

The revolt of the naval officers in Bombay was of special significance in the context of existing circumstances. This was the first time since 1857 that a section of the Defence Forces had openly rebelled against the British on a political issue. The rebellion was not an isolated event, for earlier there had been the formation of the Indian National Army under Subhas Chandra Bose out of Indian prisoners of war. This army had attacked India in 1944 and was at one stage on the point of capturing Imphal. After the surrender of Japan, the British reoccupied Burma and many officers of the Indian National Army were taken prisoner. They did not repent of their action in having joined the Indian National Army and some of them were now facing trial for treason. All these developments convinced the British that they could no longer rely on the Armed Forces unless the political problem of India was satisfactorily solved.

I first heard of the capture of the officers of the Indian National Army when I was in Gulmarg after the Simla Conference. Mr. Pratap Singh, a judge of the Punjab High Court, came to me one day in great excitement and reported that some Indian officers who had fought the British under Subhas Chandra Bose had been arrested. I think that one of his relations was involved in the affair and he was greatly worried about the fate of these young men. His own mentality was that of the traditional civil servant. He, therefore, felt that any interference by the Congress would prejudice the case of these prisoners. He suggested that the Congress should take no interest in the affairs of the Indian National Army, for he argued that this would keep the trial out of politics. I told him that his views were entirely wrong. If the Congress took no interest in the matter, the Government would punish the I.N.A. officers and, in some cases, mete out the extreme penalty. These officers included some of our finest young men and their imprisonment or death would be a serious national loss. I decided straightaway that Congress should undertake the defence of the I.N.A. officers and immediately issued a statement to this effect.

As I viewed the matter, I felt that the British Government could not complain of the conduct of these officers. A part of the Indian Army had been sent to Burma and Singapore. When Japan occupied these regions, the British Government left the Indian Army to its fate. In fact, it was a British officer who handed over the Indian Army to the Japanese. If the Indians had remained supine, as prisoners of war they would still have been compelled to undertake the construction of roads or other work in factories which would help the Japanese war effort. They would thus have become playthings in the hands of the Japanese and might well have been the instruments for capturing India for Japan. They adopted a different attitude and decided they would themselves fight for Indian freedom. So long as they were prisoners in Japanese hands the British Government could not help them in any way. If they had sided with the Japanese under duress, even such action could have been justified. In fact they did better. Their action in organizing a separate army which maintained its identity as the Liberation Army of India was the best course of action in the circumstances. In this way they ensured that, if the British were driven out of India, the country would be occupied, not by Japanese armies, but by an Indian National Army. I therefore saw no reason why members of the I.N.A. should be prosecuted.

The Congress held that if the Government proposed to prosecute the officers of the I.N.A., the trial should be public and the Congress should make the necessary arrangements for their legal defence. I wrote to Lord Wavell in this connection and pressed that he should accept the Congress view. Lord Wavell agreed and issued orders that a public trial of the officers should be held in the Red Fort. The trials excited great public enthusiasm and continued for several months. In the end, all the officers were released, either on the orders of the court or as an act of clemency by the Viceroy.

There were a few officers who were not at first released or in whose cases the decision was withheld. This led to great public resentment and demonstrations were held in different parts of the country. When I went to Lahore in connection with the formation of the Punjab Ministry, the students brought out a huge procession. They marched through the city and came to the house where I was staying. I had felt from the beginning that these demonstrations were not justified. I spoke strongly to the students and told them that the demonstrations were completely out of place in view of the attitude the Congress had adopted. We had decided to defend the prisoners and secure their release. All legal and constitutional methods were being utilized for the purpose and unauthorized demonstrations instead of helping harmed the cause. The whole political future of India was under discussion. A new Government had been formed in Britain with an absolute majority of the Labour party in Parliament. They had promised to find out a solution for the Indian problem and they must be given an opportunity of taking the necessary action. Congress had accordingly decided that there should be no movement for the present. The country should therefore wait and see what directives the Congress issued.

I have said that the demonstrations were held in different parts of India. In Calcutta, there was violence during some of these demonstrations. In Delhi, the people tried to set fire to Government buildings and destroyed public property. When I returned to Delhi and met Lord Wavell, he referred to these incidents and said that they were not consistent with the assurance of the Congress that the political problem of India would be solved in a peaceful atmosphere. I could not but admit that the complaint was justified. I sent for all the Congress workers in Delhi and told them that a grave crisis faced the Congress. In all national movements, a stage is reached when the leaders have to decide whether they should lead or follow the masses. It seems that in India we had now reached that stage. If Congress believed that the Indian problem could be solved only through peaceful methods, Congressmen must be prepared to carry that message to the people and act in accordance with it. I told them that I for one was not prepared to follow the line of least resistance and acquiesce in whatever the masses did. What had happened in

Delhi was in my opinion wrong. I said I would try to guide and direct public opinion and not merely follow the wishes of the mob. If they did not like my attitude, then they would have to find someone else to lead them.

Before I close this chapter I should like to comment on certain developments which led to the exclusion of Bhulabhai Desai from the newly elected Congress party in the Central Legislature. Many were surprised at the time that he was left out but few knew all the details of the case. I am afraid that the inner history may remain unknown unless I place on record all the relevant facts.

Bhulabhai Desai was one of the most successful legal practitioners in Bombay and in course of time became known as one of the foremost lawyers of India. He was not originally an active Congress worker but when the Government of India Act 1935 was passed and Congress decided to contest the elections, he was returned to the Central Assembly on the Congress ticket. He was elected the leader of the Congress party in the Central Assembly and carried out his duties with great distinction. His ability and enthusiasm soon earned him a place in the inner ranks of the Congress. He became a member of the Working Committee and was counted among its first-rank leaders. This, however, made some of the older members of the Congress jealous of him and they felt that so much importance should not be given to a man who was a comparatively recent recruit.

Bhulabhai Desai did not enjoy good health and I had not, therefore, included him in my new Working Committee. He was not arrested in 1942 and was one of the few top men in the Congress who remained outside. I have already referred to the developments which took place after Gandhiji's release in 1944. He had earlier opposed India's participation in the war effort but after his release he had offered Indian cooperation in return for the recognition of Indian freedom. His efforts did not succeed and the stalemate continued. Some people in Delhi thought that the deadlock might be broken if a settlement was negotiated, not between the Congress and the Moslem League, but between the Congress party and the League party in the Central Assembly. Such an arrangement would obviously be *ad hoc* and temporary, but, even if it could be made for the duration of the war, it might make a permanent settlement between Congress and the League easier to achieve after the end of hostilities.

Mutual friends approached Liaqat Ali [who was later Prime Minister of Pakistan], Deputy Leader of the Moslem League party, and Bhulabhai Desai. Liaqat Ali agreed that exploratory talks should take place and there was a meeting between him and Bhulabhai Desai.

Bhulabhai Desai was interested in the proposal but made it clear that he could not take any step without the approval of the Congress. He insisted that the understanding must be not only between the parties in the Legislature but between the two organizations. All the Congress leaders were, however, in jail and it was not possible to consult them. He then suggested that he would approach Gandhiji and seek his advice.

Bhulabhai Desai met Gandhiji and reported to him his discussions with Liaqat Ali and other friends. Gandhiji used to observe every Monday as a day of silence and, since Bhulabhai met him on a Monday, Gandhiji wrote out a reply in Gujrati [which was Gandhi's mother tongue, spoken in Bombay and other parts of west India]. The purport of his advice was that Bhulabhai should go ahead and, after ascertaining the details, report back to him.

Armed with Gandhiji's authority Bhulabhai continued the negotiations and an agreement was reached that the Executive Council should be reconstituted to include members of the Congress party and the League party. The negotiators desired that, as leader of the Congress party, Bhulabhai should join the Executive Council but, if this was not possible, Abdul Qayyum Khan, who was then the Deputy Leader of the Congress party, should enter the Council. Bhulabhai reported this development to Gandhiji but for various reasons the negotiations failed and the matter was dropped.

When we all came out of jail in 1945, these incidents were reported to us and led to a good deal of discussion among Congressmen. Unfortunately the discussions ignored the fact that whatever Bhulabhai did was with Gandhiji's knowledge and permission. Sardar Patel took a special interest in the matter and somehow the impression was created that Bhulabhai had tried to enter into the Executive Council behind the back of the Congress by reaching an understanding with Liaqat Ali. I have already said that many Congressmen were jealous of Bhulabhai Desai's rapid advance in the organization and they were now enraged by what they thought of as his lack of loyalty. Bhulabhai's opponents were also successful in turning Gandhiji against him by making certain allegations against Bhulabhai's private life. Many of these charges were false, but the propaganda was sustained for several months and did Bhulabhai permanent damage.

There were some people who sought to influence Gandhiji's judgment by working upon his close associates. They used to report various incidents to them in the expectation that these would reach Gandhiji's ears. Gandhiji generally had the capacity to ignore such insinuations and innuendoes but there were times when his judgment was affected if something was continually repeated to him by those who belonged to his personal circle. I remember an occasion when Gandhiji's mind had been poisoned in this way against Motilal Nehru. Jawaharlal had also once been the object of such a campaign. But in both these cases when Gandhiji came to know the facts he was able to take a fair and objective view of the whole matter. In the case of Bhulabhai this unfortunately did not happen and Gandhiji was accordingly estranged from him.

I have already mentioned that it was upon Gandhiji's day of silence that Bhulabhai sought his permission to negotiate with the Moslem League so that Gandhiji had given his reply in writing. Bhulabhai had preserved this note and showed it to Sardar Patel and others. He pointed out that he had carried out the negotiations with Gandhiji's knowledge and consent and could not therefore be blamed.

There was in fact no reply to Bhulabhai's defence. Unfortunately his protests were not heeded and reports continued to circulate that he had entered into an intrigue with the League. Feeling against him became so strong that when the General Elections were held in the winter of 1945–46 he was not offered a Congress ticket.

This shocked Bhulabhai and affected his health. He had suffered from heart attacks even before, but now the attacks became more frequent. He felt that he had served the Congress faithfully and suffered in its cause and his only reward was rejection and disgrace.

I visited Bombay about this time and as usual stayed with Bhulabhai. He was in bed and when I asked him how he felt he was so moved that he began to weep. His deepest regret was that Gandhiji, who knew all the facts, had not defended him against his critics. I tried to offer him consolation but it was of no avail. I described the incident to Gandhiji but I found that by now he had heard so much against Bhulabhai that his heart was turned against him. Soon after this Bhulabhai died of heart failure. I cannot but feel a deep regret whenever I remember the incident, for Bhulabhai had served the Congress well and was condemned without any justification.

CHAPTER 12

The British Cabinet Mission

AS I surveyed the political situation in India in February 1946, it was clear to me that the country had undergone a complete transformation. An absolutely new India had been born. The people, whether officials or nonofficials, were fired with a new desire for freedom. There was also a change of spirit on the British side. As I had expected from the beginning, the Labour Cabinet was studying the Indian situation from the right angle. Soon after the assumption of power, it sent a Parliamentary Delegation to India. This delegation visited the country in the winter of 1945–46. I was satisfied from my conversations with its members that they had sensed the change of temper in the country. They were convinced that Indian freedom could not be long delayed and their report to Government must have strengthened the Labour Cabinet in its resolve to effect an early and friendly settlement.

I was listening to the radio at 9:30 in the evening on 17 February 1946 when I heard the report of the new British decision. Lord Pethick-Lawrence [Secretary of State for India in Attlee's Cabinet] had announced in Parliament that the British Government would send a Cabinet Mission to India to discuss with the representatives of India the question of Indian freedom. This was also announced in the program outlined in the Viceroy's speech on the same date. The Mission was to consist of Lord Pethick-Lawrence, Secretary of State for India, Sir Stafford Cripps, the President of the Board of Trade and Mr. A. V. Alexander, the First Lord of the Admiralty.

Within half an hour, a representative of the Associated Press arrived and asked me about my reactions.

I told him that I was glad that the Labour Government had taken a decisive step. I was also pleased that the Mission which was coming included Sir Stafford Cripps, who had already carried on negotiations with us and was therefore an old friend.

I added that one thing seemed absolutely clear to me. The new British Government was not shirking the Indian problem but facing it boldly. This was a very important change.

On 15 March 1946, Mr. Attlee made a statement in the House of Commons on the Indian situation. This statement had no precedent in the history of Indo-British relations. He frankly admitted that the situation had completely changed and demanded a new approach. His declaration that any attempt to persist with old methods would lead not to a solution, but a deadlock, created a great impression in India.

Some of the points which Mr. Attlee made in his speech deserve special mention. He admitted that there had been faults on both sides and added that they should now look to the future rather than harp on the past. He explained that it was no good applying the formulas of the past to the present situation, for the temper of 1946 was not the temper of 1920, 1930 or even 1942. He went on to say that he did not wish to stress the differences between Indians, for, in spite of all differences and divisions, Indians were united in their desire for freedom. This was the underlying demand of all the Indian people whether they were Hindus or Moslems, Sikhs or Marathas, politicians or civil servants. Mr. Attlee frankly admitted that the conception of nationalism had continually grown stronger and it now permeated even the soldiers who had rendered splendid service in the war. He also said that if there were social and economic difficulties in India these could be resolved only by Indians. He concluded by announcing that the Cabinet Mission was going out in a positive mood and with the resolve to succeed.

The Cabinet Mission arrived in India on 23 March. Mr. J. C. Gupta, a prominent Congressman of Bengal, had acted as host to

Sir Stafford Cripps when he came to India on an earlier occasion. He told me he was going to Delhi to meet Cripps. I gave him a letter for Sir Stafford welcoming him back to India.

I reached Delhi on 2 April 1946. It seemed to me that the most important subject for consideration at this stage was not the political issue between India and Britain but the communal question in India. The Simla Conference had convinced me that the political question had reached a stage of settlement. The communal differences were still unresolved. One thing nobody could deny. As a community, the Moslems were extremely anxious about their future. It is true that they were in a clear majority in certain provinces. At the provincial level they had therefore no fears in these areas. They were, however, a minority in India as a whole and were troubled by the fear that their position and status in independent India would not be secure.

I gave continuous and anxious thought to this subject. All over the world, the tendency was for the decentralization of power. In a country so vast as India and with people so diverse in language, customs and geographical conditions, a unitary government was obviously most unsuitable. Decentralization of power in a federal government would also help to allay the fears of the minorities. Ultimately I came to the conclusion that the Constitution of India must, from the nature of the case, be federal. Further, it must be so framed as to ensure autonomy to the provinces in as many subjects as possible. We had to reconcile the claims of provincial autonomy with national unity. This could be done by finding a satisfactory formula for the distribution of powers and functions between the central and the provincial governments. Some powers and functions would be essentially central, others essentially provincial and some which could be either would be provincially or centrally exercised by consent. The first step was to devise a formula by which a minimum number of subjects should be declared as essentially the responsibility of the Central Government. These must belong to the Union Government compulsorily. In addition, there should be a list of subjects which could be dealt with centrally if the provinces so desired. This might be called the optional list for the Central Government and any province which so wished could delegate its powers in respect of all or any of these subjects to the Central Government.

It was clear to me that defence, communications and foreign affairs were subjects which could be dealt with adequately only on an all-India basis. Any attempt to deal with them on a provincial level would defeat the purpose and destroy the very basis of a federal government. Certain other subjects would be equally obviously a provincial responsibility, but there should be a third list of subjects where the provincial legislature would decide whether to retain them as provincial subjects or delegate them to the Centre.

The more I thought about the matter, the clearer it became to me that the Indian problem could not be solved on any other lines. If a constitution were to be framed which embodied this principle, it would ensure that in the Moslem majority provinces, all subjects except three could be administered by the province itself. This would eliminate from the minds of the Moslems all fears of domination by the Hindus. Once such fears were allayed, it was likely that the provinces would find it an advantage to delegate some other subjects as well to the Central Government. I was also satisfied that, even apart from communal considerations, this was the best political solution for a country like India. India is a vast country with a large population divided into more or less homogeneous units which live in different provinces. It was necessary to assure to the provinces the largest possible measure of autonomy even on general considerations of constitutional propriety and practical administration.

This picture had gradually formed in my mind and had become quite clear by the time the Cabinet Mission came to India though I had not so far discussed it with my colleagues. I thought that I should state my position in clear and unambiguous terms when the proper time came.

I met the members of the Cabinet Mission for the first time on 6 April 1946. The Mission had framed some questions for discussion. The first one dealt with the communal problem in India. When the Mission asked me how I would tackle the communal situation, I indicated the solution I had already framed. As soon as I

said that the Centre should have a minimum list of compulsory subjects and an additional list of optional ones, Lord Pethick-Lawrence
said, "You are in fact suggesting a new solution of the communal
problem."

Sir Stafford Cripps took special interest in my suggestion and
cross-examined me at great length. In the end, he also seemed to
be satisfied with my approach.

The Working Committee met on 12 April when I reported on
my discussions with the Cabinet Mission. I described in somewhat
greater detail the solution of the communal problem I had suggested.
This was the first time that Gandhiji and my colleagues had an opportunity of discussing my scheme. The Working Committee was
initially somewhat skeptical about the solution and members raised
all kinds of difficulties and doubts. I was able to meet their objections and clarified doubtful points. Finally the Working Committee
was convinced about the soundness of the proposal and Gandhiji
expressed his complete agreement with the solution.

Gandhiji in fact complimented me by saying that I had found a
solution of a problem which had till then baffled everybody. He
said that my solution should allay the fear of even the most communal among the Moslem Leaguers and at the same time it was
inspired by a national and not a sectional outlook. Gandhiji was
emphatic that only a federal constitution could work in a country like
India. From this point of view also, he welcomed my solution and
said that, while it did not introduce any novel principle, it brought
out clearly the implications of federalism in the Indian context.

Sardar Patel asked me whether the Central Government would be
restricted to three subjects alone. He said that there were certain
subjects like currency and finance which must from the nature of the
case belong to the Central sphere. He held that trade and industry
could be developed only on an all-India basis and the same thing
applied to commercial policy.

I did not have to reply to his objections. Gandhiji himself took up
my point of view and answered Sardar Patel. He said that there was
no reason to assume that provincial governments would differ from

the Centre on questions like currency or customs. It would be in their own interest to have a unified policy in these matters. It was not therefore necessary to insist that currency or finance must be included in the compulsory list of Central subjects.

The Moslem League had for the first time spoken of a possible division of India in its Lahore Resolution.[1] This later on came to be known as the Pakistan Resolution. The solution I suggested was intended to meet the fears of the Moslem League. Now that I had discussed my scheme with my colleagues and members of the Cabinet Mission, I felt that the time had come to place it before the country. Accordingly on 15 April 1946, I issued a statement dealing with the demands of Moslems and other minorities. Now that the division of India is a fact and ten years have passed, I again look at the statement and find that everything I had then said has come about. As this statement contains my considered views on the solution of the Indian problem, I feel I should quote it. This is what I said then and would still say:

I have considered from every possible point of view the scheme of Pakistan as formulated by the Muslim League. As an Indian, I have examined its implications for the future of India as a whole. As a Muslim I have examined its likely effects upon the fortunes of Muslims of India.

Considering the scheme in all its aspects I have come to the conclusion that it is harmful not only for India as a whole but for Muslims in particular. And in fact it creates more problems than it solves.

I must confess that the very term Pakistan goes against my grain. It suggests that some portions of the world are pure while others are impure.[2] Such a division of territories into pure and impure is un-Islamic and a repudiation of the very spirit of Islam. Islam recognises no such division and the Prophet says, "God has made the whole world a mosque for me."

Further, it seems that the scheme of Pakistan is a symbol of defeatism and has been built up on the analogy of the Jewish demand for a national home. It is a confession that Indian Muslims cannot hold their own in India as a whole and would be content to withdraw to a corner specially reserved for them.

One can sympathise with the aspiration of the Jews for such a national home, as they are scattered all over the world and cannot in any region

[1] Adopted in 1940, it was a demand for an independent country: Pakistan.
[2] The word "Pakistan" was translated "Land of the Pure."

have any effective voice in the administration. The condition of Indian Muslims is quite otherwise. Over 90 millions in number they are in quantity and quality a sufficiently important element in Indian life to influence decisively all questions of administration and policy. Nature has further helped them by concentrating them in certain areas.

In such context, the demand for Pakistan loses all force. As a Muslim, I for one am not prepared for a moment to give up my right to treat the whole of India as my domain and to share in the shaping of its political and economic life. To me it seems a sure sign of cowardice to give up what is my patrimony and content myself with a mere fragment of it.

As is well known Mr. Jinnah's Pakistan scheme is based on his two-nation theory. His thesis is that India contains many nationalities based on religious differences. Of them the two major nations, the Hindus and Muslims, must as separate nations have separate states. When Dr. Edward Thompson [a professor at Oxford University] once pointed out to Mr. Jinnah that Hindus and Muslims live side by side in thousands of Indian towns, villages and hamlets, Mr. Jinnah replied that this in no way affected their separate nationality. Two nations according to Mr. Jinnah confront one another in every hamlet, village and town, and he, therefore, desires that they should be separated into two states.

I am prepared to overlook all other aspects of the problem and judge it from the point of view of Muslim interests alone. I shall go still further and say that if it can be shown that the scheme of Pakistan can in any way benefit Muslims I would be prepared to accept it myself and also to work for its acceptance by others. But the truth is that even if I examine the scheme from the point of view of the communal interests of the Muslims themselves, I am forced to the conclusion that it can in no way benefit them or allay their legitimate fears.

Let us consider dispassionately the consequences which will follow if we give effect to the Pakistan scheme. India will be divided into two states, one with a majority of Muslims and the other of Hindus. In the Hindustan State there will remain 3½ crores of Muslims scattered in small minorities all over the land. With 17 per cent in the U.P., 12 per cent in Bihar and 9 per cent in Madras, they will be weaker than they are today in the Hindu majority provinces. They have had their homelands in these regions for almost a thousand years and built up well-known centres of Muslim culture and civilization there.

They will awaken overnight and discover that they have become aliens and foreigners. Backward industrially, educationally and economically, they will be left to the mercies of what would then become an un-adulterated Hindu *raj*.

On the other hand, their position within the Pakistan State will be vulnerable and weak. Nowhere in Pakistan will their majority be comparable to the Hindu majority in the Hindustan State.

In fact, their majority will be so slight that it will be offset by the economical, educational and political lead enjoyed by non-Muslims in these areas. Even if this were not so and Pakistan were overwhelmingly Muslim in population, it still could hardly solve the problem of Muslims in Hindustan.

Two States confronting one another offer no solution of the problem of one another's minorities, but only lead to retribution and reprisals by introducing a system of mutual hostages. The scheme of Pakistan therefore solves no problem for the Muslims. It cannot safeguard their rights where they are in a minority nor as citizens of Pakistan secure them a position in Indian or world affairs which they would enjoy as citizens of a major State like the Indian Union.

It may be argued that if Pakistan is so much against the interest of the Muslims themselves, why should such a large section of Muslims be swept away by its lure? The answer is to be found in the attitude of certain communal extremists among the Hindus. When the Muslim League began to speak of Pakistan, they read into the scheme a sinister Pan-Islamic conspiracy and began to oppose it out of fear that it foreshadowed a combination of Indian Muslims with trans-Indian Muslim States.

The opposition acted as an incentive to the adherents of the League. With simple though untenable logic they argued that if Hindus were so opposed to Pakistan, surely it must be of benefit to Muslims. An atmosphere of emotional frenzy was created which made reasonable appraisement impossible and swept away especially the younger and more impressionable among the Muslims. I have, however, no doubt that when the present frenzy has died down and the question can be considered dispassionately, those who now support Pakistan will themselves repudiate it as harmful for Muslim interests.

The formula which I have succeeded in making the Congress accept secures whatever merit the Pakistan scheme contains while all its defects and drawbacks are avoided. The basis of Pakistan is the fear of interference by the Centre in Muslim majority areas as the Hindus will be in a majority in the Centre. The Congress meets this fear by granting full autonomy to the provincial units and vesting all residuary power in the provinces. It has also provided for two lists of Central subjects, one compulsory and one optional, so that if any provincial unit so wants, it can administer all subjects itself except a minimium delegated to the Centre. The Congress scheme therefore ensures that Muslim majority provinces are internally free to develop as they will, but can at the same time influence the Centre on all issues which affect India as a whole.

The situation in India is such that all attempts to establish a centralised and unitary government are bound to fail. Equally doomed to failure is the attempt to divide India into two States. After considering all aspects of the question, I have come to the conclusion that the only solution can be on the lines embodied in the Congress formula which allows room for development both to the provinces and to India as a whole. The Congress formula meets the fear of the Muslim majority areas to allay which the scheme of Pakistan was formed. On the other hand, it avoids the defects of the Pakistan scheme which would bring the Muslims where they are in a minority under a purely Hindu government.

I am one of those who consider the present chapter of communal bitterness and differences as a transient phase in Indian life. I firmly hold that they will disappear when India assumes the responsibility of her own destiny. I am reminded of a saying of Gladstone that the best cure for a man's fear of the water is to throw him into it. Similarly India must assume responsibility and administer her own affairs before fears and suspicions can be fully allayed.

When India attains her destiny, she will forget the present chapter of communal suspicion and conflict and face the problems of modern life from a modern point of view. Differences will no doubt persist, but they will be economic, not communal. Opposition among political parties will continue, but they will be based, not on religion but on economic and political issues. Class and not community will be the basis of future alignments and policies will be shaped accordingly. If it be argued that this is only a faith which events may not justify I would say that in any case the nine crores of Muslims constitute a factor which nobody can ignore and whatever the circumstances, they are strong enough to safeguard their own destiny.

The League had moved further along the path of separatism since the Lahore Resolution. It did not, however, make it clear as to what exactly was its demand. The wording was vague and capable of more than one interpretation but the general purport was clear. The Moslem League demanded that the Moslem majority provinces should have full autonomy. Sikandar Hayat Khan in his support of the Resolution had given the same interpretation but now the League leaders gave their demand a much wider connotation. They talked loosely of the partition of the country and the establishment of an independent state for the Moslem majority areas. The Cabinet Mission was not prepared to concede the demand. On the contrary, the Mission was in favor of a solution more or less on the lines I had suggested.[3]

Till almost the end of April, the negotiations continued. There were meetings with the Mission and the Mission also held discussions among themselves. In the meantime, the Mission took a recess and went to Kashmir. The summer had now set in and Delhi was getting hotter and hotter. I was anxious for a little rest and I had first thought of going to Kashmir and had written to friends there. When I found that the Mission was going to Kashmir I changed my plan. I thought that my stay in Kashmir might be interpreted to mean that I wanted to be in contact with the Mission and influence its judgment. I therefore went instead to Mussoorie.

I have already said that, after the failure of the Cripps Mission, Shri Rajagopalachari started a campaign that the Congress should accept the demands of the Moslem League. He even went to the extent of saying that partition of the country should be accepted in principle. This led to his dissociation from the Working Committee and he became unpopular with the rank and file of Congressmen. Gandhiji also did not approve of Rajaji's activities. He did not therefore wish that Rajaji should meet the Cabinet Mission during our negotiations. He asked Rajaji to remain in Madras. Rajaji felt this bitterly but for some time he kept quiet. When I went to Mussoorie during the recess, I received a letter from him and learnt for the first time that he had been prevented from coming to Delhi by Gandhiji. I felt that Gandhiji was not even now willing that Rajaji should come to Delhi. I did not therefore consult him but on my own responsibility wrote to Rajaji that if he wished, he could come. Rajaji took me at my word and arrived. Gandhiji was a little displeased but I told him that Rajaji had come only after receiving my letter. I also explained to Gandhiji that I did not consider it proper that Rajaji should be prevented from coming to Delhi in this way.

[3] The British Cabinet Mission's Plan of May 16, 1946, stated, ". . . a separate sovereign State of Pakistan on the lines claimed by the Moslem League would not solve the communal minority problem. . . . We are therefore unable to advise the British government that the power which at present resides in British hands should be handed over to two entirely separate sovereign states." Lord Wavell likewise approved the establishment of a united India.

The Mission returned to Delhi on 24 April and reviewed the constitutional negotiations in conjunction with the Viceroy. After several discussions, Sir Stafford Cripps called on me to have an informal discussion on the issues which had been raised. On 27 April, the Mission issued a statement that further informal discussions were desirable to find a basis for settlement by agreement between the main parties. The delegation therefore invited the presidents of the Congress and the Moslem League to nominate representatives of the Working Committee of the two bodies to meet the delegation and carry on negotiations at Simla. The Working Committee authorized me to appoint the representatives to confer with the Cabinet Mission. Accordingly I nominated Jawaharlal and Sardar Patel as my colleagues to represent Congress. The Government arranged for our stay in Simla. Gandhiji was not formally a member of the negotiating body, but the Mission invited him to come up to Simla so that he would be available for consultations. He acceded to their request and stayed in Manor Villa. We held informal meetings of the Working Committee there so that Gandhiji could attend.

Discussions started at Simla on 2 May and continued till 12 May. Apart from the formal conference we had many informal discussions. I was staying at the Retreat and on several occasions members of the Mission came to meet me there. I also went to meet them either individually or collectively as the occasion demanded. Asaf Ali or Humayun Kabir sometimes accompanied me during these visits.

After about two weeks we returned to Delhi. The members of the Cabinet Mission held further discussions among themselves, and framed their proposals. These were announced by Mr. Attlee in the House of Commons on 16 May. A White Paper was also issued embodying the Plan and it was stated that the British Cabinet Mission considered this to be the best arrangement to ensure the speedy setting up of a new constitution for India. I have included the Cabinet Mission Plan in the Appendix and readers who are interested may compare it to the scheme I had formulated in my statement of 15 April.

I was in favor of continuing our discussions over the Cabinet Mission Plan in Simla. I told Lord Wavell that it would be better to conclude our deliberations in Simla as the climate in Delhi was not congenial for the cool and careful consideration of the important issues involved. Lord Wavell said that the seat of government was in Delhi and work was likely to suffer if he stayed away too long. My comment was that Delhi presented no difficulty for him as the Viceregal Lodge was air-conditioned and he never moved out of it. It was, however, otherwise with the members of the Cabinet Mission and us. We would find it extremely difficult to work in the furnace which Delhi had become. Lord Wavell replied that it was a matter of only a few days.

In the end, it turned out that we passed the rest of May and the whole of June in Delhi. This year the weather was unusually hot. The members of the Cabinet Mission felt it, and most of all Lord Pethick-Lawrence, who fainted one day because of the heat. The Viceroy had arranged an air-conditioned room for me and this certainly helped, but the weather was so trying that everybody wanted to bring the discussions to an early conclusion. Unfortunately, the differences between Congress and the League could not be resolved so easily and discussions failed to indicate any solution.

We had enough headaches with the Cabinet Mission and its Plan, but a new one was added by developments in Kashmir. The National Conference under the leadership of Sheikh Abdullah [who was a socialist friend of Nehru's] had been fighting for political rights for the people of Kashmir. When the Cabinet Mission arrived he thought he would use this opportunity to press his claims. He raised the slogan of "Quit Kashmir" and placed his case before the Cabinet Mission. His demand was that the Maharaja of Kashmir should end autocracy and give self-government to the people. The Maharaja's Government replied by arresting Sheikh Abdullah and his colleagues. Some time back a representative of the National Conference had been taken into the Government and it had seemed that a compromise might be achieved. The arrest of Sheikh Abdullah and his associates dashed these hopes.

Jawaharlal had always taken a keen interest in Kashmir's struggle for representative Government. When these new developments took place, he felt that he ought to go to Kashmir. It was also thought necessary that some arrangements should be made for the legal defence of the leaders of the National Conference. I asked Asaf Ali to attend to this. Jawaharlal said that he would accompany Asaf Ali and so the two of them left. The Maharaja's Government was irritated by this decision and issued a ban against their entry into Kashmir. When they left Rawalpindi and approached the Kashmir frontier, they were stopped at Uri. They refused to obey the ban and the Kashmir Government arrested them. This naturally created a great sensation in the country.

I was not very happy about these developments. While I resented the action of the Kashmir Government, I thought that this was not the proper occasion to start a new quarrel over Kashmir. I spoke to the Viceroy and said that the Government of India should arrange that I could speak over the telephone with Jawaharlal. He had been detained in a dak bungalow [a traveler's rest house] and I succeeded in getting the connection only after some time. I told Jawaharal that I was of the view that he should return to Delhi as soon as possible. It would not be proper for him to insist on entering Kashmir at the present stage. So far as the question of Kashmir was concerned I assured him that as Congress President I would take up the matter myself. I would also work for the release of Sheikh Abdullah and his colleagues, but Jawaharlal should immediately return.

At first Jawaharlal objected, but after some discussion and on my assurance that I would myself take up the cause of Kashmir he agreed. I then requested Lord Wavell to arrange for an aeroplane to bring back Jawaharlal and Asaf Ali. It was about seven in the evening when I made this request but he sent an aeroplane that very night. It reached Srinagar at about 10:00 P.M. and returned to Delhi with Jawaharlal and Asaf Ali at two in the morning. Lord Wavell's attitude over the whole matter was extremely friendly and I greatly appreciated it.

I have already mentioned that the Cabinet Mission published its scheme on 16 May. Basically, it was the same as the one sketched in my statement of 15 April. The Cabinet Mission Plan provided that only three subjects would belong compulsorily to the Central Government. These were defence, foreign affairs and communications, which I had suggested in my scheme. The Mission, however, added a new element to the Plan. It divided the country into three zones, A, B and C, as the members of the Mission felt that this would give a greater sense of assurance to the minorities. Section B would include the Punjab, Sind, the N.W.F.P. and British Baluchistan. This would constitute a Moslem majority area. In Section C, which included Bengal and Assam, the Moslems would have a small majority over the rest. The Cabinet Mission thought that this arrangement would give complete assurance to the Moslem minority, and satisfy all legitimate fears of the League.[4]

The Mission had also accepted my view that the majority of subjects would be treated at the provincial level. Moslems in the majority provinces would thus exercise almost complete autonomy. Only certain agreed subjects would be dealt with at the sectional level. Here also the Moslems were assured of a majority in Sections B and C and would be able to satisfy all their legitimate hopes. So far as the Centre was concerned, there were only three subjects which from the nature of the case could not be provincially administered. Since the Cabinet Mission Plan was in spirit the same as mine and the only addition was the institution of the three sections, I felt that we should accept the proposal.

At first Mr. Jinnah was completely opposed to the scheme. The Moslem League had gone so far in its demand for a separate independent state that it was difficult for it to retrace its steps. The Mission had stated in clear and unambiguous terms that they could never recommend the partition of the country and the formation of an independent state. Lord Pethick-Lawrence and Sir Stafford Cripps said repeatedly that they could not see how a state like the Pakistan

---

[4] Section A would include all the predominantly Hindu territory between Section B in western India and Section C in eastern India.

envisaged by the Moslem League could be viable and stable. They felt that my formula, which gave the largest possible autonomy to the provinces and reserved only three subjects for the Central Government, offered the only solution. Lord Pethick-Lawrence said more than once that the acceptance of this formula would mean that in the beginning the Moslem majority provinces would delegate to the Central Government only three subjects and thus ensure complete autonomy for themselves. The Hindu majority provinces would on the other hand voluntarily agree to transfer to the Central Government several more subjects. The Cabinet Mission thought there was nothing wrong in this. In a true federation, the federating units must have the freedom to decide on the number and nature of the subjects to be transferred to the central government.

The Moslem League Council met for three days before it could come to a decision. On the final day, Mr. Jinnah had to admit that there could be no fairer solution of the minority problem than that presented in the Cabinet Mission Plan. In any case he could not get better terms. He told the Council that the scheme presented by the Cabinet Mission was the maximum that he could secure. As such, he advised the Moslem League to accept the scheme and the Council voted unanimously in its favor.

While I was still in Mussoorie, some members of the Moslem League had met me and expressed their sense of bewilderment and surprise. They said candidly that if the League was prepared to accept the Cabinet Mission Plan, why had it raised the cry of an independent state and led Moslems astray? I discussed the question with them in detail. In the end they were forced to admit that whatever might be the view of the Moslem League, the Moslems of India could not expect any terms better than those offered in the Cabinet Mission Plan.

In our discussions in the Working Committee, I pointed out that the Cabinet Mission Plan was basically the same as the scheme Congress had accepted. As such, the Working Committee did not have much difficulty in accepting the main political solution contained in the Plan. There was, however, the question about India's relation to the Commonwealth. I had asked the Mission to leave the decision to India. I believed that in this way alone could a right decision be reached. I had also said that it was my opinion that if the question were left to India, it was not unlikely that India might decide in favor of continuing in the Commonwealth. Sir Stafford Cripps assured me that this would be so. In the Cabinet Mission Plan, the question was left to the decision of independent India. This also made it easier for us to accept the Cabinet Mission Plan. After protracted negotiations, the Working Committee in its resolution of 26 June accepted the Cabinet Mission Plan for the future, though it found itself unable to accept the proposal for an interim Government.

I would here like to pay a tribute to the way in which the Cabinet Mission conducted the negotiations. Sir Stafford was an old friend and I have already expressed my opinion about him. I had not met Lord Pethick-Lawrence and Mr. Alexander before, but formed a very favorable impression of both of them. I was specially impressed by the spirit of sympathy and understanding displayed by Lord Pethick-Lawrence. He was an old man but he had the spirit of youth. His transparent sincerity, his deep love for India and his accurate assessment of our difficulties made us pay the greatest attention to whatever he said. Mr. Alexander did not speak much, but, whenever he made a remark, it was characterized by great shrewdness and political insight.

The acceptance of the Cabinet Mission Plan by both Congress and Moslem League was a glorious event in the history of the freedom movement in India. It meant that the difficult question of Indian freedom had been settled by negotiation and agreement and not by methods of violence and conflict. It also seemed that the communal difficulties had been finally left behind. Throughout the country there was a sense of jubilation and all the people were united in their demand for freedom. We rejoiced but we did not then know that our joy was premature and bitter disappointment awaited us.

CHAPTER 13

The Prelude to Partition

NOW that the political problems seemed to be solved, a fresh subject demanded my attention. I was elected President of the Congress in 1939. According to the constitution of the Congress, my office was for only one year. In normal circumstances, a new President would have been elected in 1940. The war intervened and soon after the individual Satyagraha Movement began. Normal activities were suspended and we were arrested in 1940 and again in 1942. Congress was also declared an illegal organization. There could therefore be no question of the election of a President to succeed me and I remained President throughout this period.

The situation had now returned to normal. The question naturally arose as to whether there should be fresh Congress elections and a new president chosen. As soon as this was mooted in the press, there was a general demand that I should be re-elected President for another term. The main argument in favor of my re-election was that I had been in charge of negotiations with Cripps, with Lord Wavell and at present with the Cabinet Mission. At the Simla Conference, I had for the first time succeeded in arriving at a successful solution of the political problem, even though the Conference finally broke on the communal issue. There was a general feeling in Congress that since I had conducted the negotiations till now, I should be charged with the task of bringing them to a successful close and implementing them. Congress circles in Bengal, Bombay, Madras, Bihar and the U.P. openly expressed the opinion that I should be charged with the responsibility of giving effect to the proposals in the Cabinet Mission Plan.

I sensed, however, that there was some difference of opinion in the inner circles of the Congress High Command. I found that Sardar Patel and his friends wished that he should be elected President. It became for me a very delicate question and I could not at first make up my mind as to what to do. I thought the matter over carefully and finally came to the conclusion that, since I had been President for seven years from 1939 to 1946, I must now retire. I therefore decided that I should not permit my name to be proposed.

The next point which I had to decide was the choice of my successor. I was anxious that the next President should be one who agreed with my point of view and would carry out the same policy as I had pursued. After weighing the pros and cons, I came to the conclusion that Jawaharlal should be the new President. Accordingly, on 26 April 1946, I issued a statement proposing his name for the presidentship and appealing to Congressmen that they should elect Jawaharlal unanimously. Gandhiji was perhaps somewhat inclined towards Sardar Patel, but, once I had proposed Jawaharlal's name, he gave no public indication of his views. Some people did propose the names of Sardar Patel and Acharya Kripalani, but in the end Jawaharlal was accepted unanimously.

I acted according to my best judgment but the way things have shaped since then has made me think that I may have been wrong and those who wanted me to continue for at least another year were perhaps in the right.

My decision caused a commotion among Congressmen all over the country. Several important leaders travelled from Calcutta, Bombay and Madras to persuade me to withdraw my statement and allow my name to be put up. Appeals in the press also appeared to the same effect. But I had already taken a decision and did not feel that I should change my view.

The Moslem League Council had accepted the Cabinet Mission Plan. So had the Congress Working Committee. It, however, needed the approval of the A.I.C.C. We thought this would be a formal matter as the A.I.C.C. had always ratified the decision of the Working Committee. Accordingly, a meeting of the A.I.C.C. was called

at Bombay on 7 July 1946. Once this decision was taken there
was no need for me to stay on in Delhi. The heat was becoming
intolerable and I returned to Calcutta on 30 June. On 4 July I left
Calcutta for Bombay. Sarat Chandra Bose was travelling in the same
train. At almost every station men assembled in large numbers and
their slogan was that I should continue as Congress President. Sarat
Babu came to my compartment at every large station and kept on
repeating, "See what the public want and yet what have you done."

The Working Committee met on 6 July and prepared draft resolutions for the consideration of the A.I.C.C. The first resolution dealt
with the Cabinet Mission Plan. I was asked to move it, as strenuous
opposition was expected from the leftist group in the Congress.

When the A.I.C.C. met, I invited Jawaharlal to take over as
Congress President from me. Sardar Patel moved a vote of thanks
for my services as Congress President during these critical years and
spoke in detail about the way many insuperable difficulties had been
overcome. Then I moved the resolution on the Cabinet Mission
Plan and briefly spoke about its main features. The leftists opposed
it with great vehemence. The Congress Socialists took the leading
part in the opposition, for it had become a cheap device to assume
an extreme position and attempt to win popularity. They adopted
an unreal and theatrical attitude. Yusuf Meharally [1] was then very
ill but they brought him on a stretcher to create greater sympathy
in the audience. He also spoke against the Cabinet Mission Plan.

In my reply I explained in detail what were the implications of
the Plan and pointed out that the Plan was in fact a great victory for
Congress. I said that this marked the achievement of independence
without a violent and bloody uprising. The British acceptance of
India's national demand as a result of nonviolent agitation and
negotiation was unprecedented in world history. A nation of forty
crores was becoming independent through discussion and settlement
and not as a result of military action. From this point of view alone,
it would be sheer lunacy to underestimate our victory. I further

---

[1] A former Mayor of Bombay who has since died of heart trouble which he
attributed to a blow on the chest received in a lathi charge.

The Education Minister and the Prime Minister of India, when the latter laid the foundation stone of the Central Institute of Education, Delhi.

PLATE V

Azad at Palam Airport on his return to India after a tour of the United Kingdom and other European countries.

At the A.I.C.C. meeting in Bombay, July 1946.

PLATE VI

Rajkumari Amrit Kaur, Lord and Lady Mountbatten, the Hon'ble
Pamela Mountbatten, Maulana Azad, and the Chinese Ambassador to
India, Dr Lo Chia Luen, during the cremation of Mahatma Gandhi.

pointed out that the Cabinet Mission Plan had accepted in all essentials the Congress point of view. The Congress had stood for the freedom and unity of India and opposed all fissiparous tendencies. It passed my understanding how people like the Congress Socialists could regard such a victory as a defeat.

My speech had a decisive influence on the audience. When the vote was taken the resolution was passed with an overwhelming majority. [The vote was 200 in favor and 51 against.] Thus the seal of approval was put on the Working Committee's resolution accepting the Cabinet Mission Plan.

After a few days, I received telegrams of congratulation from Lord Pethick-Lawrence and Sir Stafford Cripps. They were happy that the A.I.C.C. had accepted my resolution and congratulated me on my able presentation of the Cabinet Mission Plan.

Now happened one of those unfortunate events which changed the course of history. On 10 July, Jawaharlal held a press conference in Bombay in which he made a statement which in normal circumstances might have passed almost unnoticed, but, in the existing atmosphere of suspicion and hatred, set in train a most unfortunate series of consequences. Some press representatives asked him whether, with the passing of the resolution by the A.I.C.C., the Congress had accepted the Plan *in toto,* including the composition of the interim Government.

Jawaharlal stated in reply that Congress would enter the Constituent Assembly "completely unfettered by agreements and free to meet all situations as they arise."

Press representatives further asked if this meant that the Cabinet Mission Plan could be modified.

Jawaharlal replied emphatically that the Congress had agreed only to participate in the Constituent Assembly and regarded itself free to change or modify the Cabinet Mission Plan as it thought best.

I must place on record that Jawaharlal's statement was wrong. It was not correct to say that Congress was free to modify the Plan as it pleased. We had in fact agreed that the Central Government would be federal. There would be the compulsory list of three Central subjects while all other subjects remained in the provincial sphere. We had further agreed that there would be the three sections, viz., A, B and C, in which the provinces would be grouped. These matters could not be changed unilaterally by Congress without the consent of other parties to the agreement.

The Moslem League had accepted the Cabinet Mission Plan, as this represented the utmost limit to which the British Government would go. In his speech to the League Council, Mr. Jinnah had clearly stated that he recommended acceptance only because nothing better could be obtained.

Mr. Jinnah was thus not very happy about the outcome of the negotiations, but he had reconciled himself as there was no alternative. Jawaharlal's statement came to him as a bombshell. He immediately issued a statement that this declaration by the Congress President demanded a review of the whole situation. He accordingly asked Liaqat Ali Khan to call a meeting of the League Council and issued a statement that the Moslem League Council had accepted the Cabinet Mission Plan in Delhi as it was assured that the Congress had also accepted the scheme and that the Plan would be the basis of the future constitution of India. Now that the Congress President had declared that the Congress could change the scheme through its majority in the Constituent Assembly, this would mean that the minorities were placed at the mercy of the majority. His view was that Jawaharlal's declaration meant that the Congress had rejected the Cabinet Mission Plan and as such the Viceroy should call upon the Moslem League, which had accepted the Plan, to form the Government.

The Moslem League Council met at Bombay on 27 July. In his opening speech Mr. Jinnah reiterated the demand for Pakistan as the only course left open to the Moslem League. After three days' discussion, the Council passed a resolution rejecting the Cabinet Mission Plan. It also decided to resort to direct action for the achievement of Pakistan.

I was extremely perturbed by this new development. I saw that the scheme for which I had worked so hard was being destroyed through our own action. I felt that a meeting of the Working Committee must be held immediately to review the situation. The Working Committee accordingly met on 8 August. I pointed out that if we wanted to save the situation, we must make it clear that the view of the Congress was expressed by the resolution passed by the A.I.C.C. and that no individual, not even the Congress President, could change it.

The Working Committee felt that it faced a dilemma. On the one side, the prestige of the Congress President was at stake. On the other, the settlement which we had so painfully achieved was in danger. To repudiate the President's statement would weaken the organization but to give up the Cabinet Mission Plan would ruin the country. Finally, we drafted a resolution which made no reference to the press conference but reaffirmed the decision of the A.I.C.C. in the following terms:

The Working Committee regret to note that the Council of the All-India Muslim League, reversing their previous decision, have decided not to participate in the Constituent Assembly. In this period of rapid transition from dependence on a foreign power to full independence, when vast and intricate political and economic problems have to be faced and solved, the largest measure of co-operation among the people of India and their representatives is called for, so that the change-over should be smooth and to the advantage of all concerned. The Committee realise that there are differences in the outlook and objectives of the Congress and the Muslim League. Nevertheless, in the larger interests of the country as a whole and of the freedom of the people of India, the Committee appeal for the co-operation of all those who seek the freedom and good of the country, in the hope that co-operation in common tasks may lead to the solution of many of India's problems.

The Committee have noted that criticisms have been advanced on behalf of the Muslim League to the effect that the Congress acceptance of the proposals contained in the Statement of May 16th was conditional. The Committee wish to make it clear that while they did not approve of all the proposals contained in this Statement, they accepted the scheme in its entirety. They interpreted it so as to resolve the inconsistencies contained in it and fill the omissions in accordance with the principles laid down in that Statement. They hold that provincial autonomy is a

basic provision and each province has the right to decide whether to
join a group or not. Questions of interpretation will be decided by the
procedure laid down in the Statement itself, and the Congress will advise
its representatives in the Constituent Assembly to function accordingly.

The Committee have emphasised the sovereign character of the Constituent Assembly, that is its right to function and draw up a constitution
for India without the interference of any external power or authority.
But the Assembly will naturally function within the internal limitations
which are inherent in its task, and will therefore seek the largest measure
of co-operation in drawing up a constitution of free India allowing the
greatest measure of freedom and protection for all just claims and interests. It was with this object and with the desire to function in the Constituent Assembly and make it a success, that the Working Committee
passed their resolution on June 26, 1946 which was subsequently ratified
by the All-India Congress Committee on July 7, 1946. By that decision of
the A.I.C.C. they must stand, and they propose to proceed accordingly
with their work in the Constituent Assembly.

The Committee hope that the Muslim League and all others concerned,
in the wider interests of the nation as well as of their own, will join in this
great task.

We had hoped that this resolution of the Working Committee
would save the situation. Now there was no longer any doubt that
the Congress had accepted the Cabinet Mission Plan in its entirety.
If the Moslem League accepted our resolution, it could return to
the early position without any loss of prestige. Mr. Jinnah did not,
however, accept the position and held that Jawaharlal's statement
represented the real mind of Congress. He argued that, if Congress
could change so many times while the British were still in the
country and power had not come to its hands, what assurance could
the minorities have that, once the British left, Congress would not
again change and go back to the position taken up in Jawaharlal's
statement?

The resolution of the Working Committee accepted the Cabinet
Mission Plan in its entirety. This meant both the long-term plan
and the proposals for the interim Government. This unequivocal
acceptance of the Cabinet Mission Plan by the Working Committee
led to an immediate response from the Viceroy. On 12 August,

Jawaharlal was invited by him to form an interim Government at
the Centre in the following terms:

His Excellency the Viceroy, with the approval of His Majesty's Government, has invited the President of the Congress to make proposals
for the immediate formation of an interim Government and the President
of the Congress has accepted the invitation. Pandit Jawaharlal Nehru
will shortly visit New Delhi to discuss this proposal with His Excellency
the Viceroy.

Mr. Jinnah issued a statement the same day in which he said that
"the latest resolution of the Congress Working Committee passed
at Wardha on 10 August does not carry us anywhere because it is
only a repetition of the Congress stand taken by them from the
very beginning only put in a different phraseology." He rejected
Jawaharlal's invitation to cooperate in the formation of an interim
Government. Later, on 15 August Jawaharlal met Mr. Jinnah at his
house. Nothing, however, came out of their discussions and the situation rapidly deteriorated.

When the League Council met at the end of July and decided to
resort to direct action, it had also authorized Mr. Jinnah to take any
action he liked in pursuance of the program. Mr. Jinnah declared
16 August as the "Direct Action Day," but he did not make it clear
what the program would be. It was generally thought that there
would be another meeting of the Moslem League Council to work
out the details, but this did not take place. On the other hand
I noticed in Calcutta that a strange situation was developing. In
the past, political parties had observed special days by organizing
hartals, taking out processions and holding meetings. The League's
"Direct Action Day" seemed to be of a different type. In Calcutta,
I found a general feeling that, on 16 August, the Moslem League
would attack Congressmen and loot Congress property. Further
panic was created when the Bengal Government decided to declare
16 August a public holiday. The Congress party in the Bengal
Assembly protested against this decision and, when this proved
ineffective, walked out as a protest against the Government's policy

in giving effect to a party decision through the use of Government machinery. There was a general sense of anxiety in Calcutta which was heightened by the fact that the Government was under the control of the Moslem League and Mr. H. S. Suhrawardy was the Chief Minister.

The Congress Working Committee had on 9 August appointed a Parliamentary Subcommittee consisting of Sardar Vallabhbhai Patel, Dr. Rajendra Prasad and myself. On the 13th we held a meeting "to discuss a proposal to be submitted to the Viceroy for the formation of the interim Government." Jawaharlal now called a meeting of the Parliamentary Committee for the 17th. I accordingly left for Delhi by plane on the 16th.

The 16th of August was a black day in the history of India. Unprecedented mob violence plunged the great city of Calcutta into an orgy of bloodshed, murder and terror. Hundreds of lives were lost. Thousands were injured and property worth crores of rupees was destroyed. Processions were taken out by the League, which began to loot and commit acts of arson. Soon the whole city was in the grip of goondas of both communities.

Sarat Chandra Bose, the leader of the Bengal Congress, had gone to the Governor and asked him to take immediate action to bring the situation under control. He also told the Governor that he and I were required to go to Delhi for a meeting of the Working Committee. The Governor told him that he would send the military to escort us to the airport. I waited for some time but nobody arrived, I then started on my own. The streets were deserted and the city had the appearance of death. As I was passing through Strand Road, I found that a number of carters and darwans [porters] were standing about with staves in their hands. They attempted to attack my car. Even when my driver shouted that this was the car of the Congress leader, they paid little heed. However, with great difficulty I got to Dum Dum [2] just a few minutes before the plane was due to leave. I found there a large military contingent waiting in trucks.

[2] The Calcutta airport situated near the ancient munitions factory where Dum Dum bullets were first produced.

When I asked why they were not helping to restore order, they replied that their orders were to stand ready but not to take any action. Throughout Calcutta, the military and the police were standing by but remained inactive while innocent men and women were being killed.

The 16th of August 1946 was a black day not only for Calcutta but for the whole of India. The turn that events had taken made it almost impossible to expect a peaceful solution by agreement between the Congress and the Moslem League. This was one of the greatest tragedies of Indian history and I have to say with the deepest regret that it had followed inexorably from the opportunity given to the Moslem League to reopen the whole question of political and communal settlement. Mr. Jinnah took full advantage of this mistake and withdrew from the League's early acceptance of the Cabinet Mission Plan.

Jawaharlal is one of my dearest friends and his contribution to India's national life is second to none. He has worked and suffered for Indian freedom and, since the attainment of independence, he has become the symbol of our national unity and progress. I have nevertheless to say with regret that he is at times apt to be carried away by his feelings. Not only so, but sometimes he is so impressed by theoretical considerations that he is apt to underestimate the realities of a situation.

His fondness for abstract theory was responsible for his statement about the Constituent Assembly. The same theoretical bias led him to commit a similar mistake in 1937, when the first elections were held under the Government of India Act 1935. In these elections, the Moslem League had suffered a great setback throughout the country except in Bombay and the U.P. In Bengal, the Governor of the province had practically made up his mind to form a League Government but the success of the Krishak Praja [Peasant People's] party upset his calculations. In the other Moslem majority provinces like the Punjab, Sind and the N.W.F.P., the League had suffered equal setbacks. In Bombay the League had won a number of seats but it was in the U.P. that the League attained its greatest success, mainly on account of the support given to the League by the Jamiat-ul-Ulema-i-Hind.[3] The Jamiat had supported the Moslem League under the impression that, after the elections, the Moslem League would work in cooperation with the Congress.

Choudhari Khaliquzzaman and the Nawab Ismail Khan were then the leaders of the Moslem League in the U.P. When I came to Lucknow to form the Government, I spoke to both of them. They assured me that not only would they cooperate with the Congress, but would fully support the Congress program. They naturally expected that the Moslem League would have some share in the new Government. The local position was such that neither of them could enter the Government alone. Either both would have to be taken or neither. I had therefore held out hopes that both would be taken into the Government. If the Ministry consisted of seven members only, two would be Moslem Leaguers and the rest would all be Congressmen. In a cabinet of nine, the Congress majority would be still more marked. After discussion with me, a note was prepared to the effect that the Moslem League party would work in cooperation with the Congress and accept the Congress program. Both Nawab Ismail Khan and Choudhari Khaliquzzaman signed this document, and I left Lucknow for Patna as my presence was necessary for the formation of the Ministry in Bihar.

After some days, I returned to Allahabad and found to my great regret that Jawaharlal had written to Choudhari Khaliquzzaman and Nawab Ismail Khan that only one of them could be taken into the Ministry. He had said that the Moslem League party could decide who should be included, but, in the light of what I have said above, neither was in a position to come in alone. They therefore expressed their regrets and said that they were unable to accept Jawaharlal's offer.

This was a most unfortunate development. If the U.P. League's offer of cooperation had been accepted, the Moslem League party would for all practical purposes have merged in the Congress.

[3] A nationalist, noncommunal organization of Moslem theologians.

Jawaharlal's action gave the Moslem League in the U.P. a new lease of life. All students of Indian politics know that it was from the U.P. that the League was reorganized. Mr. Jinnah took full advantage of the situation and started an offensive which ultimately led to Pakistan.

I found that Purshottamdas Tandon had taken a leading part in the whole affair and influenced Jawaharlal's judgment. I did not have much respect for Tandon's views and I tried to persuade Jawaharlal to modify his stand. I told him that he had made a great mistake in not bringing the League into the Ministry. I also warned him that the result of his action would be to create new life in the Moslem League and thus bring about new difficulties in the way of Indian freedom. Jawaharlal did not agree with me and held that his judgment was right. He argued that with a strength of only twenty-six the Moslem Leaguers could not claim more than one seat in the Cabinet. When I found that Jawaharlal was adamant, I went to Wardha and sought Gandhiji's advice. When I explained the whole situation to him, he agreed with me and said he would advise Jawaharlal to modify his stand. When Jawaharlal put the matter in a different light, Gandhiji submitted to Jawaharlal and did not press the matter as he should have done. The result was that there was no settlement in the U.P. Mr. Jinnah took full advantage of this situation and turned the whole League against the Congress. After the elections, many of his supporters had been on the point of leaving Mr. Jinnah, but now he was able to win them back to his fold.

Jawaharlal's mistake in 1937 had been bad enough. The mistake of 1946 proved even more costly. One may perhaps say in Jawaharlal's defence that he never expected the Moslem League to resort to direct action. Mr. Jinnah had never been a believer in mass movement. I have myself tried to understand what brought about this change in Mr. Jinnah. He had perhaps hoped that when the Moslem League rejected the Cabinet Mission Plan, the British Government would reopen the whole question and hold further discussion. He was a lawyer and perhaps felt that if discussions were held again he could gain some more advantage by pressing his demands. His calculations, however, proved wrong. The British Government did not oblige Mr. Jinnah by initiating fresh discussions.

Sir Stafford Cripps had been in correspondence with me throughout this period. I had written to him that the Cabinet Mission had held discussion with the Congress and the Moslem League for over two months and finally framed a plan which both the Congress and the League had accepted. It was unfortunate that the League had withdrawn from that position, but that responsibility for this rested with the League. This must not, however, lead to a reopening of the whole question. If this was done, it would mean that there could never be any finality in our negotiation with the British. It would have a most adverse effect on public opinion and create fresh problems. Sir Stafford Cripps replied that he agreed with me and his view was that the Government would adopt the same attitude. Events turned out as I had expected. I have already mentioned that on 12 August 1946, the Viceroy issued a communiqué inviting Jawaharlal to form the interim Government.

We met in Delhi on 17 August under the shadow of the disturbances which were taking place in Calcutta and elsewhere. Mr. Jinnah, we knew, was not likely to accept Jawaharlal's invitation to enter the Government. In fact, his reply declining the invitation had been received on the 16th. Jawaharlal repeated his offer of cooperation and said that the door would always be open for the Moslem League, but by now things had moved too far for a friendly settlement.

CHAPTER 14

The Interim Government

I HAVE said that Congress had entrusted the Parliamentary Committee with the task of forming the interim Government. Accordingly, Jawaharlal, Patel, Rajendra Prasad and I met in Delhi on the 17th. My colleagues pressed hard that I should join the interim Government. Gandhiji was also of the same view. It was a delicate question for me but after careful consideration I came to the conclusion that I should remain outside. I therefore advised that Asaf Ali should be taken into the Cabinet. When Asaf Ali heard this, he also pressed that I should join, but I did not agree. Many of my friends held then and still hold that my decision was wrong. They felt that the interest of the country and the crucial time through which we were passing demanded my participation in the Government. I have thought over the matter since then and I am not sure today that I was right. It is possible that I might have helped the country more if I had joined the Government and not remained outside. I had thought then that I could render greater service from outside, but I now recognize that at that time membership in the Government offered greater scope.

At the time of the Simla Conference, I had pressed strongly for the inclusion of a Parsee in the Cabinet. Now that the Congress was forming the Government, I again pressed for the acceptance of my view. After some discussion my colleagues agreed. Since the Parsee community was concentrated in Bombay, we thought that Sardar Patel would be in a better position to advise us on the choice of the

Parsee representative. We accordingly left the choice to him and after some time he suggested the name of Mr. C. H. Bhabha. We later on found out that Mr. Bhabha was a friend of Sardar Patel's son and could not by any means be regarded as a leader, or even a true representative of the Parsee community. Our selection proved wrong and, after some time, he dropped out of the Government.

We also decided that the Government should include an experienced economist as the first Indian Finance Member. We selected Dr. John Matthai, though he was not in any sense a Congressman. In fact there was no rigid insistence on the inclusion of party men at the time of the formation of the interim Government.

The Moslem League was not only disappointed but enraged. It felt that it had been let down by the British. It attempted to stage a strong demonstration in Delhi and elsewhere, but its attempts failed. Nevertheless there was bitterness and trouble throughout the country and Lord Wavell felt that he must persuade the League to join the Government. He sent for Mr. Jinnah, who came to Delhi and held several meetings with him. Ultimately on 15 October the Moslem League decided to join the interim Government.

During this period, I met Lord Wavell several times. He told me that unless the League participated in the Government, the program for carrying out the Cabinet Mission Plan would be upset. He pointed out that communal troubles were continuing and were likely to continue till the League joined the Government. I told him that there had never been any objection from the Congress side to the participation of the League. In fact I had repeatedly urged the League to come into the Government. Jawaharlal, both before and after he joined the Government, had also issued an appeal to Mr. Jinnah to cooperate.

At this stage, I issued a further statement pointing out that the Cabinet Mission proposal had met all the legitimate fears of the Moslem League. It gave the Moslem League complete freedom to function in the Constituent Assembly and place its own point of view. The League had, therefore, no justification whatever to boycott the Constituent Assembly. When I met Lord Wavell next, he told me that he had greatly appreciated my stand and sent a copy of my statement to Liaqat Ali with a request to show it to Mr. Jinnah.

I must offer a few remarks at this stage about the nominees that Mr. Jinnah sent to the Executive Council. Apart from Liaqat Ali the most important and experienced leaders of the Moslem League were Khwaja Nazimuddin of Bengal and Nawab Ismail Khan of the U.P. It was taken for granted that, if ever the League accepted office, these three men would be included among the League's nominees. During the Simla Conference, these were the names that were again and again mentioned. Now that the League had decided to enter the Executive Council, Mr. Jinnah acted in a most peculiar manner. Khwaja Nazimuddin and Nawab Ismail Khan had never taken an extreme position in the disputes between the Congress and the League. This had obviously displeased Jinnah. He thought that they would refuse to be "yes men" and he therefore decided to exclude them from his list. It would, however, have created a furore in the League Council if this fact was prematurely known. He, therefore, induced the League Council to pass a resolution delegating full authority to him.

When he submitted his list to Lord Wavell, the names he included were those of Liaqat Ali, I. I. Chundrigar, Abdur Rab Nishtar, Ghaznafar Ali and Jogendra Nath Mandal. I shall have a word to say about J. N. Mandal separately. The other three nominees of the League were completely unknown. They were dark horses about whom even members of the League had little information. It is, of course, true that the League had never taken any part in the political struggle and as such had few leaders of national importance. Nevertheless, among its members there were experienced administrators like Khwaja Nazimuddin and Nawab Ismail Khan. They were all discarded in favor of Mr. Jinnah's henchmen.

On 25 October, the names of the Moslem League members of the interim Government were announced. Khwaja Nazimuddin and Nawab Ismail Khan along with other Moslem League leaders were waiting anxiously in the Imperial Hotel for the announcement. They were absolutely sure about their own inclusion and so were their supporters. Accordingly, a large number of Moslem League members had come with garlands and bouquets. When the names were announced and neither was included in the list, one can imagine their disappointment and anger. Mr. Jinnah had poured ice-cold water on their hopes.

An even more ridiculous thing the Moslem League did was to include the name of Mr. Jogendra Nath Mandal in its list. Mr. Jinnah had done his best to make the Congress nominate only Hindus, but in spite of his efforts, Congress had nominated Hindu, Moslem, Sikh, Parsee, Scheduled Caste and Christian members on the Executive Council. Mr. Jinnah felt that he must show that the League could also represent other communities and decided to include one non-Moslem among his nominees. Accordingly, he selected Mr. Jogendra Nath Mandal. It did not strike Mr. Jinnah that his action was inconsistent with his earlier claim that Congress should nominate only Hindus and the Moslem League only Moslems. Besides, the choice of his nominee caused both amusement and anger. When Mr. Suhrawardy had formed a Moslem League Ministry in Bengal, the only non-Moslem included in his Ministry was Mr. Jogendra Nath Mandal. He was then almost unknown in Bengal and had no position whatever in all-India politics. Since he was a nominee of the Moslem League and had to be given a portfolio, he was appointed Law Member. Most of the secretaries to the Government of India were then British. Mr. Mandal also had a British secretary who complained almost daily that it was difficult to work with a member like Mr. Mandal.

Now that the League had agreed to join the Government, the Congress had to reconstitute the Government and accommodate the representatives of the League. We had to decide who should leave the Government. It was felt that Mr. Sarat Chandra Bose, Sir Shafat Ahmed Khan and Syed Ali Zaheer should resign to make room for the League nominees. Regarding the portfolios, Lord Wavell had suggested that one of the major portfolios should go to a representative of the League. His own suggestion was that we should give up the Home Department, but Sardar Patel, who was then Home Member, vehemently opposed the suggestion. My view was that the issue of law and order was essentially a provincial subject. In the picture envisaged in the Cabinet Mission Plan, the Centre would have very little to do in this field. As such, the Home Ministry in the Centre would not have much importance in the new setup. I was, therefore, for accepting Lord Wavell's suggestion, but Sardar Patel was adamant. He said that, if we insisted, he would rather leave the Government than give up the Home Department.

We then considered other alternatives. Rafi Ahmed Kidwai suggested that we should offer the Finance portfolio to the Moslem League. It was no doubt one of the most important departments, but it was a highly technical subject and the League had no member who could handle it. Kidwai's view was that, because of the technical nature of the subject, the League would refuse the offer. If this happened, the Congress would lose nothing. If on the other hand the League nominee accepted the Finance portfolio, he would soon make a fool of himself. He believed that either way Congress would stand to gain.

Sardar Patel jumped at the proposal and gave it his strongest support. I tried to point out that Finance was the key to Government, and we would have to face major difficulties if Finance was under the control of the League. Sardar Patel countered by saying that the League would not be able to manage Finance and would have to decline the offer. I did not feel happy at the decision, but, since all the others agreed, I submitted. The Viceroy was therefore informed that the Congress would offer Finance to a nominee of the Moslem League.

When Lord Wavell conveyed this information to Mr. Jinnah, he said that he would give his reply the next day. It seems that at first Mr. Jinnah was a little uncertain about the offer. He had decided to nominate Liaqat Ali as the chief representative of the League in the Cabinet, but he was doubtful if Liaqat could adequately handle Finance. Chaudhary Mohammed Ali of the Finance Department heard this news and he immediately contacted Mr. Jinnah. He told him that the offer of the Congress was a real windfall and marked a great victory for the League. He had never expected that Congress would agree to hand over Finance to the Moslem League. With the control of the Department of Finance, the League would have a say in every Department of Government. He assured Mr. Jinnah that he need have no fears. He would give every help to Mr. Liaqat Ali and ensure that he discharged his duties effectively. Mr. Jinnah then accepted the proposal and accordingly Liaqat Ali became the Member for Finance. Congress soon realized that it had committed a great blunder in handing over Finance to the Moslem League.

In all countries, the Minister in charge of Finance plays a key role in the Government. In India, his position was even more important, for the British Government had treated the Finance Member as the custodian of its interests. This was a portfolio which had always been held by an Englishman specially brought to India for the purpose. The Finance Member could interfere in every Department and dictate policy. When Liaqat Ali became the Finance Member, he obtained possession of the key to Government. Every proposal of every Department was subject to scrutiny by his Department. In addition he had the power of veto. Not a Chaprasi [or messenger] could be appointed in any Department without the sanction of his Department.

Sardar Patel had been very anxious about retaining the Home Membership. Now he realized that he had played into the hands of the League by offering it Finance. Whatever proposal he made was either rejected or modified beyond recognition by Liaqat Ali. His persistent interference made it difficult for any Congress member to function effectively. Internal dissensions broke out within the Government and went on increasing.

The fact is that the interim Government was born in an atmosphere of suspicion and distrust between Congress and the League. Even before the League joined the Government, its distrust of the Congress had influenced the composition of the new Executive Council. When the Council was first constituted in September 1946, a question arose as to who should be in charge of Defence. It will be remembered that difference over the Defence portfolio was one of the reasons for the failure of the Cripps Mission. Congress wished that Defence should be held by one of its own trusted men, but Lord Wavell pointed out that this was likely to create difficulties. He wanted Defence to be kept completely outside politics. If a Congress member was in charge of Defence, this would give the League a handle for making unfounded charges. At the same time he made it clear that even if the League came into the Government, he would not agree to place Defence in charge of a nominee of the Moslem League. He suggested that the Defence Member should be neither a Hindu nor a Moslem. Sardar Baldev Singh, a Sikh, was at that time a minister in the Punjab and on Lord Wavell's suggestion we agreed that he should have charge of Defence.

I must mention here another small incident to show how far suspicion and distrust had developed in the minds of the nominees of the Moslem League. After the interim Government was formed, it had been agreed that all the members should meet informally before the formal meetings of the Cabinet. It was felt that if the members had informal discussion among themselves, it would help to develop the convention that the Viceroy was only a constitutional head. These informal meetings were held by turn in the rooms of different members of the Council, but very often Jawaharlal asked the other members to tea. Usually the invitations were sent by Jawaharlal's private secretary. After the Moslem League joined the Cabinet, the usual letter of invitation to all members of the Council, including the nominees of the Moslem League, was sent by the private secretary. Liaqat Ali took great exception to this and said that he felt humiliated that a private secretary to Jawaharlal should ask him to tea. Besides, he did not agree that Jawaharlal had any right as Vice-President of the Council to hold such informal meetings. Though he denied the right to Jawaharlal, Liaqat Ali himself started holding similar meetings with the nominees of the Moslem League. This is a small incident, but it shows the lengths to which the Moslem League representatives were prepared to go in their noncooperation with the Congress.

In the latter half of October, Jawaharlal took a step which was unnecessary and which I opposed. His nature is, however, such that he often acts on impulse. As a rule he is open to persuasion, but sometimes he makes up his mind without taking all the facts into consideration. Once he has done so, he tends to go ahead regardless of what the consequences may be.

The North West Frontier Province had an overwhelming majority of Moslems; both in 1937 and since 1946, the Ministry there was dominated by Congress. Khan Abdul Gaffar Khan and his Khudai Khidmatgars [or "Servants of God," Moslem followers of the Congress party] were mainly responsible for this happy state of affairs. In fact, we had become accustomed to depend on Khan Abdul Gaffar Khan and his brother, Dr. Khan Saheb, in all matters concerning the Frontier Province.

Soon after the interim Government was formed, orders were issued for the stopping of the aerial bombardment of tribesmen in south Waziristan. In the meantime, Jawaharlal was receiving official reports that a large section of the people in the Frontier were against Congress and the Khan brothers. Local officers repeatedly said that the Congress had largely lost local support and that the people had transferred their loyalty from Congress to the League. Jawaharlal was of the view that these reports were not correct and were fabricated by British officers who were against Congress. Lord Wavell did not agree with Jawaharlal, though he did not either accept the official reports, *in toto*. His view was that the Frontier was almost equally divided between the Khan brothers and the Moslem League. The impression in Congress circles was that the overwhelming majority of the people were with the Khan brothers. Jawaharlal said that he would tour the Frontier and assess the situation for himself.

When I heard this, I told Jawaharlal that he should not take any hasty action. It was difficult to know what the exact situation in the Frontier was. There were factions in every province and there was bound to be a group opposed to the Khan brothers. Congress had just assumed office in the Centre and had not yet consolidated its position. His tour of the Frontier at this stage would give the dissident elements an opportunity of organizing their opposition to Congress. Since a majority of the officials were also against the Congress, they would sympathize with, if not actively support, these opposition elements. It would therefore be better if he postponed his visit till a more appropriate time. Gandhiji supported my view but Jawaharlal insisted and said that, whatever be the consequences, he would go.

The Khan brothers were certainly right in claiming that a large section of the people in the Frontier supported them. They had, however, exaggerated the extent of their influence. This was natural, for one invariably overestimates one's own strength. Perhaps they also wished to impress on us that, while there were differences in other provinces, the Frontier was solidly with Congress. In fact, however, there was quite a powerful group against the Khan brothers. Dr. Khan Saheb's terms of office as Chief Minister had given additional strength to such opposition. He had the opportunity of winning over the entire province, but he had committed mistakes which had added to the strength of the opposition.

Some of the mistakes were of a purely personal and social nature. The Frontier Pathan is famous for his hospitality. He is willing to share the last piece of his bread with a guest and his table is open to everyone. He expects similar hospitality from others and especially from those who occupy any high position in society. Nothing alienates a Pathan more than miserliness and lack of generosity. Unfortunately, this was the respect in which the Khan brothers fell very short of the expectation of their followers.

The Khan brothers were well-to-do, but unfortunately they were not hospitable by temperament. They hardly ever invited anybody to their table even after Dr. Khan Saheb became Chief Minister. If people came to them at tea or dinnertime, they were never asked to stay for the meal. Their miserliness extended even to public funds spent under their direction. During the General Elections, Congress placed large amounts at their disposal, but the Khan brothers spent as little as possible out of these funds. Many candidates lost in the elections because they did not receive sufficient or timely help. Later, when they came to know that the funds were lying idle, these men became bitter enemies of the Khans.

On one occasion, some men from Peshawar came to see me in Calcutta in connection with the election funds. As it was teatime I offered them tea and biscuits. Several members of the deputation looked at the biscuits with surprise. One took up a biscuit and asked me its name. They seemed to enjoy the biscuits and then they told me that they had seen such biscuits in Dr. Khan Saheb's house, but he had never offered biscuits or even a cup of tea to any of them!

The actual position in 1946 was that the Khan brothers did not enjoy as much support in the Frontier as we in Delhi thought. When Jawaharlal reached Peshawar, this discovery came to him with an unpleasant shock. Dr. Khan Saheb was then the Chief Minister of the province and the Ministry was a Congress Ministry. I have already said that the British officers were against Congress and had aroused public feeling against the Ministry. When Jawaharlal landed at the airport, he found thousands of Pathans massed there carrying black flags and shouting anti slogans. Dr. Khan Saheb and other ministers who had come to receive Jawaharlal were themselves under police protection and proved completely ineffective. As Jawaharlal emerged, slogans were raised against him and some people in the mob tried to attack his car. Dr. Khan Saheb was so worried that he took out his revolver and threatened to shoot. Only under this threat did the crowd give way. The cars had to proceed under police escort.

The next day Jawaharlal left Peshawar for a tour of the tribal areas. He found everywhere a large section of the people against him. The Maliks [or tribal chiefs] of Waziristan were largely responsible for the demonstrations against him. In some places his car was stoned and Jawaharlal was once hit on the forehead. Dr. Khan Saheb and his colleagues seemed so completely helpless that Jawaharlal took the situation into his own hands. He exhibited neither weakness nor fear but showed the greatest courage. His intrepid conduct made a great impression on the Pathans. After his return, Lord Wavell expressed his regret for the whole affair and wanted an enquiry to be made into the conduct of the officers, but Jawaharlal did not agree that any action should be taken against them. This greatly impressed Lord Wavell and I also admired Jawaharlal's stand.

Both Congress and the Moslem League had originally accepted the Cabinet Mission Plan, which meant that both had accepted the Constituent Assembly. So far as Congress was concerned, it was still in favor of the Cabinet Mission Plan. The only objection raised from the Congress side was by certain leaders from Assam, who objected to the formation of the C group. They were possessed by an inexplicable fear of Bengal. They said that if Bengal and Assam were grouped together, the whole region would be dominated by Moslems. This objection had been raised by these Assam leaders immediately after the Cabinet Mission had announced its Plan. Gandhiji had initially accepted the Cabinet Mission Plan and declared that "the Cabinet Mission proposals contain the seed to convert this land of sorrow into one without sorrow and suffering." He went on to say in the *Harijan*, "After four days of searching examination of the State paper issued by the Cabinet Mission and the Viceroy on behalf of the British Government, my conviction abides that it is the best document that the British Government could have produced in the circumstances."

Gopinath Bardoloi, the Chief Minister of Assam, however, persisted in his opposition and submitted a memorandum to the Congress Working Committee opposing the grouping of Assam and Bengal as proposed in the Cabinet Mission statement. In the Working Committee, we felt that we should not reopen the question of grouping. In order partly to meet the objection of our colleagues from Assam but mainly on grounds of principle, we did, however, raise the question of European participation in the election of the Constituent Assembly. I wrote to the Viceroy that Congress might reject the whole of the Cabinet Mission proposals if the European members of the Bengal and Assam Legislatures participated in the elections to the Constituent Assembly, either by voting or by standing as candidates. This objection was met as the Europeans in the Bengal Assembly made a declaration that they would not seek representation. In the meantime, however, Gandhiji's views changed and he gave his support to Bardoloi. Jawaharlal agreed with me that the fears of the Assam leaders were unjustified and tried hard to impress them with his views. Unfortunately they did not listen either to Jawaharlal or me, especially since Gandhiji was now on their side and was issuing statements supporting their stand. Jawaharlal, however, remained steadfast and gave me his full support.

I have already said that the League's rejection of the Cabinet Mission Plan had caused us a great deal of anxiety. I have also mentioned the step which the Working Committee took to meet the League's objection. This we did by passing a resolution on 10 August in which it was clearly stated that in spite of our dissatisfaction with some of the proposals contained in the Cabinet Mission Plan, we accepted the scheme in its entirety. This did not, however, satisfy Mr. Jinnah. Apart from those of his arguments which I have already mentioned, he held that the Working Committee did not still state in categorical terms that the provinces would join the group envisaged in the Cabinet Mission Plan. Both the British Government and Lord Wavell agreed with the League on this particular point.

I was all the time trying to iron out the differences through discussion and Lord Wavell fully supported my efforts in this direction. This was one reason why he was anxious to bring the Moslem League into the Government, and he therefore welcomed the statement I had made in this behalf. He genuinely believed that there could be no better solution of the Indian problem than that outlined in the Cabinet Mission Plan. He repeatedly told me that, even from the point of view of the Moslem League, no better solution was possible. Since the Cabinet Mission Plan was largely based on the scheme I had formulated in my statement of 15 April, I naturally agreed with him.

Mr. Attlee was also taking a personal interest in the Indian developments. On 26 November 1946 he invited Lord Wavell and representatives of the Congress and the League to meet in London in another attempt to resolve the deadlock. At first the Congress was not willing to accept this invitation. Jawaharlal in fact told Lord Wavell that there would be no point in going to London for further discussion. All relevant issues had been thrashed out again and again and it would do more harm than good to reopen them.

Lord Wavell did not agree with Jawaharlal and discussed the matter in further detail with me. He said that if the present attitude of the Moslem League continued, not only would the administration suffer, but a peaceful solution of the Indian problem would become more and more difficult. He further argued that discussions in London would have the advantage of allowing the leaders to take a more objective and dispassionate view. They would be free from local pressure and the continual interference of their followers. Lord Wavell also stressed the point that Mr. Attlee had been a friend of India and his participation in the discussions might prove helpful.

I recognized the force of Lord Wavell's arguments and persuaded my colleagues to change their point of view. It was then decided that Jawaharlal should represent Congress. The League was represented by Mr. Jinnah and Liaqat Ali while Baldev Singh went on behalf of the Sikhs. The discussions were held from the 3rd till the 6th of December, but yielded little or no result.

The major differences concerned the interpretation of the clauses relating to grouping[1] in the Cabinet Mission Plan. Mr. Jinnah held that the Constituent Assembly had no right to change the structure of the Plan. Grouping was an essential part of the Plan and any change regarding grouping would alter the basis of the agreement. The Plan had itself provided that after the groups had framed the constitution, a province could opt out. This Mr. Jinnah said was sufficient protection for any province which did not wish to belong to the group to which it was allotted. The Congress leaders of Assam held on the other hand that a province could stay out from the beginning. It need not join the group at all and could frame its constitution independently. In other words, according to Mr. Jinnah,

[1] The grouping of provinces in the A, B and C sections of India.

the provinces must first join the group and could thereafter, if they wished, separate. According to the Congress leaders of Assam, the provinces could start as separate units and could thereafter join the group if they so wished. The Cabinet Mission had held that the interpretation of the League on this point was correct. Mr. Jinnah argued that it was on the basis of the distribution of powers among the Centre, the provinces and the groups that he had persuaded the League to accept the Plan. Assam Congress leaders did not agree, and, after some hesitation, Gandhiji, as I have already said, gave his support to the interpretation suggested by the leaders from Assam. In fairness, I have to admit that there was force in Mr. Jinnah's contention.

On 6 December, the British Cabinet issued a statement in which it upheld the point of view of the Moslem League on grouping, but this did not heal the breach between Congress and the League.

The first meeting of the Constituent Assembly was held on 11 December 1946. The question arose as to who should be President of the Assembly. Both Jawaharlal and Sardar Patel were of the view that someone not in the Government should be elected President. They both pressed me to accept the office but I did not feel inclined to agree. Several other names were then discussed but there was no agreement. Finally Dr. Rajendra Prasad was elected though he was a member of the Government. This proved a very happy choice, for he carried out the duties of President with great distinction and offered valuable suggestions and advice on many critical issues.

I have already said that when the interim Government was formed in September 1946 Gandhiji and my colleagues had pressed me to join. I had, however, felt that at least one senior Congress leader should remain outside the Government. I had thought that this would permit me to judge the situation objectively. I had, therefore, put Asaf Ali into the Government. After the League joined the interim Government, new difficulties arose inside the Executive Council. Thus the question again arose with regard to my participation in the Government. Gandhiji pressed even more strongly than before that I should join. He told me openly that, whatever might be my opinion or my personal feelings, it was my duty, in the interests of the country, to join the Government. He said that my remaining outside was proving harmful. Jawaharlal was of the same view.

Gandhiji suggested that Education would be the most appropriate subject for me and also in the true national interest. He said that the pattern of future education was a basic question for free India. Accordingly on 15 January 1947, I took over Education from Shri Rajagopalachari who had till then been the Education Member.

The policy and program in the field of Education that I followed after I assumed charge would form the subject matter of a separate study. My views on some of our educational problems have been collected and published separately. I do not therefore want to say anything about them in this volume. I will here deal only with the general political situation in the country. This was every day becoming more and more difficult and delicate, on account of the differences between Congress and the League.

I have already described the way in which the League members of the Executive Council were thwarting us at every step. They were in the Government and yet against it. In fact, they were in a position to sabotage every move we took. The powers of the Finance Member were being stretched to the limit and a new shock awaited us when the budget for the following year was presented by Liaqat Ali.

It was the declared policy of Congress that economic inequalities should be removed and a capitalist society gradually replaced by one of a socialist pattern. This was also the stand in the Congress election manifesto. In addition, both Jawaharlal and I had issued statements regarding the profits earned by businessmen and industrialists during the war years. It was open knowledge that a large part of this income had gone underground and escaped the income tax. This had meant that large resources were denied to the Government and we felt that the Government of India should take strong action to recover taxes which were due but had remained unpaid.

Liaqat Ali had framed a budget which was ostensibly based on

Congress declarations, but that was in fact a clever device for discrediting the Congress. He did this by giving a most unpractical turn to both the Congress demands. He proposed taxation measures which would have impoverished all rich men and done permanent damage to commerce and industry. Simultaneously, he brought forward a proposal for the appointment of a Commission to enquire into allegations regarding unpaid taxes and their recovery from businessmen and industrialists.

We were all anxious that there should be increasing equalization of wealth and that all tax evaders should be brought to book. We were therefore not against Liaqat Ali's proposal in principle. When Liaqat Ali raised the matter in the Cabinet, he openly said that his proposals were based on the declarations of responsible Congress leaders. He admitted that, but for the statements that Jawaharlal had made, he might never have thought about the matter. He did not, however, give details, so that on general grounds we agreed with him in principle. Having secured assent in principle, he proceeded to frame specific measures that were not only extreme, but calculated to harm the national economy.

Liaqat Ali's proposals took some of our colleagues by complete surprise. There were some who were secretly in sympathy with the industrialists. There were others who honestly felt that Liaqat Ali's specific proposals were based on political and not on economic considerations. Sardar Patel and Shri Rajagopalachari in particular were violently opposed to his budget, for they felt that Liaqat Ali was more concerned with harassing industrialists and businessmen than with serving the interests of the country. They thought that his main motive was to harm the members of the business community, the majority of whom were Hindus. Rajaji said openly in the Cabinet that he was opposed to Liaqat Ali's proposals and hinted that they were based on communal considerations. I pointed out to my colleagues that the proposals were in conformity with declared Congress objectives. We could not therefore oppose the principles but should examine them on their merits and support them wherever they were consistent with our principles.

As I have said, the situation was difficult and delicate. The Moslem League had at first accepted and then rejected the Cabinet Mission Plan. The Constituent Assembly was in session, but the League had boycotted it in spite of the fact that the whole country was united in the demand for freedom. On the one hand, the people were impatient for the attainment of independence. On the other, there seemed to be no solution of the communal problem. The Cabinet Mission Plan offered the only solution and yet we were not able to clinch the issue and so resolve our differences.

The Labour Government in Britain felt that they were faced with a dilemma. Should they allow the present state to continue or should they take a forward step on their own initiative? Mr. Attlee was of the view that a stage had been reached where suspense was most undesirable. It was necessary to take a clear-cut decision and he decided that the British Government should fix a date for the withdrawal of British power from India. Lord Wavell did not agree regarding the announcement of a date. He wished to persist with the Cabinet Mission Plan, for he held that it was the only possible solution of the Indian problem. He further held that the British Government would fail in its duty if it transferred political power before the communal question had been solved. Passions had been roused to such a peak in India that even responsible people were carried away. The withdrawal of British power in such an atmosphere would in his view lead to widespread riots and disturbances. He therefore advised that the *status quo* should be maintained and that every attempt should be made to compose the differences between the two major parties. It was his firm conviction that it would be dangerous and unworthy if the British withdrew without a previous understanding between Congress and the League.

Mr. Attlee did not agree. He held that once a date line was fixed, the responsibility would be transferred to Indian hands. Unless this was done, there would never be any solution. Mr. Attlee feared that, if the *status quo* was continued, Indians would lose their faith in the British Government. Conditions in India were such that the British could not maintain their power without an effort which the British people were not prepared to make. The only alternatives were to rule with a firm hand and suppress all disturbances, or transfer power to the Indians themselves. The Government could continue to govern, but this would require an effort which would interfere with the reconstruction of Britain. The other alternative was to fix a date for the transfer of power and thus place the responsibility squarely on Indian shoulders.

Lord Wavell was not convinced. He still argued that, if communal difficulties led to violence, history would not forgive the British. The British had governed India for over a hundred years and they would be responsible if unrest, violence and disorder broke out as a result of their withdrawal. When he found that he could not convince Mr. Attlee, Lord Wavell offered his resignation.

Looking at the events after ten years, I sometimes wonder who was right. The circumstances were so complicated and the situation so delicate that it is difficult to give a clear judgment. Mr. Attlee's decision was governed by his determination to help India to attain independence. Anyone with the slightest imperialist tendencies could easily have exploited India's weakness. In fact, Hindu-Moslem differences had always been exploited by the British Government. This had been their supreme defence against the Indian demand for independence. Mr. Attlee was resolved that the Labour Government should not adopt any policy which would lay it open to such a charge.

We must admit that if his motives had not been pure and if he had wished to exploit the differences between Congress and the League he could easily have done so. In spite of our opposition the British could have governed this country for another decade. There would, of course, have been disturbances and clashes. Indian feelings had been aroused to a level where British rule would have been challenged at every step. Nevertheless they could have, if they had so wished, continued to rule for a few more years by exploiting Indian differences. We must not forget that the French continued in Indo-China for almost ten years, even though France was much weaker than Britain. We must therefore give due credit to the motives of the Labour Government. They did not wish to exploit Indian weakness for their own advantage. History will honor them for this judgment and we must also without any mental reservation acknowledge this fact.

On the other hand, one cannot say for certain that Lord Wavell was wrong. The dangers he foresaw were real and later events proved that his reading of the situation was not incorrect. It is difficult to say which of the alternatives—the one actually adopted by Mr. Attlee or the one suggested by Lord Wavell—would have been better for India. If Lord Wavell's advice had been followed and the solution of the Indian problem deferred for a year or two, it is possible that the Moslem League would have got tired of its opposition. Even if the League had not taken a more positive attitude, the Moslem masses of India would probably have repudiated the negative attitude of the Moslem League. It is even possible that the tragedy of Indian partition might have been avoided. One cannot say for certain, but a year or two is nothing in the history of a nation. Perhaps history will decide that the wiser policy would have been to follow Lord Wavell's advice.

When it became known that Lord Wavell was leaving, I issued a statement which indicated what I thought of him. I knew that Jawaharlal and my other colleagues did not agree with me. They were against Lord Wavell but I considered it my duty to place before the public my appreciation of his contribution. This is what I said:

Mr. Attlee's statement on India has evoked mixed feelings in my mind. I am, on the one hand, gratified to find that the reading of the situation I adopted in June 1945 has been justified by events. At the same time I cannot help a feeling of regret that Lord Wavell, who was the initiator of a new chapter in the history of relations between India and England, is retiring from the scene.

There was on all hands suspicion and distrust of British intentions at the time of the Simla Conference. I confess that I was myself prejudiced and the events of the last three years had left in my mind a legacy of bitterness. It was in that mood that I went to Simla to participate in the proposed conference but when I met Lord Wavell, I experienced a sudden change of mind. I found him a rugged, straightforward soldier void of verbiage and direct both in approach and statement. He was not devious like the politician but came straight to the point and created in the mind an impression of great sincerity which touched my heart. Therefore, I felt it my duty to advise the country to adopt a constructive method for achieving its political objective. Since then in spite of a general atmosphere of doubt and opposition, I have never deviated from that course. It is common knowledge that since the first Simla Conference at least on four different occasions there were attempts both from within and outside the Congress to precipitate a movement and force Congress to resort to direct action but I was convinced that in view of the conciliatory attitude of the British Government such a course would be ill-advised.

I exerted all my influence to keep the Congress course steady, and today I feel satisfied that my reading of the situation was not wrong. The Simla Conference failed, but soon after, the general elections were held in England and the Labour Party came into power. They declared that they would carry out in practice their former professions about India. Events have since then proved that their declaration was sincere.

I do not know what communications passed between Lord Wavell and H.M.G. [His Majesty's Government in the United Kingdom] in the last two or three weeks. Obviously there were some differences which led to his resignation. We may differ from his appraisement of the situation. But we cannot doubt his sincerity or integrity of purpose. Nor can I forget that the credit for the changed atmosphere in Indo-British relations today must be traced back to the step which he so courageously took in June 1945. After the failure of the Cripps Mission Churchill's Government had made up their mind to put the Indian question in cold storage for the duration of the war. Indian opinion could also find no way out and the events after 1942 had further increased the bitterness. To Lord Wavell must belong the credit for opening the closed door. In spite of initial opposition from the Coalition Government [of the United Kingdom], he was able to persuade them to agree to make a new offer to India. The result was the Simla Conference. It did not succeed but everything that has followed since then has been a logical development of the courageous step which he took.

I am confident that India will never forget this service of Lord Wavell and when the time comes for the historian of independent India to appraise the relations of England and India, he will give Lord Wavell the credit for opening a new chapter in these relations.

There was a dinner that evening in which Lord Wavell bade farewell to members of the Viceroy's Executive Council. He was obviously touched by my statement and told to a friend, "I am glad to say that there is at least one man in India who has tried to understand my stand."

The day before he left, Lord Wavell presided over his last Cabinet meeting. After the business was over, he made a brief statement which made a deep impression on me. Lord Wavell said, "I became Viceroy at a very difficult and critical time. I have tried to discharge my responsibility to the best of my ability. A situation, however, developed which made me resign. History will judge whether I acted rightly in resigning on this issue. My appeal to you would, however, be that you should take no hasty decision. I am grateful to all of you for the cooperation I have received from you."

After this speech, Lord Wavell collected his papers quickly and walked away without giving any of us an opportunity to say anything. The next day he left Delhi.

CHAPTER 15

The Mountbatten Mission

LORD MOUNTBATTEN first became well known during the war years. He stayed for some months in India and then transferred his headquarters to Ceylon. When the war ended, he returned to Britain, but on Lord Wavell's resignation he was appointed Viceroy and Governor-General. Fully briefed by the Labour Government before he left, he came with instructions from Mr. Attlee that power must be transferred before 30 June 1948.

He reached Delhi on 22 March and was sworn in as Viceroy and Governor-General of India on the 24th. Immediately after the swearing-in ceremony, he made a short speech, in which he stressed the need for reaching a solution within the next few months.

Soon after this, I had my first interview with Lord Mountbatten. At the very first meeting he told me that the British Government was fully determined to transfer power. Before this could happen, a settlement of the communal problem was necessary and he desired that a final and decisive attempt must be made to solve the problem. He agreed with me that the differences between the Congress and the League had now been greatly narrowed down. The Cabinet Mission Plan had grouped Assam and Bengal together. The Congress held that no province should be compelled to enter a group and each province might vote whether to join the group or not. The League said that it had accepted the Cabinet Mission Plan on the basis that the group would vote as a whole and that a province could opt out only after the group had framed the constitution.

212

The League further argued that any change in the proposals of the Plan would nullify the agreement and held that Congress action had in effect done so. On this basis, the League had rejected the Cabinet Mission Plan.

Nobody can understand why the League placed so much emphasis on the question of Assam, when Assam was not a Moslem majority province. If the League's own criterion was applied, there was no valid reason for forcing Assam to join Bengal. Whatever be the reason, the League was formally right, though morally and politically its case was weak. I discussed the question with Lord Mountbatten on several occasions. I felt that the difference between the Congress and the League had reached a stage where agreement could only be attained through the mediation of a third party. My opinion was that we might leave the matter to Lord Mountbatten. Let the Congress and the League agree to refer the question to him and accept his arbitration. Neither Jawaharlal nor Sardar Patel would, however, agree to this suggestion. They did not like the idea of arbitration and I did not press the point further.

In the meantime, the situation was deteriorating every day. The Calcutta riots had been followed by risings in Noakhali and Bihar. Thereafter there was trouble in Bombay. The Punjab, which had been quiet till now, also showed signs of strain and conflict. Malik Khizir Hayat Khan had tendered his resignation as the Premier of the Punjab on 2 March. Anti-Pakistan demonstrations, which led to thirteen deaths and many injured, were held in Lahore on 4 March. Communal disturbances spread to other parts of the province and there were major disturbances in Amritsar, Taxila and Rawalpindi.

On the one hand, communal passions were mounting. On the other, the administration was becoming lax. Europeans in the services [the British civil servants] no longer had their hearts in the work. They were convinced that, within a short time, power would be transferred to Indian hands. This being so, they were no longer interested in their work and were only marking time. They told people openly that they were no longer responsible for the administration.

This led to more unrest and uncertainty among the people and created an all-round loss of confidence.

The situation was made worse by the deadlock between the Congress and the Moslem League within the Executive Council. The Central Government was paralyzed by the way in which the members of the Council pulled against one another. The League was in charge of Finance and held the key to the administration. It will be remembered that this had been entirely due to Sardar Patel, who, in his anxiety to retain the Home portfolio, had offered Finance to the Moslem League. There were some very able and senior Moslem officers in the Finance Department who gave every possible help to Liaqat Ali. With their advice Liaqat Ali was able to reject or delay every proposal put up by the Congress members of the Executive Council. Sardar Patel discovered that though he was Home Member he could not create so much as the post of a Chaprasi without Liaqat Ali's concurrence. The Congress members of the Council were at a loss and did not know what to do.

A truly pathetic situation had developed as a result of the Congress' mistake in giving Finance to the Moslem League. This had led to the deadlock which gave Lord Mountbatten the opportunity of slowly preparing the ground for the partition of India. As he began to give a new turn to the political problem, he tried to impress on Congress the inevitability of partition, and sowed the seeds of the idea in the minds of the Congress Members of the Executive Council.

It must be placed on record that the man in India who first fell for Lord Mountbatten's idea was Sardar Patel. Till perhaps the very end Pakistan was for Jinnah a bargaining counter, but, in fighting for Pakistan, he had overreached himself. The situation within the Executive Council had so annoyed and irritated Sardar Patel that he now became a believer in partition. The Sardar's had been the responsibility for giving Finance to the Moslem League. He therefore resented his helplessness before Liaqat Ali more than anybody else. When Lord Mountbatten suggested that partition might offer a solution for the present difficulty, he found ready acceptance of the idea in Sardar Patel's mind. He was convinced that he could not work with the Moslem League. He openly said that he was prepared to let the League have a part of India if only he could get rid of it.

Lord Mountbatten was extremely intelligent and could read the minds of all his Indian colleagues. The moment he found Patel amenable to his idea, he put out all the charm and power of his personality to win over the Sardar. In his private talks, he often referred to Patel as a walnut, a very hard crust outside but soft pulp once the crust was cracked.

As soon as Sardar Patel had been convinced, Lord Mountbatten turned his attention to Jawaharlal. Jawaharlal was not at first at all willing and reacted violently against the very idea of partition, but Lord Mountbatten persisted till step by step Jawaharlal's opposition was worn down. Within a month of Lord Mountbatten's arrival in India, Jawaharlal, the firm opponent of partition, had become, if not a supporter, at least acquiescent towards the idea.

I have often wondered how Jawaharlal was won over by Lord Mountbatten. Jawaharlal is a man of principle, but he is also impulsive and amenable to personal influence. The arguments of Sardar Patel must have had some effect, but could not have been decisive. Jawaharlal was also greatly impressed by Lord Mountbatten, but perhaps even greater was the influence of Lady Mountbatten. She is not only extremely intelligent, but had a most attractive and friendly temperament. She admired her husband greatly and in many cases tried to interpret his thought to those who would not at first agree with him.

Another person who probably influenced Jawaharlal on this question was Krishna Menon. Krishna Menon professed great admiration for Jawaharlal and I knew Jawaharlal often listened to his advice. I did not feel very happy about this, as I felt that Krishna Menon often gave him wrong advice. Sardar Patel and I did not always see eye to eye but we were agreed in our judgment about him. However, this I will discuss at greater length when I write the third volume of my autobiography.

When I became aware that Lord Mountbatten was thinking in terms of dividing India and had persuaded Jawaharlal and Patel, I was deeply distressed. I realized that the country was moving towards a great danger. The partition of India would be harmful not only to Moslems but to the whole country. I was and am still convinced that the Cabinet Mission Plan was the best solution from every point of view. It preserved the unity of India and gave every community an opportunity to function with freedom and honor. Even from the communal point of view, Moslems could expect nothing better. They would have complete internal autonomy in provinces in which they were in a majority. Even in the Centre they would have more than adequate representation. So long as there were communal jealousies and doubts, their position would be adequately safeguarded. I was also convinced that if the Constitution for free India was framed on this basis and worked honestly for some time, communal doubts and misgivings would soon disappear. The real problems of the country were economic, not communal. The differences related to classes, not to communities. Once the country became free, Hindus, Moslems and Sikhs would all realize the real nature of the problems that faced them and communal differences would be resolved.

I did my best to persuade my two colleagues not to take the final step. I found that Patel was so much in favor of partition that he was hardly prepared even to listen to any other point of view. For over two hours I argued with him. I pointed out that if we accepted partition we would create a permanent problem for India. Partition would not solve the communal problem but make it a permanent feature of the country. Jinnah had raised the slogan of two nations. To accept partition was to accept that slogan. How could Congress ever agree to divide the country on the basis of Hindus and Moslems? Instead of removing communal fears, partition would perpetuate them by creating two states based on communal hatred. Once states based on hatred came into existence, nobody knew where the situation would lead.

I was surprised and pained when Patel in reply said that, whether we liked it or not, there were two nations in India. He was now convinced that Moslems and Hindus could not be united into one nation. There was no alternative except to recognize this fact. In this way alone could we end the quarrel between Hindus and Moslems. He further said that if two brothers cannot stay together, they divide. After separation with their respective shares, they become friends. If on the other hand they are forced to stay together, they tend to fight every day. It was better to have one clean fight and then separate than have bickerings every day.

I now turned to Jawaharlal. He did not speak in favor of partition in the way that Patel did. In fact, he admitted that partition was by nature wrong. He had, however, lost all hopes of joint action after his experience of the conduct of the League members of the Executive Council. They could not see eye to eye on any question. Every day they quarrelled. Jawaharlal asked me in despair what other alternative there was to accepting partition.

Jawaharlal spoke to me in sorrow but left no doubt in my mind as to how his mind was working. It was clear that, in spite of his repugnance to the idea of partition, he was coming to the conclusion day by day that there was no alternative. He recognized that partition was evil, but he held that circumstances were inevitably leading in that direction.

After a few days Jawaharlal came to see me again. He began with a long preamble in which he emphasized that we should not indulge in wishful thinking, but face reality. Ultimately he came to the point and asked me to give up my opposition to partition. He said that it was inevitable and it would be wisdom not to oppose what was bound to happen. He also said that it would not be wise for me to oppose Lord Mountbatten on this issue.

I told Jawaharlal that I could not possibly accept his views. I saw quite clearly that we were taking one wrong decision after another. Instead of retracing our steps we were now going deeper into the morass. The Moslem League had accepted the Cabinet Mission Plan and a satisfactory solution of the Indian problem seemed in sight. Unfortunately, the position changed and Mr. Jinnah got a

chance of withdrawing from the League's earlier acceptance of
the Plan.

I argued that our second mistake had arisen when Lord Wavell
suggested that the Home portfolio should be given to the Moslem
League. This would not have caused any insuperable difficulty,
but, because Sardar Patel insisted on retaining Home, we had ourselves offered Finance to the Moslem League. This was the cause of
our present difficulties. I warned Jawaharlal that history would
never forgive us if we agreed to partition. The verdict would then
be that India was divided as much by the Moslem League as by
Congress.

Now that Sardar Patel and even Jawaharlal had become supporters of partition, Gandhiji remained my only hope. During this
period he was staying at Patna. He had earlier spent some months
in Noakhali, where he made a great impression on local Moslems
and created a new atmosphere of Hindu-Moslem unity. We expected
that he would come to Delhi to meet Lord Mountbatten and he
actually arrived on 31 March. I went to see him at once and his
very first remark was, "Partition has now become a threat. It seems
Vallabhbhai and even Jawaharlal have surrendered. What will you
do now? Will you stand by me or have you also changed?"

I replied, "I have been and am against partition. Never has my
opposition to partition been so strong as today. I am, however, distressed to find that even Jawaharlal and Sardar Patel have accepted
defeat and, in your words, surrendered their arms. My only hope
now is in you. If you stand against partition, we may yet save the
situation. If you however acquiesce, I am afraid India is lost."

Gandhiji said, "What a question to ask? If the Congress wishes
to accept partition, it will be over my dead body. So long as I am
alive, I will never agree to the partition of India. Nor will I, if I can
help it, allow Congress to accept it."

Later that day Gandhiji met Lord Mountbatten. He saw him
again the next day and still again on 2 April. Sardar Patel came to
him soon after he returned from his first meeting with Lord Mountbatten and was closeted with him for over two hours. What hap-

pened during this meeting I do not know. But when I met Gandhiji again, I receive the greatest shock of my life, for I found that he, too, had changed. He was still not openly in favor of partition but he no longer spoke so vehemently against it. What surprised and shocked me even more was that he began to repeat the arguments which Sardar Patel had already used. For over two hours I pleaded with him but could make no impression on him.

In despondency I said at last, "If even you have now adopted these views, I see no hope of saving India from catastrophe."

Gandhiji did not reply to my comments but said that he had already made the suggestion that we should ask Mr. Jinnah to form the Government and choose the members of the Cabinet. He said that he had mentioned this idea to Lord Mountbatten and he was greatly impressed.

I knew this was so. When I met Lord Mountbatten the day after Gandhiji had talked to him, he told me that, if Congress accepted Gandhiji's suggestion, partition could still be avoided. Lord Mountbatten agreed that such an offer on the part of Congress would convince the Moslem League and perhaps win the confidence of Mr. Jinnah. Unfortunately, this move could make no progress as both Jawaharlal and Sardar Patel opposed it vehemently. In fact they forced Gandhiji to withdraw the suggestion.

Gandhiji reminded me of this and said that the situation now was such that partition appeared inevitable. The only question to decide was what form it should take. This was the question which was now being debated day and night in Gandhiji's camp.

I thought deeply over the whole matter. How was it that Gandhiji could change his opinion so quickly? My reading is that this was due to the influence of Sardar Patel. Patel openly said that there was no way out except partition. Experience had shown that it was impossible to work with the Moslem League. Another consideration probably weighed with Sardar Patel. Lord Mountbatten had argued that Congress had agreed to a weak Centre only in order to meet the objection of the League. Provinces were, therefore, given full provincial autonomy, but in a country so divided by language, com-

munity and culture, a weak Centre was bound to encourage fissiparous tendencies. If the Moslem League were not there, we could
plan for a strong Central Government and frame a constitution
desirable from the point of view of Indian unity. Lord Mountbatten
advised that it would be better to give up a few small pieces in the
northwest and the northeast and then build up a strong and consolidated India. Sardar Patel was impressed by the argument that
cooperation with the Moslem League would jeopardize Indian unity
and strength. It seemed to me that these arguments had influenced
not only Sardar Patel but Jawaharlal. The same arguments repeated
by Sardar Patel and Lord Mountbatten had also weakened Gandhiji's
opposition to partition.

My effort throughout had been to persade Lord Mountbatten
to take a firm stand on the Cabinet Mission Plan. So long as Gandhiji
was of the same view, I had not lost hope. Now with the change in
Gandhiji's view, I knew that Lord Mountbatten would not agree to
my suggestion. It is also possible that Lord Mountbatten did not
feel so strongly about the Cabinet Mission Plan, as this was not the
child of his brain. It is therefore not surprising that, as soon as he
met with strong opposition to the Cabinet Mission Plan, he was
willing to substitute for it a plan of partition formulated according
to his own ideas.

Now that partition seemed generally accepted, the question of
Bengal and the Punjab assumed a new importance. Lord Mountbatten said that, since partition was on the basis of Moslem majority
areas and, since both in Bengal and the Punjab there were areas
where the Moslems were in a clear majority, these provinces should
also be partitioned. He, however, advised the Congress leaders not
to raise the question at this stage and assured us that he would himself raise it at the appropriate time.

Before Gandhiji left for Patna, I made a last appeal to him. I
pleaded with him that the present state of affairs might be allowed
to continue for two years. De facto power was already in Indian
hands and, if the de jure transfer was delayed for two or three years,
this might persuade the League to come to a settlement for reasons

I have already mentioned in the last chapter. Gandhiji himself had suggested this a few months ago and I reminded him that two or three years is not a long period in a nation's history. If we waited for two or three years, the Moslem League would be forced to come to terms. I realized that if a decision was taken now, partition was inevitable, but a better solution might emerge after a year or two. Gandhiji did not reject my suggestion but neither did he evince any enthusiasm for it.

By this time Lord Mountbatten had framed his own proposals for the partition of India. He now decided to go to London for discussions with the British Government and to secure their approval to his proposals. He also felt that he would be able to win the Conservatives' support for his plan. The Conservatives had opposed the Cabinet Mission proposal mainly on the grounds that it did not satisfy the Moslem League demand for the partition of India. Now that the Mountbatten proposal was based on the partition of the country, it would be natural to expect Mr. Churchill's support.

After the Congress Working Committee concluded its session on 4 May, I went up to Simla. After a few days Lord Mountbatten also came up. He wanted to have a brief vacation before his departure for London. His plan was to return to Delhi on 15 May and leave for London on the 18th. I thought I would make a last attempt to save the Cabinet Mission Plan and accordingly, on the night of 14 May, I met him at Viceregal Lodge.

We had discussions lasting for over an hour. I appealed to him not to bury the Cabinet Mission proposal. I told him that we should exercise patience, for there was still hope that the Plan would succeed. If we acted in haste and accepted partition, we should be doing permanent injury to India. Once the country was divided, no one could foresee the repercussions and there would be no chance of retracing our steps.

I also told Lord Mountbatten that Mr. Attlee and his colleagues were not likely to give up easily a plan which they had themselves formulated after so much labor. If Lord Mountbatten also agreed and emphasized the need for caution, the Cabinet was not likely to raise any objection. Till now, it was the Congress which had been insisting that India should be freed immediately. Now it was the Congress which asked that the solution of the political problem might be deferred for a year or two. Surely no one could blame the British if they conceded the Congress request. I also drew Lord Mountbatten's attention to another aspect of the question. If the British acted hastily now, independent and impartial observers would naturally conclude that the British wanted to give freedom to India in conditions where Indians could not take full advantage of this development. To press on and bring partition against Indian desires would evoke a suspicion that British motives were not pure.

Lord Mountbatten assured me that he would place a full and true picture before the British Cabinet and that he would report faithfully all that he had heard and seen during the last two months. He would also tell the British Cabinet that there was an important section of the Congress which wanted postponement of the settlement by a year or two. He assured me that he would tell Mr. Attlee and Sir Stafford Cripps what my views on the matter were. The British Government would have all these materials before them when they came to a final decision.

I also asked Lord Mountbatten to take into consideration the likely consequences of the partition of the country. Even without partition, there had been riots in Calcutta, Noakhali, Bihar, Bombay and the Punjab. Hindus had attacked Moslems and Moslems had attacked Hindus. If the country was divided in such an atmosphere, there would be rivers of blood flowing in different parts of the country and the British would be responsible for the carnage.

Without a moment's hesitation Lord Mountbatten replied, "At least on this one question I shall give you complete assurance. I shall see to it that there is no bloodshed and riot. I am a soldier, not a civilian. Once partition is accepted in principle, I shall issue orders to see that there are no communal disturbances anywhere in the country. If there should be the slightest agitation, I shall adopt the sternest measures to nip the trouble in the bud. I shall not use even the armed police. I will order the Army and the Air Force to act and I will use tanks and aeroplanes to suppress anybody who wants to create trouble."

Lord Mountbatten gave me the impression that he was not going to London with a clear-cut picture of partition, nor that he had completely given up the Cabinet Mission Plan. Later events made me change my estimate of the situation. The way he acted afterwards suggests that he had perhaps already made up his mind and was going to London to persuade the British Cabinet to accept his plan of partition.

The whole world knows what was the sequel to Lord Mountbatten's brave declaration. When partition actually took place, rivers of blood flowed in large parts of the country. Innocent men, women and children were massacred. The Indian Army was divided and nothing effective was done to stop the murder of innocent Hindus and Moslems. That is why in the preceding chapter I have said that perhaps Lord Wavell was right.

CHAPTER 16

The End of a Dream

I HAD a lingering hope that the Labour Cabinet would not easily accept the rejection of the Cabinet Mission Plan. It was framed by three members of the Cabinet who were also important members of the Labour Movement. It was true that Lord Pethick-Lawrence had by this time resigned from the office of Secretary of State for India, but Sir Stafford Cripps and Mr. Alexander were still members of the British Cabinet. It was thus my hope that they would make a last effort to save their plan. It was therefore with regret that I heard soon after Lord Mountbatten reached London that the British Cabinet had accepted the scheme proposed by him.

The details of Lord Mountbatten's Plan were not yet published, but I guessed that it would entail the partition of India. He returned to Delhi on 30 May and on 2 June held discussions with the representatives of the Congress and the Moslem League. On the 3rd of June a White Paper was issued which gave all the details of the Plan. The statement of the British Government will be found in the Appendix and I need only say that my worst fears were realized. The price for freedom was the partitioning of India into two states.

The publication of this statement meant the end of all hopes for preserving the unity of India. This was the first time that the Cabinet Mission Plan was discarded and partition accepted officially. In trying to explain why the Labour Government changed its attitude, I came to the painful conclusion that its action was governed more by consideration of British than Indian interests. The Labour party had always sympathized with Congress and its leaders and had many times openly declared that the Moslem League was a reactionary body. Its surrender to the demands of the Moslem League was in my opinion due more to its anxiety to safeguard British interests than to its desire to please the Moslem League. If a united India had become free according to the Cabinet Mission Plan, there was little chance that Britain could retain her position in the economic and industrial life of India. The partition of India, in which the Moslem majority provinces formed a separate and independent state, would, on the other hand, give Britain a foothold in India. A state dominated by the Moslem League would offer a permanent sphere of influence to the British. This was also bound to influence the attitude of India. With a British base in Pakistan, India would have to pay far greater attention to British interests than she might otherwise do.

It had for long been an open question whether India would remain in the Commonwealth after attaining her freedom. The Cabinet Mission Plan left the choice to free India. I had told Sir Stafford Cripps at the time that free India might of her own free will elect to remain in the Commonwealth. The partition of India would materially alter the situation in favor of the British. A new state formed according to the Moslem League demand was bound to remain in the Commonwealth. If Pakistan did so, India would be compelled to follow suit. All these factors must have weighed with the Labour Government. They had pledged their support for Indian freedom, but they could not forget that, during the political struggle, Congress had always opposed the British and the League had always supported them. When Lord Mountbatten proposed the partition of India and the creation of a new state to satisfy the Moslem League, the proposal found a sympathetic response from many of the members of the Labour Cabinet.

My reading is that Lord Mountbatten must have stressed this point when he met the Conservative party. Mr. Churchill had never been in favor of the Cabinet Mission Plan. He found the Mountbatten Plan much more to his taste and threw his weight in favor of it. This fact may also have weighed with the Labour Government, as Conservative support would make the passage of the Indian Independence Bill much easier.

The Congress Working Committee met on 3 June and considered the new situation. One of the first points which came up for discussion was the future of the North West Frontier Province. The Mountbatten Plan had created a strange situation for the Frontier. Khan Abdul Gaffar Khan and his party had always supported Congress and opposed the Moslem League. The League regarded the Khan brothers as its mortal enemies. In spite of the League opposition, the Khan brothers had been able to form a Congress Government in the Frontier and this Government was still functioning. Partition would place the Khan brothers and the Congress party in a most awkward situation. In fact, it would throw the Khan brothers and their party of Khudai Khidmatgars on the mercy of the League.

I have already said that Gandhiji's conversion to the Mountbatten Plan had been a cause of surprise and regret to me. He now spoke in the Working Committee in favor of partition. As I had already had an inkling into his mind, this did not take me by surprise, but one can imagine the reaction of Khan Abdul Gaffar Khan. He was completely stunned and for several minutes he could not utter a word. He then appealed to the Working Committee and reminded the Committee that he had always supported the Congress. If the Congress now deserted him, the reaction on the Frontier would be terrible. His enemies would laugh at him and even his friends would say that, so long as the Congress needed the Frontier, they supported the Khudai Khidmatgars. When, however, the Congress wished to come to terms with the Moslem League, it gave up its opposition to partition without even consulting the Frontier and its leaders. Khan Abdul Gaffar Khan repeatedly said that the Frontier would regard it as an act of treachery if the Congress now threw the Khudai Khidmatgars to the wolves.

Gandhiji was moved by the appeal and said that he would raise the matter with Lord Mountbatten. He did so when he met the

Viceroy and told him that he would not be able to support the plan for partition till he was satisfied that the Moslem League would deal fairly with the Khudai Khidmatgars. How could he desert those who had always stood by the Congress in the days of difficulty and stress?

Lord Mountbatten said that he would discuss the matter with Mr. Jinnah. As a result of his conversation, Mr. Jinnah expressed the wish to meet Khan Abdul Gaffar Khan. They met in Delhi but the talks were inconclusive. This was not surprising. Once Congress had accepted partition, what future could there be for Khan Abdul Gaffar Khan and his party? The Mountbatten Plan was based on the principle that the Moslem majority provinces should be separated and formed into a separate state. Moslems were in an overwhelming majority in the Frontier. As such, it was bound to be included in Pakistan. Geographically also the Frontier was within the proposed territories of Pakistan. In fact it would have no point of contact with India.

Lord Mountbatten had said that the provinces would be given a chance to opt. He declared that the Frontier would also be given the opportunity to decide its fate on the basis of self-determination. Accordingly, he suggested that a referendum might be held to decide whether the Frontier would join Pakistan or India. Dr. Khan Saheb, who was still the Chief Minister of the Frontier, joined the meeting of the Working Committee at this stage. Lord Mountbatten had told him about his plan to hold a plebiscite and asked Dr. Khan Saheb if he had any objection. Dr. Khan Saheb was the Chief Minister, as he claimed to have the support of the majority. As such he could not object to the proposal for a plebiscite. He had, however, raised a new issue. He said that if there was to be a plebiscite, the Pathans of the Frontier should have also the right to opt for Pakhtoonistan, a state of their own.

The fact was that the Khan brothers were not so strong in the Frontier as Congress had thought. Their influence had waned after the beginning of the agitation for partition. Now that Pakistan was in sight and the Moslem majority provinces had been promised the opportunity of forming an independent state, an emotional upheaval swept through the Frontier. The movement for Pakistan was further strengthened by the activity of the British officers, who openly supported Pakistan and persuaded the majority of the tribal chiefs in the Frontier to side with the Moslem League. Dr. Khan Saheb saw that his only chance of retaining the leadership of the Frontier was to raise the demand for Pakhtoonistan. Many Pathans would prefer a small state of their own as they feared the domination of the Punjab. Lord Mountbatten was not, however, prepared to listen to any new demand. He wanted to push through his scheme as fast as possible and the question of a free Pakhtoonistan was not even discussed in detail.

Since this was the last occasion on which the Khan brothers took part in discussions with the Congress, I may at this stage briefly record what happened to them immediately before and after partition. When they found that the Congress was now committed to partition, they did not know what to do. They could not possibly refuse the plebiscite. It would be an admission that they did not enjoy the support of their people. They returned to Peshawar and, after consulting their friends, they raised the slogan of independence for the Frontier.

The Congress Working Committee had endorsed the decision of the Frontier Congress authorizing Khan Abdul Gaffar Khan to take whatever action he thought necessary to deal with the situation in the province. The Frontier Congress now demanded the creation of a free Pathan State with a constitution framed on the basis of the Islamic conception of democracy, equality and social justice. Explaining his stand, Khan Abdul Gaffar Khan said that the Frontier Pathans had their own distinct history and culture, and these could not be preserved unless they had full freedom to maintain and develop their own institutions. They therefore claimed that the plebiscite should not be on the basis of a choice between Pakistan and India, but that there should be the third alternative of an independent Pakhtoonistan. This alone would make the plebiscite fair and truly representative of the peoples' will. If this was not done, the plebiscite would become meaningless, as the Pakhtoons would be submerged by the other elements in Pakistan. There are reasons to think that if the plebiscite had included the issue of free Pakhtoonistan, a large number of the Frontiersmen might have voted for it. They were afraid of being swallowed up by the Punjab and this fact alone might have swayed them to vote against Pakistan.

Neither Mr. Jinnah nor Lord Mountbatten was, however, prepared to accept this demand. Lord Mountbatten made it clear that the Frontier could not form a separate and independent state, but must be included either in India or Pakistan. The Khan brothers then declared that their party could take no part in the plebiscite and called on the Pathans to boycott it. But their opposition was of no avail. The plebiscite was held and a large proportion of the people voted in favor of Pakistan. If the Khan brothers had not boycotted the plebiscite and their supporters had worked earnestly, it would have been known what proportion of the Pathans were against Pakistan. However, the result went in favor of the Moslem League and the British Government immediately accepted it.

After partition actually took place, the Khan brothers modified their attitude in conformity with the demands of the situation. They declared that their demand for a free Pakhtoonistan did not mean the creation of a separate state but the recognition of full autonomy for the Frontier as a unit of Pakistan. They explained that what they stood for was a constitution of Pakistan which would be truly federal, which would guarantee full provincial autonomy to its units and would thus secure the social and cultural life of the Pathans. Without such constitutional safeguards, the Punjabis would dominate the whole of Pakistan and might deny the legitimate rights of Pathans and other minorities.

One must admit that this demand of the Khan brothers was eminently reasonable. It was also in conformity with the resolution which the Moslem League itself had passed in Lahore and which it had never modified. Mr. Jinnah had therefore no justification when he accused the Khan brothers of wanting to break away from Pakistan. In fact, Khan Abdul Gaffar Khan had several interviews with him at Karachi and at one stage it seemed that an understanding would be reached. Some observers in Pakistan said that Mr. Jinnah was impressed by Khan Abdul Gaffar Khan's sincerity and planned to go to Peshawar to meet him and his fellow workers. This, however, did not materialize and very soon the political enemies of the Khan brothers poisoned Mr. Jinnah's mind against them. Khan Abdul Qayyum Khan, who had formed the Ministry in the Frontier, was naturally opposed to any reconciliation between Mr. Jinnah and the Khan brothers. He therefore behaved in a way which made any understanding impossible. In fact his Government acted without any sense of decency or justice and harassed the Khudai Khidmatgars by adopting all kinds of illegal and unfair measures. Democracy was crushed and force became the order of the day. Khan Abdul Gaffar Khan, Dr. Khan Saheb and all other leaders of the Khudai Khidmatgars were sent to jail where they languished for almost six years without any legal charge or trial. Khan Abdul Qayyum Khan's vendetta became so bitter that even a section of the Moslem League was disgusted and said that either the Khan brothers should be prosecuted or released. All such efforts were, however, of no avail. Lawless oppression was perpetrated in the name of the law.

The A.I.C.C. met on 14 June 1947. I have attended many meetings of the A.I.C.C. but this was one of the strangest that it was my misfortune to attend. Congress, which had always fought for the unity and independence of India, was now considering an official resolution for the division of the country. Pandit Govind Ballabh Pant moved the resolution and, after Sardar Patel and Jawaharlal had both spoken on it, Gandhiji himself had to intervene.

It was impossible for me to tolerate this abject surrender on the part of the Congress. In my speech I said clearly that the decision which the Working Committee had reached was the result of a most unfortunate development. Partition was a tragedy for India and the only thing that could be said in its favor was that we had done our best to avoid division, but we had failed. We must not, however, forget that the nation is one and its cultural life is and will remain

one. Politically we had failed and were therefore dividing the
country. We should accept our defeat, but we should at the same
time try to ensure that our culture was not divided. If we put a stick
in the water, it may appear that the water has been divided but the
water remains the same and the moment the stick is removed, even
the appearance of division disappears.

Sardar Patel did not like my speech. He spent almost the whole
of his speech in trying to refute what I had said. He argued that the
resolution for the division of the country did not arise out of weakness or compulsion but that it was the only true solution in the
existing circumstances in India.

There were elements of comedy even in the midst of this great
tragedy. There have always been in Congress some men who have
posed as nationalists but who are in fact utterly communal in outlook. They have always argued that India has no unified culture and
have held that, whatever Congress may say, the social life of the
Hindus and the Moslems was entirely different. It was surprising to
find that members with these views had suddenly appeared on the
platform as the greatest upholders of Indian unity.

They opposed the resolution vehemently and the grounds they
gave were that the cultural and national life of India could not be
divided. I agreed with what they were saying, and had no doubt
that what they now said was true. I could not, however, forget that
they had all their lives opposed such a view. It was strange that
now at this eleventh hour they should be the persons to raise the
cry for an undivided India.

After the first day's debate, there was a very strong feeling against
the Working Committee's resolution. Neither Pandit Pant's per-
suasiveness nor Sardar Patel's eloquence had been able to persuade
the people to accept this resolution. How could they, when it was
in a sense the complete denial of all that Congress had said since its
very inception? It therefore became necessary for Gandhiji to intervene in the debate. He appealed to the members to support the
Congress Working Committee. He added that he had always opposed partition and no one could deny this fact. He felt, however,

that a situation had now been created where there was no alternative. Political realism demanded the acceptance of the Mountbatten Plan and he would appeal to the members to accept the resolution moved by Pandit Pant.

When the resolution was put to the vote, 29 voted for it and 15 against. Even Gandhiji's appeal could not persuade more members to vote for the partition of the country!

The resolution was no doubt passed, but what was the condition of the people's mind? All hearts were heavy at the idea of partition. Hardly anyone could accept the resolution without mental reservations. Even those who accepted partition had all their feelings against it. This was bad enough. What was worse was the kind of insidious communal propaganda which was gaining ground. It was being openly said in certain circles that the Hindus in Pakistan need have no fear, as there would be 45 millions of Moslems in India and, if there was any oppression of Hindus in Pakistan, the Moslems in India would have to bear the consequences.

In the meeting of the A.I.C.C., the members from Sind opposed the resolution vehemently. They were given all kinds of assurances. Though not on the public platform, in private discussion they were even told by some people that if they suffered any disability or indignity in Pakistan, India would retaliate on the Moslems in India.

When I first became aware of such suggestions, I was shocked. I immediately saw that this was a dangerous sentiment and could have most unfortunate and far-reaching repercussions. It implied that partition was being accepted on the basis that, in both India and Pakistan, the minority would be looked upon as hostages in order to safeguard the security of the minority in the other state. The idea of retaliation as a method of assuring the rights of minorities seemed to me barbarous. Later events proved how justified my apprehensions were. The rivers of blood which flowed after partition on both sides of the new frontier grew out of this sentiment of hostages and retaliation.

Some members of the Congress realized how dangerous such theories were. I remember in particular Kiran Shankar Roy, one of the Congress leaders of Bengal, who first brought this to my notice. He also spoke to Acharya Kripalani, who was then the President of Congress, and pointed out that it was a most dangerous theory. Once such a feeling was allowed to grow, it would lead to the oppression and murder of Hindus in Pakistan and of Moslems in India. Nobody, however, paid any attention to Kiran Shankar Roy. In fact, many ridiculed him for his fears. They also told him that once India was divided, we must accept the theory of hostages. They argued that it was only in this way that the Hindus of Pakistan could be protected. Kiran Shankar Roy was not convinced and he came to me almost in tears. He never accepted the assurance which some of the Congress leaders had held out and he lived to see the fulfilment of his worst fears.

The British Government had originally fixed a period of fifteen months for the completion of the arrangements for the transfer of power. Mr. Attlee had in fact explicitly stated on 20 February 1947 that it was the definite intention of the British Government to effect the transfer of power to responsible Indian hands by a date not later than June 1948. A great deal had happened between 20 February and 3 June 1947. Now that the plan for partition was accepted, Lord Mountbatten declared that the scheme should be brought into effect as quickly as possible. His motives were perhaps mixed. On the one hand, he wished that the British should transfer the responsibility to Indian hands as early as possible. On the other, he probably had apprehensions that delay might bring up new impediments to the new plan. The fate of the Cabinet Mission Plan had shown that the delay in its implementation had given rise to second thoughts and had ultimately led to the rejection of the Plan.

Lord Mountbatten set for himself a period of three months during which to carry out the task of partitioning India. It was not an easy task and I openly expressed my doubts about the possibility of carrying out so complicated a plan in such a short time. I must pay a tribute to Lord Mountbatten for the efficiency and ability with which he presided over his task. He had such a mastery of detail and such quick grasp that in less than three months all the problems were solved and, on 14 August 1947, India was divided into two states.

I will give one or two examples of the expedition and assurance with which Lord Mountbatten handled the various intricate problems that arose in connection with the creation of two states. As soon as it became known that India was going to be partitioned, the Hindus and the Moslems began to put up inflated claims. There were sporadic disturbances throughout the country. The great Calcutta killings in 1946 had been followed by trouble in Noakhali and Bihar. Riots had started in the Punjab in March. Originally confined to Lahore, the disturbances spread and soon large areas in and around Rawalpindi were torn with strife. Lahore in fact became the battleground for which communalists among Hindus and Moslems fought. Representatives of Hindus and Sikhs tried hard to persuade Congress that Lahore must be retained in India. They pointed out that the political and economic life of the Punjab was centred in Lahore and, if it went to Pakistan, the Punjab would be permanently crippled. Many, therefore, pressed that Congress should make an issue of Lahore. Congress did not agree to their suggestion and held that the question should be decided in accordance with the wishes of the population.

Some sections among the Moslems and the Hindus as well as the Sikhs thought that the issue of Lahore could be decided by resorting to violence. Generally speaking, the Hindus were the property-owning classes in and around Lahore. Some Moslems thought that they could hurt the Hindus most by destroying their property and attacking them on the economic front. They therefore burnt factories and houses and looted the property of non-Moslems indiscriminately. Some sections of the Hindus in Lahore retaliated by killing Moslems. They had wealth and felt that such attacks might drive Moslems away from Lahore and assure them a Hindu majority. It was openly said that in this conflict—in which one side attacked property and the other life—important leaders of the communal parties were directly or indirectly involved. Thus it was widely reported and generally believed that leaders of the Moslem League, both central

and provincial, were organizing attacks on Hindus. Similarly, the
Hindu Mahasabha leaders were accused of inciting the Hindus
against the Moslems.

An almost parallel situation had developed in Calcutta. The supporters of the Moslem League insisted that Calcutta should go to
Pakistan, while all those against the League were anxious that Calcutta should remain with India.

It was in this situation that the question of the partition of the
Punjab and Bengal was taken up by Lord Mountbatten. It had been
decided that there would be a vote in the Provincial Assembly to
decide whether the provinces should be partitioned at all or as a
whole join India or Pakistan. Both the Bengal and the Punjab
Assemblies voted for partition and it became necessary to decide
what would be the boundary of the two new provinces. Lord Mountbatten appointed a Boundary Commission to go into this question
and asked Mr. Radcliff to undertake the task. Mr. Radcliff was then
in Simla. He accepted the appointment, but suggested that he
would start his survey in early July. He pointed out that it would be
an almost impossible task to undertake a field survey in the Punjab
in the heat of June and in any case July meant a delay of only three
or four weeks. Lord Mountbatten told him that he was not prepared
for even one day's delay and any suggestion of three or four weeks'
postponement was simply out of question. His orders were carried
out. This offers an example of the expedition and despatch with
which Lord Mountbatten worked.

A second problem which faced Lord Mountbatten was the partition of the secretariat and assets of the Government of India.
There were difficulties even about the provinces which went wholly
to one state or the other. Records dealing with the provinces which
went to Pakistan had to be separated and sent to Pakistan. In the
case of provinces which were divided the task was even more difficult. Lord Mountbatten personally supervised most of the arrangements and the committee which he appointed for the purpose
settled every question as soon as it arose.

Even more difficult were the problems of dividing the finances of the country and partitioning the Army but no obstacle proved too great for Lord Mountbatten's ingenuity and drive. The most complicated issues in finance were decided within the allotted date.

Regarding the Army, it was decided that Pakistan should have one-fourth of the Army and India three-fourths. The question arose whether the Army should be divided immediately, or should serve under a unified command for two or three years. The Army commanders advised that the general staff should remain common during this period. I was impressed by their arguments and supported them. I had my own reasons, apart from those advanced by Lord Mountbatten. I was afraid that partition would be followed by disturbances and riots. I felt that, in such a context, a unified army could serve India well. I was clear in my mind that we should not bring communal divisions within the Army if the situation was to be saved. Till now there had never been any communal feelings within the Army. If the Army was kept outside politics, their discipline and neutrality could be assured. I, therefore, pressed for a unified command and I wish to bring on record that Lord Mountbatten fully supported the stand. I am convinced that if the Army had remained unified we would have avoided the rivers of blood which flowed immediately after independence.

I regret to say that my colleagues did not agree with me and opposed me. What surprised me most was the opposition of Dr. Rajendra Prasad. He was a pacifist and wedded to nonviolence. He now took the lead in insisting on a division of the Army. He said that if India was divided into two states, a unified army should not and indeed could not continue for a day.

I think it was a dangerous decision. It divided the Army on the basis of communities. The Moslem units mostly went to Pakistan and the Hindu and Sikh units remained wholly in India. This injected communal poison into an army which till then had been free from it. When, after 15 August, the blood of innocent men and women flowed on both sides of the frontier, the Army remained passive spectators. What is worse, in some cases military men even joined in the strife.

Lord Mountbatten said to me more in sorrow than in anger that Indian members of the Army wanted to take part in killing Moslems in East Punjab but the British officers restrained them with great difficulty. This was Lord Mountbatten's report and I am not quite sure how far this statement about the British officers is correct. This, however, I know from personal knowledge—that some members of the former undivided Indian Army killed Hindus and Sikhs in Pakistan and Moslems in India. The wonderful tradition of the Indian Army was disturbed and a slur was cast on what till then had been a proud record.

Regarding the [civil] services, I suggested that they should not be divided on a communal basis. Political necessity had compelled us to accept partition of the country, but there was no reason why officials should be uprooted from their own areas. I felt that all service men should be retained in their own provinces. Thus officials from West Punjab, Sind or East Bengal, whatever their community, should remain in Pakistan. Similarly service men who belonged to the Indian provinces should serve India regardless of whether they were Hindus or Moslems. My idea was that if we could keep communal passions out of at least the services, a better atmosphere could be maintained in both states. Administration would thus be free of communal poison and the minorities in each state would feel a greater sense of security. I regret to say that my pleadings proved vain. It was decided that all service men would be given the right to opt for India or Pakistan. The result was that almost without exception Hindus and Sikhs opted for India and Moslems for Pakistan.

I discussed this question with Lord Mountbatten in great detail. I pointed out how dangerous it was to divide the Army and the services on a communal basis. Lord Mountbatten agreed with me and did his best to support my stand. So far as the Army was concerned he had no success at all. With regard to the civilians, the only result of his efforts was that officials were given the right to opt permanently or provisionally. There would be no question about those who opted permanently. Those who exercised their option provisionally were given the right to revise their decision within a period of six months. Both the states gave a guarantee of taking back those who revised their option in this manner. I have to say with great regret that though this solemn assurance was given, the unfortunate individuals who exercised their option provisionally did not generally receive fair treatment from either state.

I also regret to say that the Moslem League acted foolishly and blindly even in the matter of the exercise of option. It incited all Moslem officials to opt for Pakistan and leave India. At that time, a large number of key positions in the Central Secretariat were held by Moslems. The Moslem League pressed all of them to leave India. Those who did not readily agree were frightened by all kinds of reports as to what their fate would be once Congress came into undisputed power. As such rumors were causing a certain amount of nervousness among Moslem employees, I pressed the Government of India to issue a circular clarifying its stand. Lord Mountbatten and Jawaharlal supported me fully and a circular was actually issued reassuring service men from Moslem and other minority communities that, if they remained to serve in India, not only would they be given their rights but they would be treated generously.

The result of this circular was that a number of Moslem officers in the Central Secretariat regained their confidence and decided to stay on in India. When the Moslem League leaders came to know this, they started to canvass the officers who wished to remain. These Moslem officers were already nervous about what the future might hold in store for them. They were now threatened that if they remained in India, the Moslem League and the Pakistan Government would regard them as enemies and harass them in every possible way.

Many of these officers came from provinces which were to become parts of Pakistan. When they found that the Moslem League authorities proposed to retaliate against their property and their relations in Pakistan, most of these officers became highly disturbed. In my own Ministry, there were several Moslem officers holding high positions. They had opted for India on the strength of my assurances, but, when the Moslem League held out threats against their families and their property, some of them came to me in tears and said, "We had decided to stay in India but now after the threat held out by the Moslem League it is impossible to do so. Our families are in West Punjab and we cannot allow them to suffer. We are therefore compelled to opt for Pakistan."

The action of the Moslem League in driving almost all the Moslem officers out of India was not only foolish but harmful. In fact it was more harmful to the Moslems than to India as a whole. Now that partition had been accepted and Pakistan was being established, it was clear that the Moslems would get every advantage in the new state. If, in addition, some Moslems could have served in India, this would not only have been of personal advantage to them but would have been a great gain for the community as a whole. The presence of Moslems in some responsible positions would have given assurance to the community and allayed many unreasonable fears. I have already said how foolishly the League had acted in insisting on partition. The League's attitude towards Moslem officers was another example of the same foolishness.

It was decided that the Indian Dominion would come into existence on 15 August 1947. The Moslem League decided that Pakistan should be constituted a day earlier on 14 August. There was an unpleasant incident even with regard to the birth of the two dominions. The convention had grown in the British Commonwealth that a dominion could choose its own Governor-General and some dominions had appointed their own nationals to this post. India was, therefore, free to choose an Indian to be the first constitutional Governor-General of India. We, however, decided that it would be better not to make a sudden change and felt that the appointment of Lord Mountbatten would give continuity of policy and administration. It was also thought that in the initial stages there would be one Governor-General for the two dominions and any change could be carried out later. It was generally thought that Pakistan would be influenced by the same considerations.

We accordingly announced that Lord Mountbatten was our choice for the Governor-General. We expected the League to select him, but at the last moment the League caused a surprise by proposing that Mr. Jinnah should be appointed the first Governor-General of Pakistan. As soon as Lord Mountbatten heard this news, he told us that this changed the whole situation. He suggested that we should reconsider our decision and appoint an Indian. We, however, saw no reason to change our choice and reiterated that Lord Mountbatten would be the first Governor-General of the Indian Dominion.

CHAPTER 17

Divided India

I HAVE now reached the final chapter of the story I want to tell in this volume. On 14 August 1947 Lord Mountbatten went to Karachi to inaugurate the Dominion of Pakistan. He returned the next day and, at 12 midnight on 15 August 1947, the Indian Dominion was born.

The country was free, but, before the people could fully enjoy the sense of liberation and victory, they woke up to find that a great tragedy had accompanied freedom. We also realized that we would have to face a long and difficult journey before we could relax and enjoy the fruits of liberty.

Congress as well as the Moslem League had accepted partition. Since the Congress represented the entire nation and the Moslem League had considerable support among the Moslems, this would normally have meant that the whole country had accepted partition. The real position was, however, completely different. When we looked at the country immediately before and after partition, we found that the acceptance was only in a resolution of the All India Congress Committee of the Congress and on the register of the Moslem League. The people of India had not accepted partition. In fact, their hearts and souls rebelled against the very idea. I have said that the Moslem League enjoyed the support of many Indian Moslems, but there was a large section in the community who had always opposed the League. They had naturally been deeply cut by the decision to divide the country. As for the Hindus and the Sikhs, they were to a man opposed to partition. In spite of Congress acceptance of the Plan their opposition had not abated in the least. Now, when partition had become a reality, even the Moslems who were the followers of the Moslem League were horrified by the result and began to say openly that this was not what they had meant by partition.

In reviewing the situation after ten years, I find that events have confirmed what I said at that time. It was even then clear to me that the Congress leaders had not accepted partition with free and open minds. Some had accepted it out of sheer anger and resentment and others out of a sense of despair. Men when they are swayed by indignation or fear cannot judge objectively. How could the advocates of partition who acted under the stress of passion see the implications of what they were doing?

Among Congressmen the greatest supporter of partition was Sardar Patel, but even he did not believe that partition was the best solution of the Indian problem. He threw his weight in favor of partition out of irritation and injured vanity. He found himself frustrated at every step by the veto put on his proposals by Liaqat Ali Khan as Finance Minister. It was therefore in sheer anger that he decided that, if there was no other alternative, partition should be accepted. He was also convinced that the new State of Pakistan was not viable and could not last. He thought that the acceptance of Pakistan would teach the Moslem League a bitter lesson. Pakistan would collapse in a short time and the provinces which had seceded from India would have to face untold difficulty and hardship.

The real test of the people's attitude towards the partition of the country came on 14 August 1947 when independent Pakistan was formed. If the people of India had willingly accepted partition, surely the Hindus and Sikhs of the Punjab, the Frontier, Sind and Bengal would have rejoiced in the same way as the Moslems of those regions. Reports which we received from all these provinces showed how hollow was the claim that the Congress acceptance of partition meant its acceptance by the Indian people.

The 14th of August was for the Moslems of Pakistan a day of rejoicing. For the Hindus and the Sikhs, it was a day of mourning.

This was the feeling not only of most people, but even of important leaders of Congress. Acharya Kripalani was then President of the Congress. He is a man of Sind. On 14 August 1947, he issued a statement that it was a day of sorrow and destruction for India. This feeling was expressed openly by Hindus and Sikhs throughout Pakistan. It was surely a strange situation. Our national organization had taken a decision in favor of partition, but the entire people grieved over it.

One question naturally arises here. If partition evoked such feelings of anger and sorrow in the hearts of all Indians, why did the Indian people accept it? Why was there not greater opposition to it? Why was there such a hurry to take a decision which almost everybody regarded as wrong? If the right solution of the Indian problem could not be found by 15 August, why take a wrong decision and then grieve over it? I had again and again said that it was better to wait till a correct solution was found. I had done my best, but my friends and colleagues unfortunately did not support me. The only explanation I can find of their strange blindness to facts is that anger or despair had clouded their vision. Perhaps also the fixation of a date—15 August—acted like a charm and hypnotized them into accepting whatever Lord Mountbatten said.

The situation was one in which tragedy and comedy were inextricably mixed. After partition, the most ridiculous position was that of the Moslem League leaders who remained in India. Jinnah left for Karachi with a message to his followers that now that the country was divided they should be loyal citizens of India. This parting message created in them a strange sense of weakness and disillusion. Many of these leaders came to see me after 14 August. Their plight was pathetic. Every one of them said with deep regret and anger that Jinnah had deceived them and left them in the lurch.

I could not at first understand what they meant by saying that Jinnah had deceived them. He had openly demanded partition of the country on the basis of Moslem majority provinces. Partition was now a reality and both in the west and in the east Moslem majority areas formed parts of Pakistan. Why then should these spokesmen of the Moslem League say that they had been deceived?

As I talked to them I realized that these men had formed a picture of partition which had no relevance to the real situation. They had failed to realize the real implications of Pakistan. If the Moslem majority provinces formed a separate state, it was clear that the provinces in which the Moslems were in a minority would form part of India. The Moslems of the U.P. and Bihar were a minority and would remain so even after partition. It is strange, but the fact is that these Moslem Leaguers had been foolishly persuaded that, once Pakistan was formed, Moslems, whether they came from a majority or a minority province, would be regarded as a separate nation and would enjoy the right of determining their own future. Now, when the Moslem majority provinces went out of India and even Bengal and the Punjab were divided and Mr. Jinnah left for Karachi, they at last realized that they had gained nothing but in fact lost everything by the partition of India. Jinnah's parting message came as the last straw on the camel's back. It was now clear to them that the only result of partition was that their position as a minority was much weaker than before. In addition, they had through their foolish action created anger and resentment in the minds of the Hindus.

These members of the Moslem League kept on repeating that they were now at the mercy of the Hindu majority. It was such an obvious thing that their grief over these developments evoked hardly any pity for them. I reminded them of what I had said during the Cabinet Mission Plan. In my statement of 15 April 1946, I had warned the Indian Moslems in unambiguous words. I had then said that if partition ever became a reality, they would one day wake up to find that, after the majority of Moslems had gone away to Pakistan, they would still remain in India but as a small and insignificant minority.

A special program for marking the dawn of independence had been arranged for 15 August. The Constituent Assembly met at midnight and declared that India was now free and an independent state. Next day the Assembly met again at 9:00 A.M. and Lord Mountbatten delivered the inaugural speech. The whole city was in a state of tumultuous joy. Even the pangs of partition were for the moment forgotten. Millions from the city and the surrounding countryside assembled to hail the advent of freedom. The flag of free India was to be hoisted at 4:00 P.M. In spite of the burning August sun, millions gathered and in fact had been waiting in the gruelling heat for hours. The crowd was so great that Lord Mountbatten could not get out of his car at all and had to make his speech from it.

The joy was almost delirious but lasted hardly forty-eight hours. The very next day news of communal troubles began to cast deep gloom in the capital. It was the news of murder, death and cruelty. It was learnt that in the East Punjab, Hindu and Sikh mobs had attacked Moslem villages. They were burning houses and killing innocent men, women and children. Exactly the same reports came from the West Punjab. Moslems there were killing indiscriminately men, women and children of the Hindu and the Sikh communities. The whole of the Punjab, East and West, was becoming a graveyard of destruction and death. Events followed in quick succession. One East Punjab minister after another came rushing up to Delhi. They were followed by local Congress leaders who were outside the Government. All of them were horrified by the developments that were taking place. They were also stunned by the magnitude of the carnage and said in despair that perhaps nothing could stop it. We asked them why they had not called upon the military. In despair they said that the troops stationed in the Punjab were no longer reliable and not much help could be expected from them. They demanded that military help should immediately be sent to the Punjab from Delhi.

There were no disturbances in Delhi in the beginning, but with the country all round aflame with such a murderous upheaval, it was not possible to deplete the small military reserve held in Delhi. We decided to send for troops from outside but, before they could arrive, trouble reached the capital. As news of murders in the Punjab

was followed by the trickle of refugees who were coming away
from the West Punjab, violence broke out in Delhi. Murder stalked
the town. Trouble was not confined to the refugees or even to the
general public. Even the areas where only Government servants
lived were involved. When the reports of massacres in the West
Punjab reached Delhi, Moslems in the city were attacked by mobs
of unruly men. Some Sikhs took a leading part in organizing these
murderous attacks in Delhi.

I have already said how much I had been disturbed by loose talk
of the dangerous doctrine of reprisals and hostages. In Delhi we
now had a gruesome application of that doctrine. If the Moslems of
the West Punjab were guilty of the murder of Hindus and Sikhs,
why should there be retaliation on innocent Moslems in Delhi?
This theory of hostages and reprisals is so atrocious that no sane or
decent human being can say a word in its defence.

The attitude of the Army now became a critical issue. Before
partition, the Army had been free from communal hatred. When
the country was divided on a communal basis, the communal virus
entered the Army. The majority of troops in Delhi were Hindus and
Sikhs. In a few days it became clear that it might prove too great
a strain on them if strong action was to be taken for the restoration
of law and order in the city. We therefore took measures to bring
more soldiers from the South. They had not been affected by the
partition of the country and retained their sense of soldierly discipline. The soldiers of the South played a great part in bringing the
situation under control and restoring order in the capital.

Apart from the city proper, there were suburbs such as Karolbagh,
Lodhi Colony, Subzi Mandi and Sadar Bazar, which had a large
Moslem population. In all these areas, life and property were no
longer safe. Nor was it possible in the existing circumstances to
provide them with complete military protection. At one stage, the
situation in these areas became so bad that no Moslem householder
could go to sleep at night with the confidence that he would be
alive next morning.

During these days of arson, murder and rioting, I toured different parts of Delhi in the company of army officers. I found the Moslems completely demoralized and suffering from a sense of utter helplessness. Many asked for shelter in my house. Rich and well-known families of the city came to me completely destitute and with no earthly possessions left except the clothes they were wearing. Some did not dare to come by daylight and were brought under military protection at midnight or in the early hours of the morning. My house was soon full and I put up tents in my compound. Men and women of all kinds and condition—rich and poor, young and old— huddled together in sheer fear of death.

It soon became clear that it would take some time before law and order could be restored. It was not possible to protect isolated houses in different parts of the city. If we arranged for guards in one area, the attack started elsewhere. We therefore decided that Moslems should be brought together and placed in protected camps. One such camp was established at the Purana Qila or the old Fort. It has no building left but only the bastions. These were soon full. A large number of Moslems were assembled in the Fort and lived in these bastions throughout almost the whole of the winter.

Several special magistrates were appointed during these disturbances to maintain law and order and restore peace. I regret to say that the selections were not always very happy and that some of these magistrates failed in their duty. I remember distinctly the case of one magistrate to whom a Hindu member of the Congress came for help. He reported that there was danger of attack on a Moslem locality and some Moslem families were living in fear of death. This magistrate, instead of taking necessary action, accused the Congressman of what he called his lack of feeling. He said he was surprised that a Hindu should come out to help Moslems.

This incident is revealing of the way different people reacted to the crisis. Some of the special magistrates and a few Congressmen failed but the majority of Congressmen in Delhi rose to great heights during these difficult times. Hindu as well as Sikh members of the Congress stood steadfast and remained true to the principles of nationalism in spite of the taunts and insults of their communal-minded coreligionists.

I have criticized Lord Mountbatten for the way in which he helped to bring about partition. I must now pay him a tribute for the manner in which he handled the crisis which faced us. I have already referred to the energy and vigor with which he carried out the intricate and difficult task of partitioning India. He now acted with even greater vigor and energy to restore law and order in the country. His military training now stood us in very good stead. Without his leadership and experience of military tactics, it is doubtful if we could have got over the difficulties with such expedition and efficiency. He said that it was a war situation and must be treated as such. During war, war councils work round the clock. We must also set up a Council of Action which would take decisions on the spot and see that the decisions were carried out. An Emergency Board was set up, consisting of some members of the Cabinet and some high civil and military officers. The Board met daily at 9:30 A.M. in the Cabinet Room of the Government. Lord Mountbatten presided. We reviewed the orders given during the last twenty-four hours and the action taken. This Board worked without a break till peace was fully restored. The reports which came to the Board every morning gave us an insight into the dangers of the situation.

One of the first signs of a true administrator is that he can rise above personal likes and dislikes and guarantee security of life and property to all. During the terrible days of 1946 and 1947, Jawaharlal displayed in a signal manner these qualities of a true administrator. From the first day that he joined Government, he realized that the State must not discriminate between citizens and that it must treat Hindus and Moslems, Sikhs and Christians, Parsees and Buddhists equally. Whoever was an Indian citizen had equal claims in the eye of the law.

The first evidence of his quality as an administrator was seen in 1946. The Calcutta killings had been followed by riots in Noakhali, where Hindus had suffered greatly. The Hindus of Bihar then attacked local Moslems in retaliation for the Noakhali riots and widespread disturbances broke out throughout the province. The Provincial Government found it difficult to cope with the situation and the Government of India had to take strong action. I was then staying in Patna for almost two weeks and was impressed by the firmness and strength with which Jawaharlal sought to check these attacks on life and property. All of us were working to the same end, but there can be no denying that the most effective part in this task was played by Jawaharlal Nehru.

During the whole of this period, Gandhiji was living in terrible mental anguish. He strained every nerve to restore good feeling between the communities and to secure the life and property of Moslems. It caused him great distress and suffering to find that his efforts did not meet with the expected success. Often he sent for Jawaharlal, Sardar Patel and me and asked us to describe the situation in the city. It added to his distress when he found that there were differences among us even regarding what was actually happening.

The truth is that there was a difference of attitude between Sardar Patel on the one hand and Jawaharlal and me on the other. This was affecting local administration and it was becoming clear that the officers were divided into two groups. The larger group looked up to Sardar Patel as Home Minister and acted in a way which they thought would please him. A smaller group looked to Jawaharlal and me and tried to carry out Jawaharlal's orders. The Chief Commissioner of Delhi was a Moslem officer, Khurshed Ahmed, son of Sahebzada Aftab Ahmed. He was not a strong officer. In addition, he was afraid that if he took strong action he might be regarded as favoring the Moslems. The result was that he was only the nominal head of the administration and all action was being taken by the Deputy Commissioner on his own initiative. This was an officer who was a Sikh but did not follow many of the Sikh customs and conventions. He had shaved off his beard and cut his hair and many Sikhs regarded him as almost a heretic. He had been Deputy Commissioner in Delhi even before partition, and some time

before 15 August there was a suggestion that, since he had served
his term, he might be returned to the Punjab. Many leading citizens
of Delhi, especially a large section of Moslems, represented strongly
against this proposal. They said that he was a fair-minded and
strong officer, and that during these difficult days it would be hard
to find suitable replacement.

The Deputy Commissioner was accordingly retained, but it
seems that under the stress of the communal tension which was
sweeping through the Punjab he could not maintain his former
attitude. I received many reports that he was not taking sufficiently
strong or effective action against the miscreants. The very Moslems
who a year ago had pleaded for his retention now came and said
that he was not giving the necessary protection to the Moslem
citizens of Delhi. This was reported to Sardar Patel but he paid
hardly any attention to such complaints.

Sardar Patel was the Home Minister, and as such the Delhi administration was directly under him. As the lists of murder and arson
grew longer, Gandhiji sent for Patel and asked him what he was
doing to stop the carnage. Sardar Patel tried to reassure him by
saying that the reports which he was receiving were grossly exaggerated. In fact Patel went to the extent of saying that the Moslems
had no cause for complaint or fear. I distinctly remember one
occasion when the three of us were sitting with Gandhiji. Jawaharlal
said with deep sorrow that he could not tolerate the situation in
Delhi, where Moslem citizens were being killed like cats and dogs.
He felt humiliated that he was helpless and could not save them.
His conscience would not let him rest, for what answer could he
give when people complained of these terrible happenings? Jawaharlal repeated several times that he found the situation intolerable
and that his conscience would not let him rest.

We were completely taken aback by Sardar Patel's reaction. At
a time when Moslems were being murdered in Delhi in open
daylight, he calmly told Gandhiji that Jawaharlal's complaints were
completely incomprehensible. There may have been some isolated
incidents, but Government was doing everything possible to protect

the life and property of Moslems and nothing more could be done. In fact he gave vent to his dissatisfaction that Jawaharlal as the Prime Minister should express disapproval of what his Government was doing.

Jawaharlal remained speechless for some moments and then turned to Gandhiji in despair. He said that, if these were Sardar Patel's views, he had no comments to make.

Another incident which occurred about this time revealed clearly how Sardar Patel's mind was working. He may have felt that some explanation was necessary for the attacks on Moslems which were taking place every day. Accordingly he put out the theory that deadly weapons had been recovered from the Moslem quarters of the city. His suggestion was that the Moslems of Delhi had collected arms in order to attack the Hindus and the Sikhs, and, if the Hindus and the Sikhs had not taken the first offensive, the Moslems would have destroyed them. The police did recover some arms from Karolbagh and Subzi Mandi. By Sardar Patel's orders, these were brought to the Government House and kept for our inspection in the antechamber of the Cabinet Room. When we assembled for our daily meeting, Sardar Patel said that we should first go to the antechamber and inspect the captured arms. On our arrival we found on the table dozens of kitchen knives that were rusted, pocketknives and penknives, with or without handles and iron spikes which had been recovered from the fences of old houses and some cast-iron water pipes. According to Sardar Patel, these were the weapons which the Moslems of Delhi had collected in order to exterminate the Hindus and the Sikhs. Lord Mountbatten took up one or two of the knives and said with a smile that those who had collected this material seemed to have a wonderful idea of military tactics if they thought that the city of Delhi could be captured with them.

I have already said that the large majority of Moslems of the city had been collected in the Purana Qila. Winter was now approaching. Thousands who lived under the open sky suffered terribly from the cold. There were no proper arrangements for food or drinking water. What was worse, the conservancy arrangements were either nonexistent or thoroughly inadequate. One morning, Dr. Zakir Husain gave evidence before the Emergency Board and described the terrible conditions in the old Fort. He said that these poor men and women had been rescued from sudden death to be buried in a living grave. The Board asked me to inspect the arrangements and suggest necessary measures. At its next meeting, the Board decided that immediate arrangements should be made for drinking water and sanitation. The Army was also asked to lend as many tents as possible, so that the people could at least live under canvas.

Gandhiji's distress was increasing every day. Formerly, the whole nation had responded to his slightest wish. Now it seemed that his most fervent appeals were falling on deaf ears. At last he could no longer tolerate this state of affairs and sent for me to say that he had no weapon left but to fast till peace was restored in Delhi. When it became known that Gandhiji would fast until peace and order were restored in Delhi, many who had till then remained inactive were shamed into action. They felt that at his age and his state of health, he must be prevented from undergoing the fast. They appealed to him to give up the idea but he remained adamant.

One thing which weighed heavily on Gandhiji's mind was the attitude of Sardar Patel. Sardar Patel belonged to Gandhiji's inner circle, and was very dear to him. In fact, Sardar Patel owed his entire political existence to Gandhiji. Among the important leaders of the Congress, many had had a political life even before Gandhiji appeared on the scene. There were, however, two, Sardar Patel and Dr. Rajendra Prasad, who were entirely the creation of Gandhiji. Before the Noncooperation Movement, Sardar Patel was one of the many lawyers of Gujerat with hardly any interest or place in the public life of the country. When Gandhiji settled in Ahmedabad, he picked out Patel and step by step built him up. Patel became his wholehearted supporter and I have already mentioned how, on many occasions, he merely echoed Gandhiji's wishes. It was Gandhiji who made him a member of the Congress Working Committee. Again, it was because of Gandhiji that he became President of the

Congress in 1931. It hurt Gandhiji deeply that Patel should now be following a policy which was quite contrary to everything for which he himself stood.

Gandhiji said that he saw Moslems of Delhi being killed before his very eyes. This was being done while his own Vallabhbhai was the Home Member of the Government of India and was responsible for maintaining law and order in the capital. Patel had not only failed to give protection to Moslems, but he lightheartedly dismissed any complaint made on this account. Gandhiji said that he had now no option but to use his last weapon, namely, to fast until the situation changed. Accordingly, he began his fast on 12 January 1948. In a sense, the fast was directed against the attitude of Sardar Patel and Patel knew that this was so.

We had done our best to dissuade Gandhiji from undertaking his fast. On the evening of the first day's fast Jawaharlal, Sardar Patel and I were sitting by Gandhiji's side. Sardar Patel was leaving for Bombay the next morning. He spoke to Gandhiji in a formal manner and complained that Gandhiji was fasting without any justification. He also complained that there was no real reason for such a fast. In fact, his fast would lead to charges against the Government and particularly against Sardar Patel. He said in some bitterness that Gandhiji was acting as if Sardar Patel was responsible for the murder of the Moslems.

Gandhiji replied in his usual calm manner, "I am not in China now but in Delhi. Nor have I lost my eyes and ears. If you ask me to disbelieve the testimony of my own eyes and ears, and tell me that Moslems have no cause for complaint, I surely cannot convince you nor can you convince me. Hindus and Sikhs are my brothers. They are flesh of my flesh and, if they are now blind with rage, I will not blame them. I must, however, expiate through my own suffering and I hope that my fast will open their eyes to real facts."

Sardar Patel got up without a word and made as if he would go away. I stopped him and said that he should cancel his program and stay on in Delhi. Nobody could say what turn events might take and he should not leave while Gandhiji was fasting.

Patel almost shouted back, "What is the use of my staying? Gandhiji is not prepared to listen to me. He seems determined to blacken the names of the Hindus before the whole world. If this is his attitude, I have no use for him. I can't change my program and I must go to Bombay."

Sardar Patel's tone even more than his words deeply grieved me. What, I thought, would be their effect on Gandhiji? We felt that it was useless saying anything more and Patel left.

Sardar Patel had hardened his heart against Gandhiji, but not so the people of Delhi. The moment it was known that he had started his fast, not only the city but the whole of India was deeply stirred. In Delhi the effect was electric. Groups which had till recently openly opposed Gandhiji came forward and said that they would be prepared to do anything in order to save Gandhiji's precious life.

Different people came and told Gandhiji that they would work to bring peace back to Delhi, but Gandhiji was not influenced by their words. Two days of feverish activity passed. On the third day, a public meeting was called to consider the situation and to devise measures so that Gandhiji could be persuaded to give up his fast.

I went to Gandhiji on my way to the meeting. I said that he should lay down conditions for breaking his fast. We would then place them before the people and say that, provided he was satisfied on these points, he would give up his fast.

Gandhiji said, "This is talking business. My first condition is that all Moslems who have been compelled to leave Delhi because of these attacks by Hindus and Sikhs would be invited to come back and they must be resettled in their own homes."

This was a fine and noble gesture, but I knew it was not a practical proposition. After partition, life in both the Punjabs had been disrupted. Millions of refugees had come to India from West Punjab and millions had left East Punjab for Pakistan. Thousands had left Delhi and many of the refugees from West Punjab had occupied the houses which were left vacant by Moslems. If it had been a

matter of a few hundreds, perhaps Gandhiji's wishes could have
been carried out. When the men and women involved ran into tens
of thousands, any attempt to carry out Gandhiji's wishes would
only have created fresh problems. Hindus and Sikhs who had come
away from West Punjab had been uprooted once but they had now
found some kind of home in Delhi. If they were asked to vacate
their present houses, where would they go? Besides, the Moslems
who had left Delhi for Pakistan were probably scattered in different
places. How could they be brought back? Moslems could not be
brought back nor could Hindus and Sikhs be asked to leave the
houses they were occupying. To try for such a settlement would
in fact mean that, in place of the first eviction which had driven
out Moslems, we would now have a second to drive out Hindus and
Sikhs.

I caught hold of Gandhiji's hands and pleaded with him that he
should give up this point. It would be neither practical nor perhaps
morally justifiable to ask Hindus and Sikhs who had now found a
home in Delhi to become wanderers once again. I appealed to him
not to insist on this point but to lay down as his first condition that
murder and arson should immediately cease. He could also insist
that Moslems who were still in India should be able to live in honor
and peace and that friendly relations should be restored among all
the communities. At first Gandhiji would not agree and kept insisting on his own conditions. Finally, however, he relented and said
that, if the conditions I had suggested satisfied me, he also would
accept them. I thanked him for his consideration for my views and
begged him to accept my suggestions.

Gandhiji then suggested that Moslem shrines and places of wor-
ship which had been broken or violated should be restored and
repaired. The occupation of such places by non-Moslems was a
cause of terror for Moslems. Gandhiji wanted an assurance that
there would be no recurrence of any attack on such places sacred
to any community.

Gandhiji then dictated his conditions for giving up the fast. They
were as follows:—

1. Hindus and Sikhs must forthwith stop all attacks against Muslims and must reassure Muslims that they would live together as brothers.

2. Hindus and Sikhs would make every effort to ensure that not one Muslim should leave India because of insecurity of life and property.

3. Attacks which were taking place on Muslims in moving trains must forthwith stop and Hindus and Sikhs who were taking part in such attacks must be prevented from doing so.

4. Muslims who lived near the shrines and Dargahs like Nizamuddin Aulia, Khwaja Qutubuddin Bakhtiar Kaki and Nasiruddin Chiragh Dehlvi had left their homes in distress. They must be brought back to their own locality and re-settled.

5. The Dargah Qutubuddin Bakhtiar had been damaged. Government could of course restore and repair the shrine but this would not satisfy Gandhiji. He insisted that the restoration and repairs must be done by Hindus and Sikhs as an act of atonement.

6. Most important of all was the need for a change of heart. Fulfilment of the other conditions was not so important as this. Leaders of the Hindu and the Sikh communities must reassure Gandhiji on this point so that he would not have to fast again on such an issue.

"Let this be my last fast," he said.

I assured Gandhiji that these points could be met. I came to the meeting at 2:00 P.M. and placed the conditions before the audience. I told them that we had met to reassure Gandhiji and to request him to give up his fast. Mere resolutions would not move him, but, if the people of Delhi wanted to save his life, the conditions he had laid down must be fulfilled. I had come to find out if the people of Delhi would give him that assurance.

There were about 50,000 men and women present at the meeting. With one voice they shouted, "We shall carry out Gandhiji's wishes to the letter. We shall pledge our life and heart and shall not give him any cause for distress."

I was still speaking when various people copied out the conditions and began to secure signatures from the audience. Before the meeting was over, thousands had signed the document. The Deputy Commissioner of Delhi collected a group of Hindu and Sikh leaders and left for the shrine of Khwaja Qutubuddin to repair the damage. Simultaneously, several societies working in Delhi took a public pledge that they would work in their own circles for the fulfilment of Gandhiji's conditions. In fact, they declared that they would take the responsibility for the conditions being carried out. By the evening, I had received deputations from all parties and groups and from every quarter of Delhi assuring me that they accepted Gandhiji's conditions and urging me to request Gandhiji to give up his fast.

Next morning, I called a meeting of representative leaders of Delhi. We came to the decision that they should all go to Birla House and give their personal assurance to Gandhiji. I reached Birla House at about ten and told Gandhiji that I was now fully satisfied that his object had been fulfilled. His fast had changed the hearts of thousands and brought back to them the sense of justice and humanity. Thousands had now pledged themselves to regard the maintenance of good relations among the communities as their first task. I appealed to Gandhiji to accept the assurance and give up his fast.

Gandhiji was obviously pleased but he did not yet accede to our request. The day passed in discussion and persuasion. He had lost strength and weight and was unable to sit up. He was lying flat in his bed but he listened to every deputation which came and tried to assess how far there was a genuine change of heart. Finally he said that he would give his reply the next morning.

We all assembled in his room next day at ten o'clock. Jawaharlal was already there. Among others who came was Zahid Husain, the High Commissioner of Pakistan, who had asked for permission to see him. Gandhiji sent for him and he joined the gathering, which included the whole Cabinet except Sardar Patel. Gandhiji made a sign to indicate that those who wanted to repeat their pledge to him should do so. About twenty-five leaders of Delhi, including all schools of political thought among Hindus and Sikhs, came up one by one and vowed that they would faithfully carry out the conditions laid down by Gandhiji. He then made a sign and the men and women of his circle started to sing the *Ramdhun*. His granddaughter brought a glass of orange juice and he made a sign that she should hand the glass to me. I held the glass to his lips and Gandhiji broke his fast.

After Gandhiji began his fast, Mr. Arthur Moore, formerly editor of the *Statesman,* also began to fast in the Imperial Hotel. The Hindu-Moslem riots had moved him deeply. He told me that if the troubles did not end, he had also decided to fast unto death. He had been in India many years and adopted it as his country. As an Indian, he regarded it as his duty to put a stop to the human misery and degradation which was taking place. Death, he said, was preferable to the terrible tragedy which had overtaken India. I now sent him a message that Gandhiji had broken his fast and that he should do the same.

Even after Gandhiji broke his fast, it took several days before he slowly regained his strength. Sardar Patel returned from Bombay and went to see him. I was also present. Gandhiji's greatness never shone more clearly than on such occasions. He received Patel with great affection and kindness. There was not a trace of resentment or anger in his mien. Patel was obviously uncomfortable and his behavior was still dry and formal. He was not pleased with Gandhiji and did not approve of what Gandhiji had done in order to restore a sense of security among the Moslems.

Sardar Patel was not alone in this attitude towards Gandhiji's fast. In fact a group of Hindus had been bitter against Gandhiji ever since he had started his peace move. Their resentment increased day by day. They openly condemned him for giving away what they called the legitimate interests of Hindus. This was no secret and was widely known throughout the country. A section of Hindus under the leadership of the Mahasabha and the Rashtriya Svayam Sevak Sangh went about saying openly that Gandhiji was helping Moslems against Hindus. They organized opposition even to his prayer meetings, where, under Gandhiji's instructions, verses from the Quran and the Bible were read along with the Hindu scriptures. Some of these men organized an agitation against his prayer meetings and said that they would not allow the recitation of verses from the Quran or the Bible. Pamphlets and handbills were distributed to this effect. People were also incited against Gandhiji by propaganda that described him as the enemy of the Hindus. One pamphlet went so far as to say that, if Gandhiji did not change his ways, steps should be taken to neutralize him.

Gandhiji's fast had further exasperated this group. They now decided to take action against him. Soon after he resumed his prayer meetings, a bomb was thrown at him. Fortunately nobody was hurt, but people all over India were shocked that anybody should raise his hand against Gandhiji. Police started their investigations and it seemed very strange that they could not find out who planted the bomb and how they had succeeded in entering the garden of Birla House. It was also strange that adequate steps were not taken even after this incident to protect his life. The attack made it clear that, however small in number, there was a determined group that was trying to kill Gandhiji. It was therefore natural to expect that the police and the C.I.D. of Delhi should take special measures for Gandhiji's protection. To our eternal shame and sorrow I have to say that the most elementary precautionary measures were not taken even after this warning.

A few more days passed. As Gandhiji slowly regained his strength, he again started addressing the gathering after the prayers were over. Thousands used to attend these prayers and he felt that it was one of the most effective ways of carrying his message to the people.

On 30 January 1948, I went to Gandhiji at 2:30 P.M. There were several important things I had to discuss and I sat with him for over an hour. I then returned home but at about 5:30 I suddenly remembered that there were some important points on which I had not taken his advice. I went back to Birla House and to my surprise found that the gates were closed. Thousands were standing on the lawn and the crowd had overflowed into the street. I could not understand what was the matter, but they all made way when they saw my car. I got down near the gate and walked up to the house. The doors of the house were also bolted. An inmate saw me through the glass pane and came out to take me in. As I was entering, someone said in tears, "Gandhiji has been shot and is lying senseless."

The news was so shocking and unexpected that I could hardly comprehend the meaning of the words. I had a dazed feeling and walked up to Gandhiji's room. He was lying on the floor. His face was pale and his eyes were closed. His two grandsons held his feet and were weeping. I heard as if in a dream, "Gandhiji is dead."

CHAPTER 18

Epilogue

GANDHIJI'S assassination marked the end of an era. I cannot to this day forget how miserably we had failed in protecting the life of the greatest son of modern India. After the incident of the bomb, it was natural to expect that the police and the C.I.D. of Delhi should take special precautions for his protection. If an attempt is made on the life of even a common man, the police take special care. This is done even when threatening letters or pamphlets are received. In Gandhiji's case there were not only letters, pamphlets and public threats, but a bomb had actually been thrown. It was the question of the life of the greatest personality of contemporary India and yet no effective measures were taken. It was not that such measures were difficult. The prayer meetings were not held in an open field, but on the lawns of Birla House. This was a place surrounded on all sides by walls. Nobody could enter it except through the gate. It was the easiest thing for the police to check people as they came in or went out.

After the tragedy it was clear from the evidence of the spectators that the murderer had entered in a most suspicious way. His actions and words were such that the C.I.D. could and should have kept him under observation. If the police had taken any action, he could have been discovered and disarmed. He came with a revolver without any check. When Gandhiji had reached the prayer meeting, he got up and accosted Gandhiji, saying "You are late today." Gandhiji replied, "Yes." Before he could say another word, the three shots were fired which put an end to his precious life.

There was naturally a wave of anger once the tragedy had taken place. Some people openly accused Sardar Patel of inefficiency. Jai Prakash Narain showed considerable courage in raising this issue. In the meeting which was held in Delhi to express our sense of horror and sorrow at Gandhiji's death, he said clearly that the Home Minister of the Government of India could not escape the responsibility for this assassination. He demanded an explanation from Sardar Patel as to why no special measures had been taken where there was open propaganda inciting people to murder Gandhiji and a bomb had actually been thrown at him.

Dr. Profulla Chandra Ghosh of Calcutta raised the same issue. He also condemned the Government of India for its failure to save Gandhiji's life. He pointed out that Sardar Patel was reputed to be a strong and efficient Home Minister. How could he then explain why no effort had been made for the saving of Gandhiji's life?

Sardar Patel met these charges in his own characteristic way. He was no doubt deeply shocked, but he also resented the way in which people were openly accusing him. When the Congress Parliamentary party met, he said that enemies of the Congress were trying to divide the organization by bringing these charges against him. He reiterated his loyalty to Gandhiji and said that the party should not be affected by these charges but should stand firm and undivided in the dangerous situation which had been created by Gandhiji's death. His appeal was not without effect. Many members of the Congress party assured him that they would stand by him.

Isolated incidents in various parts of the country showed how widely the poison of communalism had spread in recent times. The country as a whole was overwhelmingly moved by the assassination, but in a few towns people distributed sweets and held celebrations as a mark of joy. This was said especially of the towns of Gwalior and Ujjain. I was shocked when I heard that, in both these towns, sweets were openly distributed and that some people had the impudence to rejoice publicly. Their joy was, however, short-lived. The nation as a whole was overwhelmed with grief and the wrath of the people turned against all who were supposed to be Gandhiji's enemies.

For two or three weeks after the tragedy, the leaders of the Hindu Mahasabha or the R.S.S. could not come out and face the public. Dr. Shyama Prasad Mookerjee was then President of the Hindu Mahasbha and a Minister in the Central Government. He dared not come out of his house and after some time resigned from the Mahasabha. Slowly, however, the situation improved and after some time the people settled down.

Godse,[1] the murderer, was prosecuted, but it took a long time to build up the case against him. The police took several months to make enquiries as it appeared that there had been a farflung conspiracy to murder Gandhiji. The public reaction to Godse's arrest offered an indication of how some Indians had been affected by the communal poison. The vast majority of Indians condemned Godse and compared him to Judas but some women from respectable families sent him a sweater they had knitted for him. There was also a movement for his release. His supporters did not openly defend his action. They said that since Gandhiji was a believer in non-violence, his murderer should not be executed. Telegrams were sent to Jawaharlal and me that the execution of Godse would be against Gandhiji's principles. The law, however, took its own course and the High Court confirmed his sentence.

Hardly two months had passed since Gandhiji's death when Sardar Patel had a heart attack. My own reading is that this was the result of the shock he had received. So long as Gandhiji was alive, Patel's anger against him remained. When Gandhiji was murdered and people openly accused Sardar Patel of neglect or inefficiency, he felt deep shock and humiliation. Besides, he could not forget that he owed everything to Gandhiji. Gandhiji's unfailing affection and consideration for Patel must have also made the situation more painful to him. All these worked on his mind and troubled him till he was attacked with thrombosis. He lived for some four more years, but never regained his health.

[1] Nathuram Vinayak Godse, then 35, editor of a Hindu Mahasabha (Hindu communal) weekly in Poona. After an extended public trial, Godse was sentenced to death and executed.

Thus India gained her freedom but lost her unity. A new state named Pakistan was called into being. Pakistan was the creation of the Moslem League. Naturally the Moslem League party became the dominant power in this new state. I have already described how the Moslem League was originally founded to oppose the Congress. The League therefore had hardly any members who had fought for the independence of the country. They had neither made any sacrifice nor gone through the discipline of a struggle. They were either retired officials, or men who had been brought into public life under British patronage. The result was that, when the new state was formed, power came into the hands of people who had no record of service or sacrifice. Many of the rulers of the new state were selfish people who had come into public life only for the sake of personal interest.

A majority of the leaders of the new state came from the U.P., Bihar and Bombay. In most cases, they could not even speak the language of the areas which now formed Pakistan. There was thus a gulf between the rulers and the ruled in the new state. These self-imposed leaders feared that, if free elections were held, most of them had very little chance of even being returned. Their aim therefore was to postpone the elections as long as possible and to build up their fortunes and their power in the country. Ten years have passed and it is only recently that a constitution has been framed. Even this does not seem final, for every now and then there are proposals for further changes in it. Nobody yet knows if and when the first elections under the new constitution will be held.

The only result of the creation of Pakistan was to weaken the position of the Moslems in the subcontinent of India. The 35 million Moslems who have remained in India have been weakened. On the other hand, there is as yet no indication that a strong and efficient government can be established in Pakistan. If one judges the question only from the point of view of the Moslem community, can anybody deny today that Pakistan has been for them a very unfortunate and unhappy development? In fact, the more I think about it the more I am convinced that the creation of Pakistan has solved no problem. One may argue that the relations between Hindus and Moslems had become so estranged in India that there was no alternative to partition. This view was held by most of the supporters of the Moslem League and after partition many of the Congress leaders have held a similar view. Whenever I discussed the question with Jawaharlal or Sardar Patel after partition, this was the argument they gave in support of their decision. If, however, we think the matter over coolly, we shall find that their analysis is not correct. I am convinced that the scheme I framed on the occasion of the Cabinet Mission, and which the Mission largely accepted, was a far better solution from every point of view. If we had remained steadfast and refused to accept partition, I am confident that a safer and more glorious future would have awaited us.

Can anyone deny that the creation of Pakistan has not solved the communal problem, but made it more intense and harmful? The basis of partition was enmity between Hindus and Moslems. The creation of Pakistan gave it a permanent constitutional form and made it much more difficult of solution. The most regrettable feature of this situation is that the subcontinent of India is divided into two states, which look at one another with hatred and fear. Pakistan believes that India will not allow her to rest in peace and will destroy her whenever she has an opportunity. Similarly India thinks that whenever Pakistan gets an opportunity, she will move against India and attack her. This has led both the states to increase their defence expenditure. After the war, undivided India spent only about a hundred crores for defence. Lord Wavell himself held that a hundred would suffice for the three wings of the Defence Forces. Then came partition. One-fourth of the undivided army went to Pakistan. In spite of this India has to spend over 200 crores for the maintenance of her defence forces. Of the revenues of the Government of India, about a third goes to meet the expenses of defence. Pakistan's position is if anything worse. In spite of the fact that she has only one-fourth of the territories and armies of India, she is spending at least 100 crores from her own revenues besides the aid she gets from the United States. If we pause to think, we shall realize what a great national wastage all this involves. If this fund could be used for economic development, the progress of the country would be greatly accelerated.

Mr. Jinnah and his followers did not seem to realize that geography was against them. Moslems in undivided India were distributed in a way which made it impossible to form a separate state in a consolidated area. The Moslem majority areas were on the northwest and the northeast. These two regions have no point of physical contact. People in these two areas are completely different from one another in every respect, except only in religion. It is one of the greatest frauds on the people to suggest that religious affinity can unite areas which are geographically, economically, linguistically and culturally different. It is true that Islam sought to establish a society which transcends racial, linguistic, economic and political frontiers. History has, however, proved that after the first few decades, or at most after the first century, Islam was not able to unite all the Moslem countries into one state on the basis of Islam alone.

This was the position in the past and this is the position today. No one can hope that East and West Pakistan will compose all their differences and form one nation. Even within West Pakistan, the three provinces of Sind, the Punjab and the Frontier have internal incompatibility and are working for separate aims and interests. Nevertheless the die is cast. The new State of Pakistan is a fact. It is to the interest of India and Pakistan that they should develop friendly relations and act in cooperation with one another. Any other course of action can lead only to greater trouble, suffering and misfortune. Some people hold that what has happened was inevitable. Others equally strongly believe that what has happened is wrong and could have been avoided. We cannot say today which reading is correct. History alone will decide whether we have acted wisely and correctly in accepting partition.

26 *January* 1958

Appendix

SIR STAFFORD CRIPPS issued the following Draft Declaration on behalf of the British Government:

His Majesty's Government having considered the anxieties expressed in this country and in India as to the fulfilment of promises made in regard to the future of India, have decided to lay down in precise and clear terms the steps which they propose shall be taken for the earliest possible realization of self-government in India. The object is the creation of a new Indian Union which shall constitute a Dominion associated with the United Kingdom and other Dominions by a common allegiance to the Crown but equal to them in every respect, in no way subordinate in any aspect of its domestic and external affairs.

His Majesty's Government therefore make the following declaration:

(a) Immediately upon cessation of hostilities, steps shall be taken to set up in India in manner described hereafter an elected body charged with the task of framing a new Constitution for India.

(b) Provision shall be made, as set out below for participation of Indian States in the constitution-making body.

(c) His Majesty's Government undertake to accept and implement forthwith the constitution so framed subject only to (i) The right of any province of British India that is not prepared to accept the new constitution to retain its present constitutional position provision being made for its subsequent accession if it so decides.

With such non-acceding provinces, should they so desire, His Majesty's Government will be prepared to agree upon a new constitution giving them the same full status as the Indian Union and arrived at by a procedure analogous to that here laid down.

(ii) The signing of a treaty which shall be negotiated between His Majesty's Government and the constitution-making body. This treaty will cover all necessary matters arising out of the complete transfer of responsibility from British to Indian hands; it will make provision, in accordance with undertakings given by His Majesty's Government for the protection of racial and religious minorities; but will not impose any restriction on the power of the Indian Union to decide in future its relationship to other member States of the British Commonwealth.

267

Whether or not an Indian State elects to adhere to the constitution it will be necessary to negotiate a revision of its treaty arrangements so far as this may be required in the new situation.

(d) The constitution-making body shall be composed as follows unless the leaders of Indian opinion in the principal communities agree upon some other form before the end of hostilities.

Immediately upon the result being known of provincial elections which will be necessary at the end of hostilities, the entire membership of the Lower Houses of Provincial legislatures shall as a single electoral college proceed to the election of the constitution-making body by the system of proportional representation. This new body shall be in number about 1/10th of the number of the electoral college.

Indian States shall be invited to appoint representatives in the same proportion as to their total population as in the case of representatives of British India as a whole and with the same powers as British Indian members.

(e) During the critical period which now faces India and until the new constitution can be framed His Majesty's Government must inevitably bear the responsibility for and retain the control and direction of the Defence of India as part of their world war effort but the task of organizing to the full the military, moral and material resources of India must be the responsibility of the Government of India with the co-operation of the peoples of India. His Majesty's Government desire and invite the immediate and effective participation of the leaders of the principal sections of the Indian people in the counsels of their country, of the Commonwealth and of the United Nations. Thus they will be enabled to give their active and constructive help in the discharge of a task which is vital and essential for the future freedom of India.

CORRESPONDENCE WITH SIR STAFFORD CRIPPS

Birla Park
New Delhi, April 10, 1942

Dear Sir Stafford,

On the 2nd April I sent you the resolution of the Working Committee of the Congress containing their views on the tentative proposals put forward by you on behalf of the British Government. In this resolution we expressed our dissent from several important and far-reaching proposals for the future. Further consideration of these proposals has only strengthened us in our conviction in regard to them, and we should like to repeat that we cannot accept them as suggested. The Working Committee's resolution gives expression to our conclusions relating to them which we reached after the most earnest consideration.

That resolution, however, emphasized the gravity of the present situation and stated that the ultimate decision that we might take would be governed by the changes made in the present. The over-riding problem before all of us, and more especially before all Indians, is the defence of the country from aggression and invasion. The future, important as it is, will depend on what happens in the next few months and years. We were therefore prepared to do without any assurances for this uncertain future, hoping that through our sacrifices in the defence of our country we would lay the solid and enduring foundations for a free and independent India. We concentrated, therefore, on the present.

Your original proposals in regard to the present, as contained in clause (e) of the proposed declaration were vague and incomplete, except in so far as it was made clear that "His Majesty's Government must inevitably bear the full responsibility for the defence of India." These proposals, in effect, asked for participation in the tasks of today with a view to ensure the "future freedom of India." Freedom was for an uncertain future, not for the present; and no indication was given in clause (e) of what arrangements or governmental and other changes would be made in the present. When this vagueness was pointed out, you said that this was deliberate, so as to give you freedom to determine these changes in consultation with others. In our talks you gave us to understand that you envisaged a National Government which would deal with all matters except Defence.

Defence at any time, and more particularly in wartime, is of essential importance and without it a National Government functions in a very limited field. Apart from this consideration it was obvious that the whole purpose of your proposals and our talks centred round the urgency of the problems created by the threat of the invasion of India. The chief functions of a National Government must necessarily be to organize Defence both intensively and on the widest popular basis and to a create a mass psychology of resistance to an invader. Only a National Government on whom this responsibility was laid could do that. Popular resistance must have a national background and both the soldier and the civilian must feel that they are fighting for their country's freedom under national leadership.

The question became one not of just satisfying our national aspiration but of effective prosecution of the war and fighting to the last any invader who set foot on the soil of India. On general principles a National Government would control defence through a Defence Minister, and the Commander-in-Chief would control the armed forces and would have full latitude in the carrying out of operations connected with the war. An Indian National Government should have normally functioned in this way. We made it clear that the Commander-in-Chief in India would have control of the armed forces and the conduct of operations and other matters connected therewith. With a view to arriving at a settlement, we were prepared to accept certain limitations on the normal powers of the Defence Minister. We had no desire to upset in the middle of the war the present military organization or arrangements. We accepted also that the higher strategy of the war should be controlled by the War Cabinet in London which would have an Indian member. The immediate object before us was to make the defence of India more effective, to strengthen it, to broad-base it on the popular will, and to reduce all red tape, delay and inefficiency from it. There was no question of our interfering with the technical and operational sides. One thing of course, was of paramount importance to us; India's safety and defence. Subject to this primary consideration there was no reason why there should be any difficulty in finding a way out of the present impasse in accordance with the unanimous desire of the Indian people, for in this matter there are no differences amongst us.

The emphasis on Defence led you to reconsider the matter and you wrote to me on the 7th April suggesting a formula for Defence.

In this letter you said: "As the Working Committee have understood, it is impossible to make any change in the existing constitution during the period of hostilities." The Working Committee's attitude in the matter has been completely misunderstood and I should like to clear this up, although we are not immediately concerned with it. The Committee do not think that there is any inherent difficulty in the way of constitutional changes during the war. Everything that helps in the war not only can be but must be done, and done with speed. That is the only way to carry on and win a war. No complicated enactments are necessary. A recognition of India's freedom and right to self-determination could easily be made, if it were so wished, together with certain other consequential but important changes. The rest can be left to future arrangements and adjustments. I might remind you that the British Prime Minister actually proposed a union of France and England on the eve of the fall of France. No greater or more fundamental change could be imagined, and this was suggested at a period of grave crisis and peril. War accelerates change; it does not fit in with static conceptions.

The formula for Defence that you sent us was considered by us together with its annexure which gave a list of subjects or departments which were to be transferred to the Defence Department. This list was a revealing one as it proved that the Defence Minister would deal with relatively unimportant matters. We were unable to accept this and we informed you accordingly.

Subsequently, a new formula for Defence was suggested to us, but without any list of subjects. This formula seemed to us to be based on a more healthy approach and we suggested certain changes pointing out that our ultimate decision would necessarily depend on the allocation of subjects. A revised formula was then sent back to us together with an indication of the functions of the War Department.

This was so widely and comprehensively framed that it was difficult for us to know what the actual allocation of subjects and departments, as between the Defence Department and the War Department, would be. A request was made on our behalf that illustrative lists of these subjects might be supplied to enable us to consider the matter. No such lists were supplied to us.

In the interview we had with you yesterday we discussed the new formula and expressed our view-point in regard to it. I need not repeat what I said then. The wording of the formula is after all a minor matter and we should not allow that to come in our way, unless some important principle is at stake. But behind that wording lay certain ideas and we were surprised to find that during the past few days we had been proceeding on wrong assumptions.

When we asked you for illustrative lists of subjects for the two departments, you referred us to the old list for the Defence Department which you had previously sent us and which we had been unable to accept. You added that certain residuary subjects might be added to this but, in effect, there was not likely to be any such subject as the allocation was complete. Thus, you said, that substantially there was no change between the old list and any new one that might be prepared. If this was so, and we were to go back ultimately to the place we started from, then what was the purpose of our searching for a new formula? A new set of words meaning the same thing made no difference. In the course of our talks many other matters were also cleared up, unfortunately to our disadvantage. You had referred both privately and in the course of public statements to a National Government and a "Cabinet" consisting of "ministers." These words have a certain significance and we had imagined that the new Government would function with full powers as a cabinet, with the Viceroy acting as a constitutional head. But the new picture that you placed before us was really not very different from the old, the difference being one of degree and not of kind. The new Government could neither be called except vaguely and inaccurately, nor could it function as a

National Government. It would just be the Viceroy and his Executive Council with the Viceroy having all his old powers. We did not ask for any legal changes but we did ask for definite assurances and conventions which would indicate that the new Government would function as a free government the members of which act as members of a cabinet in a constitutional Government. In regard to the conduct of the war and connected activities the Commander-in-Chief would have freedom, and he would act as War Minister.

We were informed that nothing can be said at this stage, even vaguely and generally, about the conventions that should govern the Government and the Viceroy. Ultimately there was always the possibility of the members of the Executive Council resigning or threatening to resign if they disagreed with the Viceroy. That sanction or remedy is of course always open, but it is curious that we should base our approach to a new government on the probability of conflict and resignation at the very outset.

The picture therefore placed before us is not essentially different from the old one. The whole object which we, and I believe you have in view —that is, to create a new psychological approach to the people, to make them feel that their own national government had come, that they were defending their newly-won freedom—would be completely frustrated when they saw this old picture again, with even the old labels on. The continuation of the India Office which has been a symbol of evil to us, would confirm this picture. It has almost been taken for granted for some time past that the India Office would soon disappear as it was an anachronism. But now we are told that even this undesirable relic of a past age is going to continue.

The picture of the government, which was so like the old in all essential features, is such that we cannot fit into it. Normally we would have had little difficulty in disposing of this matter for it is so far removed from all that we have striven for, but in the circumstances of today we were prepared to give full consideration to every proposal which might lead to an effective organization of the defence of India. The peril that faces India affects us more than it can possibly affect any foreigner, and we are anxious and eager to do our utmost to face it and overcome it. But we cannot undertake responsibilities when we are not given the freedom and power to shoulder them effectively and when an old environment continues which hampers the national effort.

While we cannot accept the proposals you have made, we want to inform you that we are yet prepared to assume responsibility provided a truly national government is formed. We are prepared to put aside for the present all questions about the future, though as we have indicated, we hold definite views about it. But in the present, the National Government must be a cabinet government with full power and must not merely be a continuation of the Viceroy's Executive Council. In regard to defence we have already stated what, in our opinion, the position should be at present. We feel that such an arrangement is the very minimum that is essential for the functioning of a National Government and for making the popular appeal which is urgently needed.

We would point out to you that the suggestions we have put forward are not ours only but may be considered to be the unanimous demand of the Indian people. On these matters there is no difference of opinion among the various groups and parties, and the difference is as between the Indian people as a whole and the British Government. Such differences as exist in India relate to constitutional changes in the future. We are agreeable to the postponement of this issue so that the largest possible measure of unity might be achieved in the present crisis for the defence of India. It would be a tragedy that even when there is this unanimity of opinion in India, the British Government should prevent a free National Government from functioning and from serving the cause of India as well as the larger causes for which millions are suffering and dying today.

Yours sincerely,
Sd/- Abul Kalam Azad

The Rt. Hon. Sir Stafford Cripps,
3, Queen Victoria Road,
New Delhi

On the 11th of April Cripps replied to me in the following terms:

3, Queen Victoria Road
New Delhi, 11th April, 1942.

My Dear Maulana Sahib,

I was extremely sorry to receive from you your letter of April 10th expressing the rejection by the Congress Working Committee of His Majesty's Government's draft declaration.

I will not deal with those points which are covered by the original resolution of your Committee which you sent me, as they were clearly not the reason for your decision.

Nor need I go into the question of the division of duties between the

Defence Minister and the Commander-in-Chief as War Member with which you deal at length. This division allotted to the Defence Minister all functions outside those actually connected with the General Head-quarters, Navy Headquarters and Air Headquarters which are under the Commander-in-Chief as head of the fighting forces in India.

In addition to these functions in the narrow field of "Defence" it was suggested that all other portfolios relating to that subject such as:

Home Department—Internal order, police, refugees etc.

Finance Department—All war finance in India.

Communications Department—Railways, roads, transport etc.

Supply Department—Supplies for all forces and munitions.

Information and Broadcasting Department—Propaganda, publicity etc.

Civil Defence Department—A.R.P. and all forms of civilian defence.

Legislative Department—Regulations and orders.

Labour Department—Man Power.

Defence Department—Administration and Indian personnel etc.— should be put in the hands of representative Indians as members of the Executive Council.

Nothing further could have been done by way of giving responsibility for Defence services to representative Indian members without jeopard-ising the immediate defence of India under the Commander-in-Chief. This defence is, as you know, a paramount duty and responsibility of His Majesty's Government, while unity of Command is essential in the interests of the Allied help to India.

The real substance of your refusal to take part in a National Govern-ment is that the form of Government suggested is not such as would enable you to rally the Indian people as you desire.

You make two suggestions. First that the constitution might now be changed. In this respect I would point out that you made this suggestion for the first time last night, nearly three weeks after you had received the proposals, and I would further remark that every other representative with whom I have discussed this view has accepted the practical impossi-bility of any such legislative change in the middle of a war and at such a moment as the present.

Second you suggest "a truly National Government" be formed, which must be a "cabinet Government with full power."

Without constitutional changes of a most complicated character and on a very large scale this would not be possible, as you realize.

Were such a system to be introduced by convention under the existing circumstances, the nominated cabinet (nominated presumably by the major political organizations) would be responsible to no one but itself,

could not be removed and would in fact constitute an absolute dictatorship of the majority.

This suggestion would be rejected by all minorities in India, since it
would subject all of them to a permanent and autocratic majority in the
Cabinet. Nor would it be consistent with the pledges already given by
His Majesty's Government to protect the rights of those minorities.

In a country such as India where communal divisions are still so deep
an irresponsible majority Government of this kind is not possible.

Apart from this, however, until such time as the Indian people frame
their new constitution, His Majesty's Government must continue to carry
out its duties to those large sections of the Indian people to whom it has
given its pledges.

The proposals of His Majesty's Government went as far as possible
short of a complete change in the constitution which is generally acknowledged as impracticable in the circumstances of today.

While therefore both I and His Majesty's Government recognize the
keen desire of your Working Committee to carry on the war against the
enemy by every means in their power, they regret that your Working
Committee has not seen its way to join in the war effort upon the conditions sincerely offered as the only conditions which could have brought
together all the different communities and sections of the Indian people.

Yours sincerely,
Sd/- Stafford Cripps

I propose to publish this answer.

Maulana Abul Kalam Azad,
Birla House,
New Delhi

I wrote back to him on the same day:

Birla House
Albuquerque Road
New Delhi
April 11, 1942

Dear Sir Stafford,

I have just received your letter of April 10th and I must confess that
my colleagues and I were considerably surprised to read it. I am sending

you this reply immediately and can only deal briefly here with some of the points you have raised.

The points covered by our original resolution are important and represent my Committee's well-considered views on the British proposal as a whole. But we pointed out to you that so far as the proposals relate to the future they might be set aside, as we were anxious to assume responsibility for India's government and defence in this hour of danger. This responsibility could only be undertaken, however, if it was real responsibility and power.

As regards the division of functions between the Defence Minister and the War Minister you did not give illustrative lists, as requested by us, and referred us to the previous list of the Defence Minister's function which, as you know, we had been wholly unable to accept. In your letter under reply you mention certain subjects, directly or indirectly related to the war, which will be administered by other departments. So far as the Defence Minister is concerned, it is clear that his functions will be limited by the first list that you sent.

No one has suggested any restrictions on the normal powers of the Commander-in-Chief. Indeed we went beyond this and were prepared to agree to further powers being given to him as War Minister. But it is that the British Government's conception and ours in regard to defence differ greatly. For us it means giving it a national character and calling upon every man and woman in India to participate in it. It means trusting our own people and seeking their full co-operation in this great effort. The British Government's view seems to be based on an utter lack of confidence in the Indian people and in withholding real power from them. You refer to the paramount duty and responsibility of His Majesty's Government in regard to defence. That duty and responsibility cannot be discharged effectively unless the Indian people are made to have and feel their responsibility, and the recent past stands witness to this. The Government of India do not seem to realize that the war can only be fought on a popular basis.

Your statement that we have for the first time after three weeks suggested a change in the constitution is hardly correct. In the course of our talks reference was made to it, but it is true that we did not lay stress on it as we did not want to introduce new issues. But when you stated explicitly in your letter that we had agreed that no constitutional changes could be made during the war, we had to deny this and correct your impression.

It is the last part of your letter that has especially surprised and pained us. It seems that there has been a progressive deterioration in the British

Government's attitude as our negotiations proceeded. What we were told in our very first talk with you is now denied or explained away. You told me then that there would be a National Government which would function as a Cabinet and that the position of the Viceroy would be analogous to that of the King in England vis-à-vis his Cabinet. In regard to the India Office, you told me, that you were surprised that no one had so far mentioned this important matter, and that the practical course was to have this attached or incorporated with the Dominion's Office.

The whole of this picture which you sketched before us has now been completely shattered by what you told us during our last interview.

You have put forward an argument in your letter which at no time during our talks was mentioned by you. You refer to the "absolute dictatorship of the majority." It is astonishing that such a statement should be made in this connection and at this stage. This difficulty is inherent in any scheme of a mixed cabinet formed to meet an emergency, but there are many ways in which it can be provided for. Had you raised this question we would have discussed it and found a satisfactory solution. The whole approach to this question has been that a mixed cabinet should be formed and should co-operate together. We accepted this. We are not interested in the Congress as such gaining power, but we are interested in the Indian people as a whole having freedom and power. How the Cabinet should be formed and should function was a question which might have been considered after the main question was decided; that is, the extent of power which the British Government would give up to the Indian people. Because of this we never discussed it with you or even referred to it. Nevertheless you have raised this matter for the first time, in what is presumably your last letter to us, and tried most unjustifiably to sidetrack the real issue between us.

You will remember that in my very first talk with you, I pointed out that the communal or like questions did not arise at this stage. As soon as the British Government made up its mind to transfer real power and responsibility, the other questions could be tackled successfully by those concerned. You gave me the impression that you agreed with this approach.

We are convinced that if the British Government did not pursue a policy of encouraging disruption, all of us, to whatever party or group we belonged, would be able to come together and find a common line of action. But, unhappily, even in this grave hour of peril, the British Government is unable to give up its wrecking policy. We are driven to the conclusion that it attaches more importance to holding on to its rule in India, as long as it can, and promoting discord and disruption here with that end in view, than to an effective defence of India against the aggression and invasion that overhang us. To us, and to all Indians, the dominant consideration is the defence and safety of India, and it is by that test that we judge.

You mention that you propose to publish your letter to me. I presume that you have no objection now to our publishing our original resolution, your letters to us, and our letters to you.

Yours sincerely,
Sd. Abul Kalam Azad

The Right Hon'ble Sir Stafford Cripps,
3, Queen Victoria Road,
New Delhi

QUIT INDIA

The All-India Congress Committee has given the most careful consideration to the reference made to it by the Working Committee in their resolution dated July 14, 1942, and to subsequent events, including the development of the war situation, the utterances of responsible spokesmen of the British Government, and the comments and criticisms made in India and abroad. The Committee approves of and endorses that resolution and is of opinion that events subsequent to it have given it further justification, and have made it clear that the immediate ending of British rule in India is an urgent necessity, both for the sake of India and for the success of the cause of the United Nations. The continuation of that rule is degrading and enfeebling India and making her progressively less capable of defending herself and of contributing to the cause of world freedom.

The Committee has viewed with dismay the deterioration of the situation on the Russian and Chinese fronts and conveys to the Russian and Chinese peoples its high appreciation of their heroism in defence of their freedom. This increasing peril makes it incumbent on all those who strive for freedom and who sympathise with the victims of aggression, to examine the foundations of the policy so far pursued by the Allied Nations, which have led to repeated and disastrous failure. It is not by adhering to such aims and policies and methods that failure can be converted into success, for past experience has shown that failure is inherent in them. These policies have been based not on freedom so much as on the domination of subject and colonial countries, and the continuation of the imperialist tradition and method. The possession of empire, instead of adding to the strength of the ruling Power, has become a burden and a curse. India, the classic land of modern imperialism, has become the crux of the question, for by the freedom of India will Britain and the United Nations be judged, and the peoples of Asia and Africa be filled with hope and enthusiasm. The ending of British rule in this country is thus a vital and immediate issue on which depend the future of the war and the success of freedom and democracy. A free India will assure this success by throwing all her great resources in the struggle for freedom and against the aggression of Nazism, Fascism and Imperialism. This will not only affect materially the fortunes of the war, but will bring all subject and oppressed humanity on the side of the United Nations, and give these Nations, whose ally India would be, the moral and spiritual leadership of the world. India in bondage will continue to be the symbol of British imperialism and the taint of that imperialism will affect the fortunes of all the United Nations.

The peril of today, therefore, necessitates the independence of India and the ending of British domination. No future promises or guarantees can affect the present situation or meet that peril. They cannot produce the needed psychological effect on the minds of the masses. Only the glow of freedom now can release that energy and enthusiasm of millions of people which will immediately transform the nature of the war.

The A. I. C. C. therefore repeats with all emphasis the demand for the withdrawal of the British Power from India. On the declaration of India's independence, a Provisional Government will be formed and Free India will become an ally of the United Nations, sharing with them in the trials and tribulations of the joint enterprise of the struggle for freedom. The Provisional Government can only be formed by the co-operation of the principal parties and groups in the country. It will thus be a composite government, representative of all important sections of the people of India. Its primary functions must be to defend India and resist aggression with all the armed as well as the non-violent forces at its command, together with its Allied powers, to promote the well-being and progress of the workers in the fields and factories and elsewhere to whom essentially all power and authority must belong. The Provisional Government will evolve a scheme for a Constituent Assembly which will prepare a constitution for the Government of India acceptable to all sections of the people. This constitution, according to the Congress view should be a federal one, with the largest measure of autonomy for the federating units, and with the residuary powers vesting in these units. The future relations between India and the Allied Nations will be adjusted by representatives of all these free countries conferring together for their mutual advantage and for their co-operation in the common task of resisting aggression. Freedom will enable India to resist aggression effectively with the people's united will and strength behind it.

The freedom of India must be the symbol of and prelude to the freedom of all other Asiatic nations under foreign domination. Burma, Malaya, Indo-China, the Dutch Indies, Iran and Iraq must also attain their complete freedom. It must be clearly understood that such of these countries as are under the Japanese control now must not subsequently be placed under the rule or control of any other colonial power.

While the A. I. C. C. must primarily be concerned with the independence and defence of India in this hour of danger, the Committee is of opinion that the future peace, security and ordered progress of the world demand a World Federation of free nations, and on no other basis can the problems of the modern world be solved. Such a World Federation would ensure freedom of its constituent nations, the prevention of aggression and exploitation by one nation of another, the protection of national minorities, the advancement of all backward areas and peoples, and the pooling of the world's resources for the common good of all. On the establishment of such a World Federation, disarmament would be practicable in all countries, national armies, navies and air forces would no longer be necessary, and a World Federal Defence Force would keep the world peace and prevent aggression.

An independent India would gladly join such a World Federation and co-operate on an equal basis with other nations in the solution of international problems.

Such a Federation should be open to all nations who agree with its fundamental principles. In view of the war, however, the Federation must inevitably, to begin with, be confined to the United Nations. Such a step taken now will have a most powerful effect on the war, on the peoples of the Axis countries, and on the peace to come.

The Committee regretfully realizes, however, that despite the tragic and overwhelming lessons of the war and the perils that overhang the world, the governments of few countries are yet prepared to take this inevitable step towards World Federation. The reactions of the British Government and the misguided criticisms of the foreign press also make it clear that even the obvious demand for India's independence is resisted, though this has been made essentially to meet the present peril and to enable India to defend herself and help China and Russia in their hour of need. The Committee is anxious not to embarrass in any way the defence of China or Russia, whose freedom is precious and must be preserved or to jeopardise the defensive capacity of the United Nations. But the peril grows both to India and these nations, and inaction and submission to a foreign administration at this stage is not only degrading India and reducing her capacity to defend herself and resist aggression, but is no answer to that growing peril and is no service to the peoples of the United Nations. The earnest appeal of the Working Committee to Great Britain and the United Nations has so far met with no response, and the criticisms made in many foreign quarters have shown an ignorance of India's and the world's need, and sometimes even hostility to India's freedom, which is significant of a mentality of domination and racial superiority which cannot be tolerated by a proud people conscious of their strength and of the justice of their cause.

The A. I. C. C. would yet again, at this last moment, in the interest of world freedom, renew this appeal to Britain and the United Nations. But the Committee feels that it is no longer justified in holding the nation back from endeavouring to assert its will against an imperialist and authoritarian government which dominates over it and prevents it from functioning in its own interest and in the interest of humanity. The Committee resolves, therefore, to sanction, for the vindication of India's inalienable right to freedom and independence, the starting of a mass struggle on non-violent lines on the widest possible scale, so that the country might utilise all the non-violent strength it has gathered during the last twenty-two years of peaceful struggle. Such a struggle must inevitably be under the leadership of Gandhiji and the Committee request him to take the lead and to guide the nation in the steps to be taken.

The Committee appeals to the people of India to face the dangers and hardships that will fall to their lot with courage and endurance, and instructions as disciplined soldiers of Indian freedom. They must remember that non-violence is the basis of this movement. A time may come when it may not be possible to issue instructions or for instructions to reach our people, and when no Congress Committee can function. When this happens, every man and woman, who is participating in this movement must function for himself or herself within the four corners of the general instructions issued. Every Indian who desires freedom and strives for it must be his own guide urging him on along the hard road where there is no resting place and which leads ultimately to the independence and deliverance of India.

Lastly, whilst the A. I. C. C. has stated its own view of the future government under free India the A. I. C. C. wishes to make it quite clear to all concerned that by embarking on mass struggle it has no intention of gaining power for the Congress. The power, when it comes, will belong to the whole people of India.

BRITISH GOVERNMENT'S STATEMENT OF 3 JUNE

1. On February 20th, 1947, His Majesty's Government announced their intention of transferring power in British India to Indian hands by June 1948. His Majesty's Government had hoped that it would be possible for the major parties to co-operate in the working out of the Cabinet Mission's Plan of May 16th, 1946, and evolve for India a Constitution acceptable to all concerned. This hope has not been fulfilled.

2. The majority of the representatives of the Provinces of Madras, Bombay, the United Provinces, Bihar, Central Provinces and Berar, Assam, Orissa and the North-West Frontier Provinces, and the representatives of Delhi, Ajmer-Merwara and Coorg have already made progress in the task of evolving a new Constitution. On the other hand, the Muslim League Party, including in it a majority of the representatives of Bengal, the Punjab and Sind as also the representative of British Baluchistan, has decided not to participate in the Constituent Assembly.

3. It has always been the desire of His Majesty's Government that power should be transferred in accordance with the wishes of the Indian people themselves. This task would have been greatly facilitated if there had been agreement among the Indian political parties. In the absence of such agreement, the task of devising a method by which the wishes of the Indian people can be ascertained has devolved upon His Majesty's Government. After full consultation with political leaders in India, His Majesty's Government have decided to adopt for this purpose the plan set out below. His Majesty's Government wish to make it clear that they have no intention of attempting to frame any ultimate Constitution for India; this is a matter for the Indians themselves nor is there anything in this plan to preclude negotiations between communities for a united India.

4. It is not the intention of His Majesty's Government to interrupt the work of the existing Constituent Assembly. Now that provision is made for certain provinces specified below, His Majesty's Government trust that, as a consequence of this announcement, the Muslim League representatives of those provinces, a majority of whose representatives are already participating in it, will now take their due share in its labour. At the same time it is clear that any constitution framed by this Assembly cannot apply to those parts of the country which are unwilling to accept it. His Majesty's Government are satisfied that the procedure outlined below embodies the best method of ascertaining the wishes of the people of such areas on the issue whether their Constitution is to be framed:

    (a) in the existing Constituent Assembly; or

(b) in a new and separate Constituent Assembly consisting of the representatives of those areas which decide not to participate in the existing Constituent Assembly.

When this has been done, it will be possible to determine the authority or authorities to whom power should be transferred.

5. The Provincial Legislative Assemblies of Bengal and the Punjab (excluding the European members) will, therefore, each be asked to meet in two parts, one representing the Muslim majority districts and the other the rest of the province. For the purpose of determining the population of districts the 1941 census figures will be taken as authoritative. The Muslim majority districts in these two provinces are set out in the Appendix to this announcement.

6. The members of the two parts of each Legislative Assembly sitting separately will be empowered to vote whether or not the province should be partitioned. If a simple majority of either part decides in favour of partition, division will take place and arrangement will be made accordingly.

7. Before the question as to partition is decided, it is desirable that the representative of each part should know in advance which Constituent Assembly the province as a whole would join in the event of the two parts subsequently deciding to remain united. Therefore, if any member of either Legislative Assembly so demands, there shall be held a meeting of all members of the Legislative Assembly (other than Europeans) at which a decision will be taken on the issue as to which Constituent Assembly the province as a whole would join if it were decided by the two parts to remain united.

8. In the event of partition being decided upon, each part of the Legislative Assembly will, on behalf of the areas they represent, decide which of the alternatives in paragraph 4 above to adopt.

9. For the immediate purpose of deciding on the issue of partition, the members, of the legislative assemblies of Bengal and the Punjab will sit in two parts according to Muslim majority districts (as laid down in the Appendix) and non-Muslim majority districts. This is only a preliminary step of a purely temporary nature as it is evident that for the purposes of final partition of these provinces a detailed investigation of boundary questions will be needed; and as soon as a decision involving partition has been taken for either province a boundary commission will be set up by the Governor-General, the membership and terms of reference of which will be settled in consultation with those concerned. It will be instructed to demarcate the boundaries of the two parts of the Punjab on the basis of ascertaining the contiguous majority areas of

Muslims and non-Muslims. It will also be instructed to take into account other factors. Similar instructions will be given to the Bengal Boundary Commission. Until the report of a boundary commission has been put into effect, the provisional boundaries indicated in the Appendix will be used.

10. The Legislative Assembly of Sind (excluding the European members) will at a special meeting also take its own decision on the alternatives in paragraph 4 above.

11. The position of the North-West Frontier Province is exceptional. Two of the three representatives of this province are already participating in the existing Constituent Assembly. But it is clear, in view of its geographical situation and other considerations, that if the whole or any part of the Punjab decided not to join the existing Constituent Assembly, it will be necessary to give the North-West Frontier Province an opportunity to reconsider its position. Accordingly, in such an event a referendum will be made to the electors of the present Legislative Assembly in the North-West Frontier Province to choose which of the alternatives mentioned in paragraph 4 above they wish to adopt. The referendum will be held under the aegis of the Governor-General and in consultation with the provincial Government.

12. British Baluchistan has elected a member, but he has not taken his seat in the existing Constituent Assembly. In view of its geographical situation, this province will also be given an opportunity to reconsider its position and to choose which of the alternatives in paragraph 4 above to adopt. His Excellency the Governor-General is examining how this can most appropriately be done.

13. Though Assam is predominantly a non-Muslim province, the district of Sylhet which is contiguous to Bengal is predominantly Muslim. There has been a demand that, in the event of the partition of Bengal, Sylhet should be amalgamated with the Muslim part of Bengal. Accordingly if it is decided that Bengal should be partitioned, a referendum will be held in Sylhet District under the aegis of the Governor-General and in consultation with the Assam Provincial Government to decide whether the district of Sylhet should continue to form part of Assam Province or should be amalgamated with the new province of Eastern Bengal, a boundary commission with terms of reference similar to those for the Punjab and Bengal will be set up to demarcate the Muslim majority areas of Sylhet District and contiguous Muslim majority areas of adjoining districts, which will then be transferred to East Bengal. The rest of Assam Province will in any case continue to participate in the proceedings of the existing Constituent Assembly.

14. If it is decided that Bengal and the Punjab should be partitioned,

it will be necessary to hold fresh elections to choose their representatives on the scale of one for every million of population according to the principle contained in the Cabinet Mission's Plan of May 16, 1946. Similar election will also have to be held for Sylhet in the event of it being decided that this district should form part of East Bengal. The number of representatives to which each area would be entitled is as follows:—

Province	General	Muslims	Sikhs	Total
Sylhet District	1	2	nil	3
West Bengal	15	4	nil	19
East Bengal	12	29	nil	41
West Punjab	3	12	2	17
East Punjab	6	4	2	12

15. In accordance with the mandates given to them, the representatives of the various areas will either join the existing Constituent Assembly or form the new Constituent Assembly.

16. Negotiations will have to be initiated as soon as possible on the administrative consequences of any partition that may have been decided upon:—

(a) Between the representatives and the respective successor authorities about all subjects now dealt with by the Central Government including defence, finance, and communications.

(b) Between different successor authorities and His Majesty's Government for treaties in regard to matters arising out of the transfer of power.

(c) In the case of provinces that may be partitioned, as to the administration of all provincial subjects, such as the division of assets and liabilities, the police and other services, the high courts, provincial institutions etc.

17. Agreements with tribes of the North-West Frontier of India will have to be negotiated by the appropriate successor authority.

18. His Majesty's Government wish to make it clear that the decisions announced above relate only to British India and that their policy towards Indian States contained in the Cabinet Mission's memorandum of 12th May, 1946 remains unchanged.

19. In order that the successor authorities may have time to prepare themselves to take over power, it is important that all the above processes should be completed as quickly as possible. To avoid delay, the different provinces or parts of provinces will proceed independently as far as practicable within the conditions of this plan. The existing Constituent Assem-

bly and the new Constituent Assembly (if formed) will proceed to frame
constitutions for their respective territories; they will, of course, be free
to frame their own rules.

20. The major political parties have repeatedly emphasized their desire
that there should be the earliest possible transfer of power in India. With
this desire His Majesty's Government are in full sympathy and they are
willing to anticipate the date of June 1948, for the handing over of power
by the setting up of an Independent Indian Government or Governments
at an even earlier date. Accordingly, as the most expeditious, and indeed
the only practicable way of meeting this desire, His Majesty's Government propose to introduce legislation during the current session for the
transfer of power this year on a Dominion Status basis to one or two
successor authorities according to the decisions taken as a result of this
announcement. This will be without prejudice to the right of the Indian
Constituent Assemblies to decide in due course whether or not the part
of India in respect of which they have authority will remain within the
British Commonwealth.

His Excellency the Governor-General will from time to time make
such further announcements as may be necessary in regard to procedure
or any other matters for carrying out the above arrangements.

The Muslim majority districts of the Punjab and Bengal according to
the 1941 (census):—

1. THE PUNJAB

Lahore Division—Gujranwala, Gurdaspur, Lahore, Sheikhupura, Sialkot.
Rawalpindi Division—Attock, Gujrat, Jhelum, Mianwali, Rawalpindi
                    Shahpur.
Multan Division—Dera Ghazi Khan, Jhang, Lyallpur, Montgomery,
                    Multan, Muzaffargarh.

2. BENGAL

Chittagong Division—Chittagong, Noakhali, Tipperah.
Dacca Division—Bakerganj, Dacca, Faridpur, Mymensingh.
Presidency Division—Jessore, Murshidabad, Nadia.
Rajshahi Division—Bogra, Dinajpur, Malda, Pabna Rajshahi, Rangpur.

Index